Joan McElroy's
DOLLS' HOUSE FURNITURE BOOK

Joan McElroy's
DOLLS' HOUSE
FURNITURE BOOK

Alfred A. Knopf   New York   1976

ACKNOWLEDGMENTS

My special thanks to Joseph McElroy for his continual encouragement. Also special thanks to Robert Tynes for his invaluable imaginative and practical help.

I would like to thank the following people for their encouragement and assistance: Betty Dodson, Angus Dowling, Doug Johns, Fredelle Maynard, Joyce Maynard, Hanna McElroy, Robert Milne, John Noble, Hanna Singer, Bill Wilson, and Victoria Wilson.

Library of Congress Cataloging in Publication Data
McElroy, Joan.
Joan McElroy's dolls' house furniture book.
Bibliography: p.
Includes index.
1. Doll furniture.   I. Title.   II. Title: Dolls' House furniture book.
TT175.5.M28 1976.   745.59′23   76–13703
ISBN 0–394–40057–7

For Joe

CONTENTS

Joan McElroy's
DOLLS' HOUSE FURNITURE BOOK

INTRODUCTION

I never had a dolls' house. None of my friends had dolls' houses either, and I don't think I saw one until I was in my teens. When I was a child it was wartime in London, and toys for children were very low on the list of priorities. Houses were being bombed, and I played out my fantasies, with my friends, in the ruins of abandoned houses. One house, our favorite, had most of its fourteen rooms intact, but there was no roof. We felt that it was our territory, with no adults to tell us what we could or could not do. In my imagination, I put back the roof and furnished the house in minute detail.

I can't remember a time when I wasn't fascinated by small things. Just after World War II, a friend of my parents brought me from Paris a three-piece set of miniature furniture made of Limoges china. There was a chair, a sofa, and a table, all of delicate white china, decorated in pastel colors with flowers. And there was a couple in eighteenth-century costume gazing tenderly at each other. About six months after I received this exquisite and cherished gift, Mirna Fireman said, "If you don't give me your china furniture, I won't be your friend." Like most children, and especially only children, I would have done anything not to lose a friend. And though I cried in private, I bravely handed over my best toy. To this day I regret it. I do not remember what Mirna Fireman looked like; but I do remember in every detail that set of furniture.

When I was about twelve years old, we lived in a large, rather shabby Victorian house. Our furniture—a few antiques, most of it quite tasteful—was in my eyes dull and drab. Why couldn't we live, like some of my friends, in a newly built suburb with brightly painted modern houses? I envied their furniture too, which was new and glamorous. When Ideal produced the Petite

Princess line of deluxe plastic-and-glitter dolls' house furniture in 1964, I was delighted. There it is, the furniture I envied in my friends' houses when I was a child, reduced to miniature size but quite identifiable. I have bought most of the pieces. There are Mrs. Bennett's china cabinet and dining room set; the Turners' pale pink satin-covered bedspreads, and tufted pale pink matching headboards. And my friend Marilyn's mother had the kidney-shaped vanity table, with movable side-mirrors, so you could admire your nose in profile and see the curls at the back of your head. But no one had a piano quite so grand as the Petite Princess grand piano. Seeing the Petite Princess furniture made me realize how much my taste in furniture has changed, going from eighteenth-century French via Hollywood reproductions to Danish modern and back to "drab" antiques.

The art school I went to was about three-quarters of an hour's bus ride from my house. It would have been quicker to go by underground train, but I loved to sit on the top deck of a red double-decker bus and daydream. I had two types of daydream. One involved meeting, by a series of unlikely circumstances, Tyrone Power (sometimes Kirk Douglas), who became enchanted by my wit and strange, elusive beauty, and hand in hand we walked into the sunset. The other daydream, which was more frequent, showed me saving an old lady just as she was about to step off the curb in front of a car to certain death. After the old lady had recovered from the shock, she would say to me, "How can I reward you, my child, for saving my life? I am very rich, and you may have anything you want." Without hesitation I would answer, "A house, and enough money to furnish it." The rest of the journey I would spend converting and modernizing a

Georgian or Victorian house. I would pull down walls, take away ceilings to make a room high enough to have a balcony with a small spiral staircase leading to it. I would build a conservatory, and even decide what plants I would grow in it. Then I would start furnishing each room. I would decide on a color scheme, then change my mind. The task was never completed, and each bus ride I would start anew.

In my mid-twenties I left London with my American husband, and moved to a small New England university town. The second week we were there, old friends of my husband invited us for dinner. I was unsure of myself and uncomfortable in my new roles of bride and faculty wife. On my second trip to the bathroom upstairs I noticed that the door to one of the bedrooms was open, and a girl was sitting on the floor playing with little dolls and dolls' house furniture. I asked if I could join her—and that is how I became friends with Joyce when she was eight and I was twenty-five. A friendship grew out of our mutual interest in dolls' houses.

In the years that followed, on return visits after I'd moved away from the town, I would find an excuse to leave the adult company and go and play with Joyce. I remember once saying, "Don't you wish you had a real dolls' house, rather than converted bookshelves?" And Joyce said, "But it *is* a real dolls' house."

The dolls' house and its tenants underwent changes and additions. But what I remember best was the period when the "house" became a girls' boarding school. The girls were Barbie dolls, the early types, which were made out of hard plastic, with high-heeled shoes molded onto the feet. The house was run on the most strict army-style discipline. Lists were posted everywhere throughout the house with exact orders and schedules. These lists were tiny, of course, and therefore quite hard to read: 6 a.m.—everyone get up. 6:30—Cindy sweep bedrooms, Angie dust, Samantha make breakfast. Every minute of the girls' day was ordered and accounted for. Even what courses they were taking, and their class timetables. Although Joyce was undisciplined, and her room was often a mess, the dolls' house was always neat and orderly.

When Joyce was eleven and visiting us in New York with her mother and sister, I took her to visit Angus Dowling, a friend of my mother-in-law. Angus worked for the telephone company, and, as he put it, making miniature furniture was his hobby.

I had never seen (or at least never been allowed to handle) small furniture such as Angus makes. The chairs, tables, chests, and beds are not dolls' house furniture; they are perfect reproductions of antiques, scaled down to one inch to the foot. Every measurement and detail is precise, from the dovetailing in the drawers to the size of the grain of the wood and the delicate brass drawer knobs. This was not a "hobby," but a true art, created out of the love of furniture.

I was not disappointed in Joyce's reaction when she saw the miniatures. Usually a talkative girl, she was quite speechless, except for inarticulate gasps. As we said good-by, Angus gave Joyce a tiny hammer-and-peg toy, which he had copied many years before from one his daughter had had as a child.

* * *

It was Joyce's idea to write a book on how to make dolls' house furniture, and she asked me to collaborate on it with her. But as my enthusiasm increased, hers lessened, and she became involved in other things. I continued alone, and became so absorbed with the making of dolls' house furniture that what had always interested me now took over to the exclusion of practically everything else. I have seen my noncollector friends' eyes glaze, as I would manage to bring every conversation round to dolls' house furniture.

I remember buying my first dolls' house furniture—a Victorian desk and a Victorian chest of drawers—at an antique shop in Devon in 1963. But I don't remember ever making a decision to begin collecting.

The start of one famous collection—that of Vivien Greene, the dolls' house historian—was three tiny air-twist glasses, which were given to her when she was nine years old. They can still be seen at the Rotunda, a museum in Oxford that she had specially designed and built to display her eighteenth- and nineteenth-century dolls' houses. Recently I asked Mrs. Greene when she started collecting dolls' houses and why. She said that at the beginning of World War II she and her children left their house in London and went to Oxford, where she had lived before. At first they stayed with friends, and Mrs. Greene felt that she had nothing of her own. No house, nothing to decorate or furnish. And because she felt that she had nothing of her own, she bought her first dolls' house.

I have a friend whose income is very small. He lives in a shabby, cold-water tenement apartment. But this dingy apartment is an Aladdin's cave full of treasures. From floor to ceiling it is packed with dolls, dolls' house furniture, dolls' houses. Every available surface is covered with "the collection." Through this apartment there is a path like a beaten jungle track, where, if you are not too fat, and either keep your arms pinned to your sides or hold them up above your head, you can just manage to walk. And although I have gone along this track many times, each time I find something new—a rag doll or a tiny cradle or a toy piano that I overlooked on my previous trips.

My friend seems to exist on cigarettes and very sweet tea, spending most of the money he earns either on craft supplies or on dolls and dolls' house furniture. He makes beautiful cloth and clothespin dolls, and is always either constructing a new fireplace for one of his houses, or mending a leg on a miniature Victorian sofa. My friend has said, "I know when a dolls' house room is perfect and needs nothing more to be added to it." And when a room is finished, he leaves it and sometimes doesn't touch the arrangement of the furniture for years. I am reminded of Miss Havisham, but when I look at one of my friend's "finished" rooms, I can see what he means. The curtains are hung on tiny brass rods and are meticulously lined; each fold falls naturally. The embroidered towels are carefully arranged and draped over the towel rack, within easy reach of the basin and pitcher. A small china doll, wearing an ankle-length voluminous floral dress, sits comfortably in a rocking chair. There is a feeling of opulence, order, and calm. Everything is in its place. Nothing will disturb the calm. The mailman will not come bringing bills that are hard to pay. The telephone will not ring with news of an accident or a death.

If my friend sold only a quarter of his valuable collection, he would be able to afford at least two of the things I have heard him express a desire for—a trip to Europe and several months' rent on a new and better apartment. But nothing would persuade him to sell a piece from his collection; not one of his tiny graters would he part with, even after admitting that no one needs six. The hold his collection has over him is stronger than his desire to make his life materially more comfortable. His collection is his family, and his security. More important, he has the pleasure of finding, after years of search, just the right footstool to complete a dolls' house room. He has the pleasure of knowing that he can make a patchwork quilt for a six-inch-long brass bed, or reconstruct a broken bamboo dolls' house chair.

The first piece of wooden dolls' house furniture I made was a chest of drawers. Delighted with my achievement, I called a friend and excitedly shouted down the receiver, "I've made a chest of drawers!"

"How clever of you. Is it in your bedroom?" my friend asked.

"Yes, of course," I said. And we went on to talk about other things.

Some weeks later, my friend came to visit us. She looked around our bedroom, and asked where was the chest of drawers I had made. Sometimes I forget that not everyone thinks about four-inch-high chests of drawers; yes, and that most people when they go into antique shops never ask, "Do you have any dolls' house furniture?"

I feel my dream dolls' house always just eludes me. It was sold at an auction I could not attend. Or it stood, covered in dust, hidden away at the back of an antique shop, and was bought by someone the day before I visited the shop. I have trained my friends on two continents to be on the lookout when they visit antique shops, fairs, and auctions. Several years ago friends called long distance to say they had seen a fully furnished Victorian dolls' house in an antique shop in Maine. It was in good condition and cost $60, and did I want it? Of course I wanted it. When they returned to the shop the next day, it had been sold. The feeling of loss and disappointment and anger that I felt could not be justified by what had actually happened. The night I heard my dolls' house had been sold, I couldn't sleep. When I think of it even now, those irrational feelings quickly come back.

The real, big world is hard to live in and manage: the boiler can break, the sink clog up, the cake fall, the soot blow down the chimney, and you expect six guests for dinner. Inside a dolls' house the environment is easily controllable and can become even comfortingly static. Sometimes when I am so busy and preoccupied that I want to be left alone, and my family makes justifiable demands on my time, I have thought how nice it would be to give them a swig of Alice's bottle to shrink them to dolls' house size. I could then put them comfortably on a little sofa, and leave them there until the following Wednesday. The people in the dolls' house can be manipulated, they do not resist. You control their every movement, whether they sit or stand, or are moved from one room to another.

You make their histories and decide their fate. They do not age, die, or go away. In Mrs. Greene's Belgravia House (1850–60) a mother clutching her rosary is in the process of dying, after having been delivered of her fifth child. A maid hovers by the bed, and a boy or young man (I'm not sure which—but he doesn't look like a priest) stands at the end of the bed reading from the Bible. In the other rooms of the dolls' house, the family seems unaware of the drama taking place in the bedroom. Children are busy with their games, and someone in the drawing room is playing the piano to an attentive audience. But think of it! They did not hear the sounds of childbirth, and the mother is not disturbed by the noise of children playing or the sound of a piano—because, after all, dolls' houses are silent and you hear the sounds only in your mind.

I am a compulsive eater and a compulsive dieter—a common combination. I have two little dolls that I have sat at a grossly overladen dining table. What a spread! Ham, chicken, pies, Christmas pudding, and blancmange. There the dolls sit facing each other, trapped forever, never to do anything but eat; yet they don't gain an ounce. With dolls' houses you can make your own perfect environment and create a strange kind of order.

I have yet to find my dream house, large or miniature. But just as I have made my own dolls' house furniture, I will make my own dolls' house one day (if I can ever decide on what I really want). Maybe then I will be able to let go of my fantasy of living in a fourteen-room Victorian house in London.

*   *   *

Although dolls' houses are most absorbing toys, their attraction is not only as playthings. They are historical objects beautifully illustrating tastes and modes in domestic life at different periods.

I should stress *domestic*. You will learn nothing about the battlefields of Dunkirk by looking at Faith Eaton's Churchill House, but you will see exactly how houses looked in London in 1942. Bins filled with sand, in case of fire. Windows crisscrossed with tape, to lessen the chance of broken glass scattering. Black blackout curtains. And the brave, grim little doll, with her gas-mask bag over her shoulder, perhaps about to leave the house to do her air-raid warden duty. And if a Victorian dolls' house creator has been particularly conscientious, you may notice, hung on the post of a bed, a little drawstring bag, which was used to put pocket watches in at night.

In Vivien Greene's Balustraded House (circa 1775) there is a hedgehog under the kitchen table. A notice attached to the house reads, "Hedgehogs were often kept in country kitchens to keep down the black beetles. Town kitchens just had black beetles."

Dolls' houses record the evolution of common domestic objects: for instance, the different types of brooms in early dolls' houses, the carpet sweeper in the twenties, and now miniature vacuum cleaners; or the victrola, the gramophone, and now the stereo. In a large collection of dolls' houses, one may be able to trace the changes in, say, methods of lighting or heating over a period of two hundred years.

I can more easily absorb and understand the decorative style and way of life when I look at an 1830 dolls' house than if I were to walk through an actual 1830 house. I can stand still, and let my eyes wander back and forth from room to room, and see the whole picture complete, from the servants below stairs, to the ladies in the drawing room sitting behind long-poled fire screens protecting their delicate complexions from the blaze of the open fire.

An old dolls' house with its original dolls and furniture is a treasure. When I look at it I am not only getting a history lesson, I am learning about the person who created the house.

It is important to put your own taste and feelings into the arrangement and furnishing of a dolls' house, so that it reflects you, and is perhaps a submerged autobiography. (The kitchen in my house should have a minute diet sheet taped to the refrigerator door.) Two of my favorite dolls' houses do reflect their creators and are one-of-a-kind. They are Faith Bradford's house, which is on exhibition in the Smithsonian Institution in Washington, D.C., and Carrie Stettheimer's house, which is in the Museum of the City of New York. As both these houses are not very old, and their histories are well known, you can be sure that their creators are responsible for most of the design and decoration.

Faith Bradford's dolls' house is architecturally of no interest; it looks like bookshelves which have been partitioned with vertical pieces of wood to make rooms. An illusion of depth is given by a hallway which runs the entire length of each floor and can be seen through the doorways. But all Miss Bradford's thought has gone into the dolls and the decoration and furnishing of the rooms. She began with a small collection which was given to her when she was a child, and over the years she added to it until it reached its present size.

Including attics, there are twenty-three rooms on five floors. There are fourteen members of the family in residence—mother, father, ten children (two sets of twins), and visiting grandparents. They are cared for by five devoted servants. There is a menagerie of dogs, cats, goldfish, and a canary in a cage.

Despite its size the house is cozy. It reflects a rather smug respectability, and offers an idealized picture of upper-middle-class Edwardian life. It is a well-regulated house; meals are always on time, the servants know their place, the children are all in bed by seven, and the father is shown his due respect. It is a very lived-in house, though never untidy. Care and attention have been given to detail, and consideration has been shown for the comfort of the inhabitants. The old-fashioned telephone has pad and pencil next to it for messages. In the night nursery a little stool is provided to make it easier for the smaller children to climb into the rather high beds. There is a toilet bag on the chair in the guest bathroom, which adjoins the guest room where the grandparents are temporary occupants. Miss Bradford's book, *The Dolls' House*, is well worth reading. It has many photographs, and the author tells you about each member of the family and staff—not just what they look like but their characters, too. And of course every room and its furnishings are described.

In contrast to the mundane respectability of the Bradford house, Carrie Stettheimer's dolls' house is glamorous, with its elevator that actually works and a terrace that looks like a set for a Fred Astaire–Ginger Rogers' movie. The house exhibits her original taste in color and interior decoration and even suggests the kind of life she led. It is the only dolls' house I have seen which could be called a work of art in the traditional sense, like a painting or a sculpture. This is not surprising, as the Stettheimer family was very much part of the 1920s intellectual life in New York. Carrie Stettheimer was surrounded by friends who were painters, sculptors, writers, musicians. One sister was a painter and the other wrote novels. The twelve-room dolls' house (built by a local carpenter under her supervision) was Carrie Stettheimer's form of creative expression. She spent years planning and decorating the rooms. She must have had an overall image of how the entire house would look when it was finished, but I think as she worked on each room it became a single unit and the focus of her artistic attention.

Although Miss Stettheimer sewed curtains, constructed lampshades, and put up shelves in her dolls' house, she made none of the furniture, which is mostly contemporary commercial dolls' house furniture. But she left nothing in its original state. She painted and gilded and glued and altered a piece until it was just right to fit her decorative plan. Each room is like an experiment in color and offbeat interior decoration. The experiments are nearly always successful.

When I look closely at Carrie Stettheimer's dolls' house, I feel I am getting messages about some aspects of her character. Studying the Noah's Ark collage frieze she made to go around the nursery walls, I discover she had humor. Amongst the procession of animals lined up waiting to board the ark—pigs, elephants, horses, snails, et cetera—there are people dressed in 1920s costumes: A man in a raincoat, cap, and galoshes holding an umbrella. Several fashionable women in fancy hats and dresses (one with a lapdog under her arm). Over their heads the women hold what are more like parasols than umbrellas. Waiting behind a pig is a woman in a striped swimsuit, in a fashion model's pose.

Looking at the nursery wallpaper, one can guess that Miss Stettheimer was painstakingly patient when she wanted to get a particular decorative effect. She cut tiny diamond and triangle shapes from pieces of colored paper and then stuck each piece onto a white background, making an all-over pattern. When she found a motif that she liked, she became quite compulsive. There is a short staircase on one side of the house that runs from the first-floor landing to the second-floor landing, which are utility areas. The paint work is off-white (was it once white?), and Miss Stettheimer has painted a floral frieze that is reminiscent of a crewel-work embroidery pattern along the top of the walls. The same flowers appear round the door frames, on the telephone, the wringer, the lampshade, and brushes and dustpans. There is a laundry basket full of linen, and the same

floral motif has been repeated on the borders of the towels. It's even on the doorknob.

Miss Stettheimer never quite finished her dolls' house, nor did she make the dolls she had planned to have as tenants. It is interesting to speculate about what the dolls would have looked like. Would she have made them from scratch? Or—which I think is more likely—would she have bought ordinary dolls and transformed them with paints and fabrics and magic? (A year or two ago, John Noble made charming character dolls for the Stettheimer dolls' house, depicting the Stettheimer family, their friends, and domestic staff.)

If you wanted quickly to describe Mrs. James Ward Thorne's famous miniature rooms to someone who had never seen them, you could say that they are scaled down to one inch to the foot, perfect examples of room settings, designed to show the changes in furniture and interior decoration over a period of nearly four hundred years. (And there you have a too brief and perhaps slightly unfair description of the Thorne rooms.)

When you look at the Bradford and the Stettheimer dolls' houses, and then at the Thorne rooms, you can clearly see the difference between dolls' house furniture and miniatures. This is made especially clear in photographs. When you see pictures of the Thorne rooms, you will find not a single gaffe or inconsistency which would make you think that they were anything other than normal-sized rooms. (Why is it that though the Thorne rooms look real, I can't imagine anyone living in them?) A dolls' house is a plaything; miniatures are to be looked at and admired—but please do not touch. Familiar as I am with the Thorne miniature rooms (which can be seen at the Chicago Art Institute and the Phoenix Art Museum), little of their creator comes through to me. Only, perhaps, that she knew the history of interiors and furniture thoroughly, that she was a perfectionist, and that she could afford to employ superb craftsmen. For years, I have looked at and even admired the room settings, but they have left me cold.

Recently I learned something about the real Mrs. Thorne. When, after years of study and work, she had completed her rooms, she was tired of them. They were finished and she wanted to forget about them and play. For her, playing meant setting up a workshop in the dilapidated basement of the Women's Exchange in Chicago. There she spent most of her time making miniature scenes in shadowboxes. These are small boxes with glassed-in fronts; the effect is of a small stage set. The shadowboxes Mrs. Thorne made were either sold at the Women's Exchange (the proceeds going to charity) or given to her family as presents. Mrs. Thorne used ordinary inexpensive dolls' house furniture for her shadowboxes (sometimes even plastic pieces), which she usually altered in some way to fit her decorating schemes. She also improvised to make things, using jar tops, jewelry findings, and bits of embossed gold paper.

For a granddaughter who shared Mrs. Thorne's love of mice, she made a series of little shadowbox rooms inhabited by humanized toy mice. Mrs. Thorne had never been content with the kind of life a woman in her social and economic class was supposed to lead. She hated ladies' lunches, canasta and bridge parties, gossiping at the beauty parlor. She loved the company of men, and envied their freedom, and always thought they had more fun than women. If Mrs. Thorne had been a young woman today she would probably have had a career as an architect or interior designer. Her little mouse rooms are a comment on her feelings about life.

Among the collections I've seen, there is an architect's office. Two mice, dressed only in stiff, white collars, black ties, and boaters, sit at a table which is littered with blueprints, a packet of Old Gold cigarettes, filled ashtrays, a container full of pencils and paintbrushes, and a bottle of whisky. One mouse is studying blueprints—a book called *Build It Yourself* at his side. The other mouse is checking a list of figures and has a pencil behind his ear. Through the window is a cityscape, as seen from perhaps the twentieth floor.

Four gambling mice in top hats are the characters in another shadowbox. Their umbrellas and scarves are hanging on a coat rack. They sit at a square table (a cheap plastic dolls' house table, the top of which has been covered in green felt) holding their little playing cards and drinking beer from glass mugs. A lamp shines directly over the table, where you can see other possibilities for money to change paws—dice and a roulette wheel. Placed between sports trophies, on the sideboard, are the refreshments—hot dogs, pork and beans, a loaf of bread. Little round pictures of golfers (actually buttons) hang on a wall. A "masculine" room, where men are having fun.

In contrast, all the room scenes that contain lady mice are super-feminine and rather frivolous. (I noticed that the sexes are segregated; there is a woman's world and a man's world.) In one room there are four overdressed lady mice in silly hats. They are turned toward each other chattering, rather than concentrating on their cards as they play bridge. On a little round table (made from a jar top on a pedestal) is a teapot and cups and some kind of sugary confection. The bridge players are being watched by a rigid plastic poodle with a big pink bow on its head.

In another shadowbox room a delicate-looking mouse in a lace-trimmed nighty is propped up in bed by pillows and is having breakfast off a tray. The morning newspaper is also on the bed (I'm sure turned to the society page), and the radio is within reach on the bedside table. A lady of leisure!

I compared the Thorne rooms that were on display in museums with the toy-mice-inhabited rooms; this helped me to decide how I wanted my small rooms to look. I wanted the rooms to appear comfortable and "lived-in" and not like museum pieces. The children's room has drawings and a crayon lying on the floor; the toy xylophone has not been put away in the toy chest. In the living room a fire burns in the grate, and if a member of the doll family should feel hungry, there is always fresh fruit in the bowl on the coffee table. The mother doll has left her hat on top of the blanket chest in the bedroom; the father always hangs his bathrobe on a hook on the bathroom door after he has had his morning shower. On top of the stove, in the kitchen, water boils in the kettle and stew is simmering in the pot. And the kitchen table is set for the evening meal.

*   *   *

In this book my subject is how to make dolls' house furniture and decorate rooms—not how to construct dolls' houses. I have found that most people like to collect and make dolls' house furniture in one-inch-to-the-foot scale; therefore, this is the size I have made my patterns. But they can be reduced or enlarged, should you prefer another size. (See the section on pattern reducing and enlarging on page 28.)

Sometimes it is effective to mix various scales of furniture, rather than keeping it all uniform. I have often seen this mixing done successfully with care and humor. One example is at the Bethnal Green Museum in London; it is Dingley Hall, built in 1874 for two schoolboys, Laurence and Isaac Currie. In the kitchen two maids are standing on chairs alarmed by a rat in the corner of the room. (This might be a bit of whimsy on the part of the curator.) But more significant, the dresser is so large compared to the rest of the furniture that the maids, once they get down from their chairs, will have to use a stepladder if they want to reach a cup or plate. Yet the dresser does not look out of place.

Mrs. Strauss's dolls' house, also in the Bethnal Green Museum, has held my attention for hours. The house was built and furnished at the beginning of this century, but many pieces were added to it well into the 1930s. The rooms seem unrelated to each other, yet it doesn't matter; the house has a strange attraction and you feel that one person has put it all together, guided by a private fantasy. The dining room is wood-paneled, dark and heavy. The dining table is covered by a dark-red plush tablecloth. The room is oppressive. In contrast, the drawing room is airy and decorated in pastel shades, has

[*Above*]
"*Scale.*" The more we look at a room in a dolls' house, the more everything seems life-size. The lemon, shell, crayon, and reel of thread remind us how small the dolls and furniture really are. Compare the lemon in the fruit bowl with the real lemon.

[*Below*]
The Bead family portrait. John, the father, and William, the son, have painted seed beads glued to their heads for hair. The mother doll, Sarah, has a painted wooden-bead bun. Jenny, the daughter, has ponytails made from seed and bugle beads. For instructions for making the dolls and furniture in every room pictured, consult the Index.

The bedroom. The "rail-fence" patchwork quilt consists of ninety-six 1-inch by ¼-inch pieces of fabric stitched together by hand. The quilt can be made in one or two days, whereas a life-size quilt would take many months to make. The rug in the foreground is made from braided strips cut from old stockings and tights. The wallpaper is specially designed and printed for dolls' houses. (See the Appendix, page 215, for dealers who stock small-scaled wallpapers.)

A corner of the bedroom. The sewing table has a lift-out tray for lace, buttons, and thread. Underneath the tray is a bag for balls of yarn. The perfume bottles on the chest of drawers are made from glass beads—the bottle tops from metallic beads held in place with pins and glue. The bed is made from brass tubing (the kind used in model-ship building) and brass beads. For detailed instructions on how to make the bed see page 74.

The kitchen. The handles on the oven door and the front of the broiler are made from pull-openers from the tops of beer cans. The burners on the top of the stove are large snaps. The fact that round toothpicks taper at each end makes them particularly useful as the spindles for the rocking chair. The floor is laid with glass tiles which are usually used for mosaic table tops. The wallpaper is a potato-block print (for instructions, see page 173).

A corner of the kitchen. The kettle on the stove is made from half an egg-shaped plastic container painted silver. The handle is plastic-covered electrical wire, and the spout is made from pieces of dowel and a tiny black bead. Real dried flowers "grow" in the toothpaste-cap flowerpot on top of the dresser. The salad bowls on the dresser shelves are varnished wooden buttons. And the salad tossers are made from flat toothpicks, stained brown to match the salad bowls.

The children's room. The two toy soldiers, one on the toy chest and the other on the floor, are adapted from birthday candle holders. The soldiers' hats are made from dowels, and their toothpick arms are painted and glued to the sides of the holders. The wallpaper is a stencil print. (For instruction on stencil printing, see page 174.) Two of the motifs from the woven braid molding were used for the wallpaper design. Notice that the same motifs are repeated on the border of the paper floor covering.

A corner of the children's room. With a fine-nibbed pen, Hanna McElroy (then seven years old) drew the pictures on the wall and the two lying on the floor. The crayon is "fake"—it is made from the top of a round toothpick. The letters glued to the frame of the blackboard came from a box of alphabet pasta. The piggy bank on top of the bookcase is molded from a special bread dough. (See page 144 for the dough recipe.)

pretty furniture, and looks lived-in and comfortable. To one side of the room, there is a crystal-beaded curtain, through which you can see a conservatory where plants are growing. The kitchen dominates the house; in height and length it is twice as large as any other room. The furniture is also proportionally large, and a giant cook (at least eight inches tall) is preparing food at the kitchen table.

The rooms I have made for this book have three walls and a floor, rather like the construction of the so-called Nuremberg kitchens, which were popular in the eighteenth century in Germany. These were single rooms, designed to be instructional toys. Every pan, pot, and utensil then in use was shown in miniature, for the housewife to instruct her little daughter on how to equip a large kitchen and how each object should be used.

In my rooms I have imagined a family living in the 1970s, and how they might have acquired their furniture. The bunk beds and other nursery furniture have been bought new, except for the cupboard and bookshelves, which the father and mother have made and painted. The bathroom fittings, the refrigerator, kitchen sink, and stove came with the house. The small, round tilt-top table and ladder-back chair are inherited family heirlooms. The standard lamp in the living room was a wedding present from an aunt, which the father has never liked but the mother insists on keeping. The brass bed was found very tarnished in the corner of a country junk store, and after hours of polishing has reached its present splendor. The quilt was made by the mother, who is fond of sewing and making things. And so on, very much in the way most of us get our furniture nowadays, which is not by going to the nearest department store and buying a houseful of furniture.

The section on matchbox and paper furniture is meant for children over eight and adults who feel they do not wish to start with the wooden furniture until they have tried something simpler. This kind of dolls' house furniture is much less time-consuming, and can be made on the corner of a kitchen table. But for the wooden furniture, you should try to have your own work area and table, however small, that can be left permanently as it is, so that you can return to half-finished projects, finding everything just as you left it.

The A-to-Z of Dolls' House Furnishings has a mixture of very simple and more difficult things to make. I have often thought that I was the sole author of a particularly brilliant idea—like making empty gelatin capsules into wine glasses—only to find that a friend had been using them for that purpose for years. People who make dolls' house furnishings are ingenious at adaptation. I hope,

even if you are familiar with some of my ideas, you will find many that are new to you.

I have always made things—crocheted pillows, cloth dolls, dough-bake Christmas tree ornaments. But until I started making the furniture for this book, I had never done any carving or carpentry. This is meant as encouragement. All you need is patience and what is called "being good with your hands"—and you can make everything for a fully furnished dolls' house yourself.

The pleasure and enjoyment I get out of first making, and then having, the finished piece of dolls' house furniture is enormous. I find the work totally absorbing, and when I am asked how long a certain piece of furniture took to make, I cannot answer, because I've been so engrossed that I've lost all sense of time.

I have discovered that making doll's house furniture is even more enjoyable than collecting it. And now that antique dolls' house furniture is not only hard to find but expensive, making your own is more economical. A friend of mine started making a dolls' house for his daughter when she was only two months old—which makes me think that he was just waiting for an excuse to make himself a dolls' house. "Look at all the dolls' house furniture Mr. Adams has made for Amy!" a neighbor said to me. One wonders, was it to give Amy pleasure? Yes, but only partly.

You can make a beautiful, tiny chair, when perhaps you cannot afford its larger counterpart; and no child is going to bounce up and down on it and break the springs. The rooms of a dolls' house can be redecorated and changed at whim, without the expense and inconvenience of redoing one of your own large rooms.

The furniture and dolls I have made for this book are meant to be just a beginning, to show how to go about making patterns and constructing pieces. My hope is that after having made some of the furniture, you will be eager to start making your own patterns and designs.

* * *

At the back of the book you will find an Appendix, which I've divided into two sections. The first section is a list of recommended books and magazines. This includes books on the history of dolls' houses, craft books, and some booklets devoted to the description (with many photographs) of a particular dolls' house. The second section gives the names and addresses of mail-order dealers who supply some of the special materials needed in making dolls' house furniture. Many of the tools and supplies I discuss in the first chapter can be bought at your local hardware, hobby, and art supply stores.

Tools and Supplies

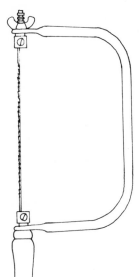

Everything you need—from knives to glue to types of wood—
precisely described, with brand names where useful.

Tools

I made a third of the wooden furniture illustrated in this book with an X-acto knife, a steel ruler, a coping saw, sandpaper, and glue. I must admit that when I bought a small jig saw it changed my life; but the only use I have found for my screwdriver is to pry open a can of varnish or shellac. Let me stress that I am not suggesting that you should buy all or even most of the tools and materials I describe—for the cost would be enormous. I think it is best to purchase supplies as you find you need them. And with that understanding I offer the following list of tools I have acquired over a period of time and have found useful. (When I mention a brand name, I do not do so because of any affiliation with the company, but because I have found the product superior, and therefore wish to recommend it.)

• *X-acto knives:*
  Blade no. 11 (which fits in handle no. 1): Use for fine cutting, trimming, angle cutting, scoring and cutting thin sheets of balsa wood.
  Blade no. 22 (which fits in handle no. 2): Use for long cuts and general shaping and whittling.
  Razor sawblade no. 035 (which fits in handle no. 5): Use for delicate sawing and cross cutting wood in a miter box.
  Keyhole sawblade no. 15 (which fits in handle No. 5): Use for small interior cuts.
  Chisel gouge A-3/16-inch (which fits in handle no. 5): Use for leveling sunken ground work in a carved object.
  V-shaped gouge C-3/16-inch (which fits in handle no. 5): Use for cutting grooves.

U-shaped gouge E-3/8-inch (which fits in handle no. 5): Use for general "gouging-out" purposes in carving. Use these three gouges also for potato cuts (see potato-cut printing on page 173).
• *Coping saw/jeweler's frame saw:* Use for making extremely fine cuts and for cutting curves. Use fine jeweler's blades in the saw.
• *Jig saw:* Dremel's Moto-shop model 57-2, series no. 3. This saw cuts wood and metal. Accessories are available such as a disc sander, which can be attached to an extension on the motor housing. Use fine-tooth blades no. 8029 for the saw.
• *Pin vise/hand drill:*
  An indispensable tool. Using a pin vise, you can drill holes smaller than the circumference of a pin. The drill operates by turning (or, more precisely, twiddling) the shank between the thumb and index finger. The pin vise chuck can be removed from its shank and then be fitted into the chuck on a power drill.
  Fine drill bits for use with a pin vise: Use an assortment, from the finest no. 80 to no. 45, which drills holes about 1/16 inch in diameter.
• *Power drill:* Preferably a model with a variable speed.
• *L-shaped square:* Use to check right angles, and to make sure a piece of furniture is squared.
• *Scissors:*
  Paper-cutting scissors.
  Fabric-cutting scissors.
  Small embroidery scissors.
• *Rulers:*
  6-inch steel ruler.
  12-inch steel ruler.
• *Compass*

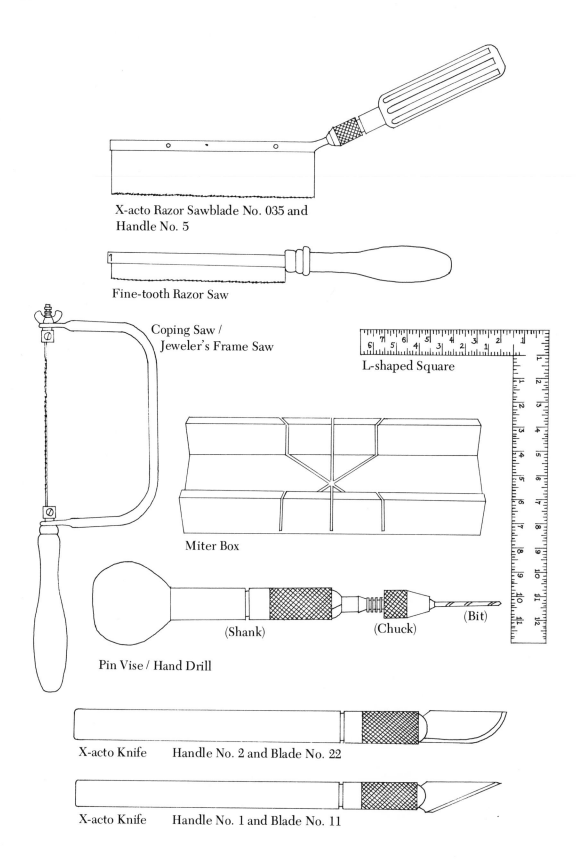

X-acto Razor Sawblade No. 035 and
Handle No. 5

Fine-tooth Razor Saw

Coping Saw /
Jeweler's Frame Saw

L-shaped Square

Miter Box

(Shank)   (Chuck)   (Bit)

Pin Vise / Hand Drill

X-acto Knife   Handle No. 2 and Blade No. 22

X-acto Knife   Handle No. 1 and Blade No. 11

- *Table vise:* Stanley's 700 model, which screws onto a work table with a clamp.
- *Tweezers*
- *Pliers:*
  X-acto's Long-nose no. 1509C.
  X-acto's Snipe-nose no. 1507C.
  X-acto's Long-nose, side cutting no. 1504C.
- *Jeweler's snip:* Use for cutting metal and wire.
- *Paper punch*
- *Needle files:* X-acto's Swiss Needle File Set no. 361C has a useful assortment of six different styles of small files, plus a handle.
- *Miter box:* A box open at the ends, with sides slotted to guide a saw in cutting miter joints (see illustration on page 22).
- *Clamps:*
  One or two small C-clamps.
  Clothespins.
  Rubber bands.
- *Awl:* I use a darning needle as an awl.

Supplies

With each project I specify all the materials which will be needed. This general list includes most of the supplies I have used throughout the book:

- *Wood:* Most lumber yards do not carry lengths of wood in thicknesses suitable for making dolls' house furniture. In the Appendix (page 216) I give a list of mail-order dealers who supply a variety of types of wood (from 1/32-inch-thick to 1/4-inch-thick and up).
- *Balsa wood:* Art and hobby supply stores usually carry balsa sheets (from 1/32-inch thick), balsa blocks, and balsa strips.
- *Wood dowel:* An assortment of thicknesses. The narrowest dowel I have found is 1/8 inch.
- *Toothpicks:* Both round and flat.
- *Wooden matches:* All sizes.
- *Sandpaper:* An assortment of fine and medium grades.
- *Emery boards:* Use for sanding.
- *Glue:*
  White glue such as Elmer's Glue-All.
  Quick-drying epoxy glue.
  Fabric glue such as Jiffy-Sew or Magic Mender.
  For gluing large areas of paper—wallpaper, for example—use wallpaper paste or bookbinder's glue.
- *Foam rubber*
- *Cotton*
- *Wood stains:* I do not use commercial wood stains for

dolls' house furniture, as I find them too intense and heavy. Instead I use a range of browns and ochres in concentrated (liquid) watercolors, and mix my own colors. Luma (Steig Products) has a good range of colors. (See the Wood Finishing section on page 32.)
- *Shellac:* White or orange depending on your preference.
- *Denatured alcohol:* Use to thin shellac.
- *Butcher's wax:* Use as a final finish for wood.
- *Artist's paintbrushes:*
  An assortment of good-quality sable brushes, from very fine to medium thicknesses.
  Cheaper brushes for applying shellac.
- *Gesso:* A ground or undercoat for paints. As a ground for acrylic paints use Liquitex's "ready-to-use" gesso.
- *Paints:*
  An assortment of colors of acrylic paints in tubes.
  An assortment of colors of Luma's concentrated (liquid) watercolors. (The watercolors come in bottles with dropper-type screw caps.)
  Gold and silver concentrated watercolors in jars.
- *Finish for acrylic paints:* Use Liquitex's gloss polymer medium as a final gloss varnish for acrylic paints. Can be diluted with water and dries quickly. There is also a matte medium.
- *Paper*
  One-ply and two-ply drawing paper.
  Thin card.
  (Throughout the book I use the word "card" as a general name for two-ply or four-ply white cardboard—e.g., Mill Blank, Oaktag, or Railroad Board.)
- *Tracing paper*
- *Graph paper*
- *Pencils:* An assortment of drawing pencils including 2B, HB, and H. (The degree of lead hardness is stamped on each pencil in a standard code. Degrees range from 7B, which is very soft, to 9H, which is extremely hard.)
- *Felt-nibbed markers*
- *Small hinges and nails:* See Appendix for mail-order dealers.
- *Brass tubing:* Various sizes of brass tubing can be bought at hobby stores that supply parts for model-ship building.
- *A 6-inch-square slab of marble:* I find this a marvelous surface to work on when cutting and trimming small pieces of wood

Found Objects

When you become interested in making dolls' house furniture, you begin to notice with a special eye every ordinary object. I now buy toothpaste not for its fluoride content, but for the shape of its cap. I have lunged across the table at a dinner party, crying out, "Don't do that!" as my now alarmed host was about to crumple the thin strip of lead which had been wrapped around a wine-bottle cork.

Conservation, recycling, and concern about ecology have led to some ingenious adaptations—for example, miniature toilets made out of the top parts of plastic fabric softener bottles and lampshades from detergent bottle caps. When the original object is still recognizable in the adaptation, then the illusion is destroyed. Therefore, if a toothpaste cap is used for a flowerpot, it should be painted and disguised so that when people look at it they see flowerpot and not toothpaste cap.

If you are a hoarder, as I am, and hate to throw anything away, now is the time when indiscriminate hoarding pays off. The following is a partial list of things to consider collecting:

Scraps of colored paper
Buttons—every shape and size
Snaps
Hooks and eyes
Beads—wooden, glass, pearl, etc.
Fabrics with small prints
Pieces of lace
Straight pins
Bead-headed pins
Push pins
Thumbtacks
Map pins
Wooden spools
Matchboxes
Scraps of embossed gold paper
Gift wrapping paper with small prints

Jewelry findings (These are the parts that are used in making jewelry, e.g., jump-rings—the connecting links that can be opened and closed to connect parts together; bell-caps—decorative metal caps for beads which have holes for stringing.)
Bottle caps
Stiff plastic wrappings
Dried-out retractable ball-point pens (Some of them when taken apart are full of useful bits, including a brass tube and a small spring.)
Clear plastic tubes (Some ball-point and felt-nibbed pen refills come packaged in narrow tubes.)
Embroidery threads
Ribbons
Odd earrings
Brooch and ring frames
Wine-bottle corks
Pieces of Styrofoam
Small plastic boxes
Small egg-shaped plastic containers that hold favors (I mean the kind that come out of vending machines and may contain a one-cent sparkling ring. My daughter is delighted to spend twenty-five cents for one of these. But I have used the containers so often that I feel as if I am getting my money's worth.)
Lengths of thin wire
Feathers
Odd leather gloves
Cigar boxes
Small lamp finials
Paper clips
Christmas cards

I have found it useful to divide my hoard of objects into categories, and to store them in various containers, such as shoe boxes, cigar boxes, and units that contain many small clear plastic drawers. I put identifying labels on the various containers, but this does not always guarantee that I will find lace in the box marked "lace."

Techniques

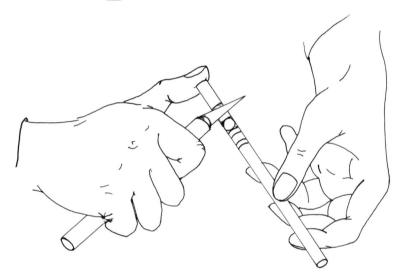

How to use the patterns. Tips on
miniature carpentry and upholstering.
Easy ways to apply a finish: stain, paint, varnish, shellac.

I am going to explain some of the techniques I have used in this book for which instructions are not readily available. (Instructions for basic skills such as knitting, crocheting, and needlepoint are easy to find in many books and women's magazines.)

Tracing and transferring patterns, enlarging and reducing patterns, drawer construction, and covering a cushion require only a simple step-by-step procedure; these techniques need no special skill, and usually turn out successfully at a first attempt. Whittling, cutting and joining, and furniture finishing are more difficult. I learned these techniques with practice, hours of trial and many errors. But don't be discouraged. After two or three attempts, the near-perfect chair leg you succeed in whittling will give you so much satisfaction you will forget the failures.

The method I use to trace and transfer patterns I learned at art school, where I studied textile designing. I still have the knife with a bone handle that I used, then, for what we called "rubbing down," when we wanted to transfer a design from tracing paper to cartridge paper.

Tracing and Transferring Patterns

1. Place a piece of tracing paper over the pattern page in the book. Hold the tracing paper in place with several strips of tape.

2. Using a sharp HB pencil, draw the patterns. Use a ruler for the straight lines.

3. Write on each of your drawn pattern pieces the name of the piece—e.g., end; the number of pieces to be cut from one pattern piece—e.g., Cut 2; and, referring to the text, the thickness of the wood—e.g., 1/8 inch.

4. Considering the grain of the wood, decide on the best layout for the patterns on the wood.

5. Reverse the tracing paper, and place it on the wood, with the penciled side *down*. Fix the tracing to the wood with strips of tape. (You may wish to cut some of the patterns from the large tracing, to make them easier to handle when transferring them to the wood. But allow for a margin around the drawn lines.)

6. As an extra aid, besides the tape, hold the tracing paper down firmly. Then, using the blunt side of a regular knife held at a slight angle, rub the surface of the back of the tracing paper. Rubbing on the back of the pencil lines will transfer the lines to the wood. With this method, a tracing can be transferred up to six times before the pencil marks become too faint. Therefore, if three identical drawer fronts are needed for a chest, just draw one. Tape and hold the drawer-front tracing on the piece of wood, and rub the tracing. Then move the tracing along, and rub it again. Move the tracing once more and transfer the drawer front a third time.

7. Trace and transfer patterns to paper or card in the same way.

Enlarging and Reducing Patterns

To reduce or enlarge a pattern proceed as follows (see scale chart).

1. Draw a rectangle around the pattern. Divide the rectangle into squares, and draw a grid.

2. To enlarge the pattern size, draw the *same* number of squares in a rectangle, but enlarge the size of each square. To reduce the pattern size, draw the same number of squares in a rectangle, but reduce the size of each square.

3. Draw the pattern (on the larger or smaller grid) square by square, referring to the original pattern as you draw.

If your original pattern is scaled 1 inch to 1 foot and the grid squares measure 1/4 inch, then the following chart may be helpful to enlarge or reduce your pattern.

Grid size:	*Scale will be:*
1/8'' squares	1/2'' to 1'
3/16'' squares	3/4'' to 1'
5/16'' squares	1-1/4'' to 1'
3/8'' squares	1-1/2'' to 1'
7/16'' squares	1-3/4'' to 1'
1/2'' squares	2'' to 1'

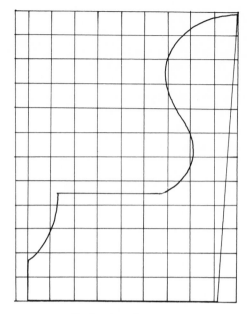

Scale: 1 Inch to 1 Foot

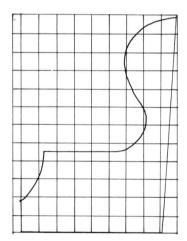

Scale: 3/4 Inch to 1 Foot

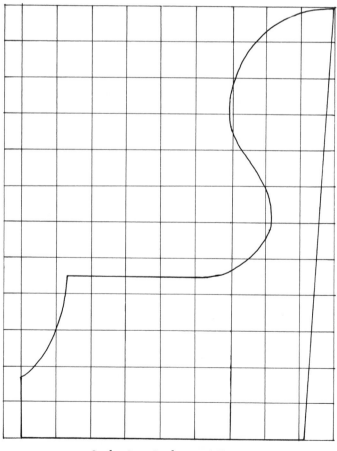

Scale: 1-1/2 Inches to 1 Foot

Whittling

Whittling is cutting small bits or paring shavings from a piece of wood. Like any other skill, it needs practice, but it is not difficult, and when you have mastered the skill, it can be fun. But don't expect to get the symmetry and perfection by whittling and hand-turning a post that you would get from making a turning on a lathe.

I will use a table leg as an example to explain my method of whittling.

1. Trace the pattern for the turning onto tracing paper, and then transfer the pattern to a length of dowel. Trace the pattern as many times as it will fit around the dowel (usually twice).

2. At each end cut the dowel an inch or two longer than the turning. This will allow for a better grip on the dowel.

3. Mark the high points on the turning, indicated by the dotted lines. These dotted lines are important as guides to retain the symmetry of each section as it is being whittled. Always carve *toward* the high points on the turning.

4. Make sure that the blade in your X-acto knife is sharp.

5. Lay the length of dowel on a flat surface. Holding the dowel with one hand, put the blade of your knife on the first line indicated by an arrow in the drawing. Put pressure on the blade, and (with the hand that is holding the dowel) roll the dowel toward you, making a cut about 1/32 inch deep on the line around the dowel. Cut the

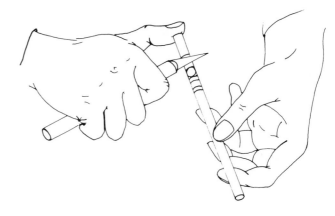

other lines around the circumference of the dowel, where the arrows indicate in the drawing.

6. Now you are ready to make the first rough cuts on the dowel. For several reasons I like the "draw" method of whittling (which means you cut *toward* your body). I find that I have more control over the knife; and with the chance of lacerating my right thumb, I gently *shave* the wood rather than making deep cuts. Take the dowel and the knife in your hands as shown in the drawing. Hold the knife as you would to peel a potato. Brace one end of the dowel against the thumb of the hand holding the knife. The other hand is the "turner," and it should hold the dowel firmly but not too tightly. Start *shaving* the wood away, cutting toward the first cut you made around the circumference of the dowel, which will act as a "brake" for your knife. As you cut, turn the dowel slowly. Continue, in this way, cutting the rough shapes of the turnings. Reverse the position of the dowel, when necessary, so that you are always cutting toward your body. When all the shapes on the turning have been cut, use an emery board and sandpaper to refine the shapes. Continue to whittle and sand, alternately, until you are satisfied with the shape of the turning. During this process, you may have to make the "brake" cuts around the circumference of the dowel deeper. Try not to cut them deeper than 1/32 inch at a time. *Note:* When applied to dolls' house furniture with its small scale, whittling should always be performed delicately and gently, with none of the vigor you might use, say, sharpening a pencil with a knife.

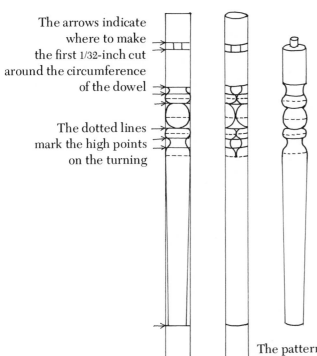

The arrows indicate where to make the first 1/32-inch cut around the circumference of the dowel

The dotted lines mark the high points on the turning

The finished turning

The Pattern

The pattern transferred to the length of dowel

Cutting and Joining

I'm only going to describe the cuts and joints I have used to make the furniture in this book (they are but a few of those used by a skilled cabinetmaker).

BEVELS
The sharp edge of the board is removed by cutting and sanding. Before cutting, make a pencil line along the top of the board where the cut will be made. For the straight bevel, cut the wood away at a 45° angle, and then sand the beveled edge smooth. For the rounded bevel, remove just a fraction of the edge with a knife, and form the curve by sanding.

DADO
A dado is a channel or flat-bottomed groove. Mark the lines that are to be cut. Using a ruler and an X-acto knife, cut along the lines to the base depth of the dado. Using a chisel blade, remove the center wood.

RABBET
A rabbet is made by cutting a rectangular strip from the edge of the board, thus forming a shoulder. Mark all the lines that are to be cut on the board, and cut the rectangle away with a sharp knife.

MORTISE AND TENON JOINTS
Two sets of mortises and tenons are illustrated. The first set is cut from dowel. Mark the lines that are to be cut on the mortise as shown in diagram A. Cut and sand the mortise to shape. (This is most easily performed in the following way: Make the cuts on the mortise; then secure the length of dowel in a table vise; using needle files, sand away the center wood.) Mark the lines that are to be cut on the tenon as shown in diagram B. Cut and sand the tenon to shape. For the other set, mark the lines to be cut on the tenon as shown in diagram C. Then cut and sand the tenon to shape. For the mortise, draw the correct-size rectangle on the top of the board. Secure the board in a table vise. Drill a hole in the center of the rectangle. Remove one end of a blade from a coping saw. Thread the free end of the blade through the hole in the board. Replace the blade in the saw, and cut the shape of the rectangle.

MITERING
A miter cut is made at an angle across the wood. In a 90° corner joint, the miter is cut at 45° on the two ends of the wood that will be joined together. Cutting miters is easier if you use a miter box (see the illustration).

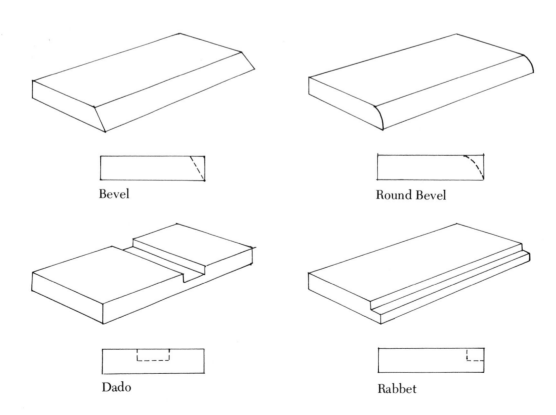

Bevel

Round Bevel

Dado

Rabbet

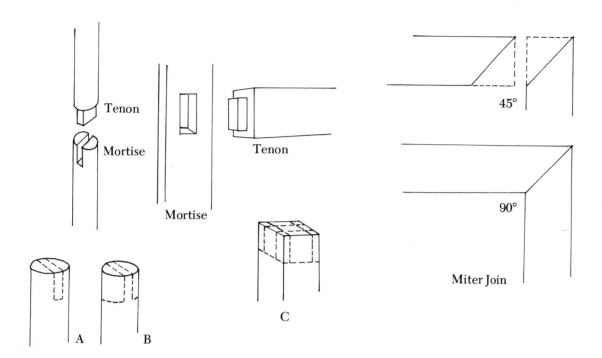

Tenon

Mortise

Mortise

Tenon

A   B

C

45°

90°

Miter Join

Basic Drawer Construction

When I made my first drawer, I copied the construction from a Victorian dolls' house chest of drawers which I have; and I have continued to make drawers in this way.

1. Cut the five sections of a drawer.
2. Glue the front to the front edge of the base.
3. Glue the sides to the top of the base.
4. Glue the back to the back edges of the sides. Note that the back is set in, and does not come parallel with the back edge of the base.
5. Cut the back corners off the base diagonally as shown in the drawing.

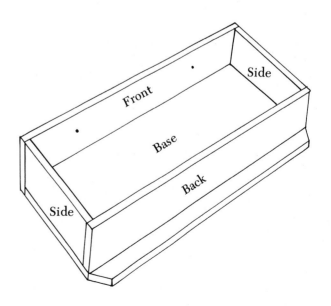

Side

Front

Base

Back

Side

Applying Furniture Finishes

After sanding, I rate the careful application of the finish second in importance. I have often seen beautifully made dolls' house furniture marred by a heavy or sticky-looking finish. Giving a professional finish takes time and patience, but it is worth the effort.

STAINS

A commercial stain, such as Minwax, which is made for staining large furniture, can be used on dolls' house furniture too. Follow the directions given on the can of stain.

I prefer not to use commercial stains as I find them too intense and difficult to control for dolls' house furniture. I use concentrated watercolors (in fact, they are transparent aniline dyes) produced by Luma or Martins, which can be bought at art supply stores. I have a selection of browns and ochres, which can be mixed together to produce colors from light oak to dark walnut. Use the following method for applying watercolor stains:

Give the piece of completed furniture a final sanding. Wipe every speck of dust from the furniture with a slightly damp cloth. Mix the stain, diluting it with water for lighter shades. Test the stain on a spare piece of wood, and let it dry so that you can judge whether the color is the correct intensity. (Stains always look darker when they are wet.) Using a medium-sized sable artist's brush, paint the stain on the piece of furniture. Do not have too much stain on the brush, and always paint in the same direction as the wood grain. Avoid streaking by not going over an area with the brush more than once. Let the stain dry, and then you can see whether a second coat is needed.

VARNISH AND SHELLAC

I usually use shellac on my furniture, but the same method of application can be used for varnish. *Note:* Thin shellac with denatured alcohol, and varnish with turpentine. Both shellac and varnish can be bought at a hardware store. Get a 3-pound-cut shellac either in white or orange, depending on your preference (orange shellac gives an "old" look to the furniture). Apply the varnish or shellac using a medium-sized brush. You may also need a small brush to get into corners. Paint with the grain, applying an even coat of varnish or shellac and trying not to go over an area more than once with the brush. Allow the finish to dry thoroughly. Sand the piece of furniture lightly with very fine grade sandpaper. Repeat the process at least two more times, always allowing the varnish or shellac to dry thoroughly between coats and sanding.

BUTCHER'S WAX

Butcher's wax is a clear paste wax for wood which can be bought at hardware stores. When applied as a final finish to furniture, it gives a satin-smooth sheen. Spread a thin, even coat of wax with a damp cloth. Allow about twenty minutes for drying, and then buff with a dry cloth.

PAINTS

I suggest that you don't use regular household paint for dolls' house furniture, because it is too dense and can be difficult to apply. Use either Flo-Paque paints or acrylic paints in a tube, such as Liquitex. For Flo-Paque use a mixture of 50 percent of their Dio-Sol thinner and 50 percent Flo-Paque Glaze as a wood sealer before painting. To cover a piece of furniture usually requires more than one coat. Sand lightly between coats, using extra-fine sandpaper. Sand after the final coat of paint, and use Crystal-Cote for a gloss finish. I use acrylic paints, and the following method for painted furniture: Apply a coat of acrylic polymer-base gesso to the piece of furniture. Gesso seals the wood and gives a good base for the paint. When the gesso is dry, sand it lightly. Then apply one or more coats of paint, sanding lightly between each coat. Finish the painted surface with a coat of gloss polymer medium (a glaze used with acrylic paints). If you prefer a matte finish, use a matte polymer medium. Take care not to use the bases or paints too thickly, or they will obscure the details in your work.

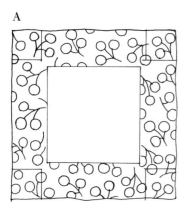

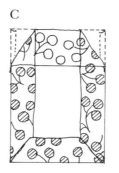
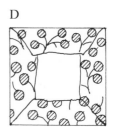

Covering a Cushion

(For the upholstered furniture in Chapter 4, "Wood and Upholstered Furniture." For a more complete list of materials needed, see directions for specific pieces.)

1. Cut the patterns of the wood, foam rubber, and fabric sections of the cushion.

2. Glue the foam rubber to the top surface of the wood, and allow it to dry.

3. Place the wood section of the cushion, foam-rubber side down, onto the fabric as shown in diagram A.

4. Fold one side of the fabric over the edge of the wood, and glue it in place. Then gently pull and fold the opposite side of the fabric over the edge and glue it in place. Cut the surplus away from the corners of the fabric (diagram B).

5. Fold the corners of the fabric at the bottom of the cushion, as you would in wrapping a parcel. Pull the fabric gently over the edge of the wood, and glue the bottom end of the fabric in place (diagram C).

6. Fold and glue the top end of the fabric in place (diagram D). The foam rubber should be compressed to about half its original thickness.

The Dolls

Step-by-step instructions (and individual patterns)
for making each doll:
Mother, Father, Sister, Brother, Baby,
and a Dolls' Doll.

One of my earliest memories (I was about seven) is of my mother bringing me a copy of the 1892 annual omnibus of *Strand Magazine* to look at when I was sick in bed. There were illustrated Sherlock Holmes stories, and pages of photographs of famous actors and actresses, oval-shaped pictures of Ellen Terry at nineteen, twenty-five, thirty-four, and "present-day." But as I looked through the book over and over again, the pages I couldn't wait to get to were the photographs and descriptions of Queen Victoria's dolls.

Written when Queen Victoria was an old lady, the article showed a selection of the more than 130 dolls that had been preserved in good condition. Queen Victoria's favorites (and now mine, too) were very small wooden-peg dolls, simple and stylized, the sharp, protruding nose distinct from the hair, cheeks, eyes, mouth, which are painted on. Part of my delight was the knowledge that they were quite unlike my own two baby-sized dolls, June and July. The peg dolls were simple—but how lavishly Victoria and her governess had dressed them. For hours I studied their beautiful costumes. How I longed to handle the dolls, touch them, lift their skirts to see if they wore underwear. Queen Victoria's dolls all had names—and such grand and exotic names— Viscountess Stuart, Mlle. Leontine Heberle, the Duchess of Parma... aristocracy, opera singers, actresses, and ballet dancers.

I started making dolls long before I made dolls' house furniture. When I was a child I made cutout paper dolls; then I progressed to puppets and quite elaborately dressed cloth dolls. When I had a little girl, she was a good excuse for me to make stuffed animals. My first attempt at small toys was a large family of dressed, domesticated bears.

I had every intention of making a house for these bears, but they remained homeless. Which may not be quite so unfortunate as the opposite situation—a dolls' house without tenants. An acquaintance of mine owns a large and unique collection of dolls' house furniture and miniatures, and also has a mail-order business in contemporary dolls' house furniture. One of his customers, an old lady, would write and tell him about her collection, and would make inquiries and want to hear about his collection too. So with the placing and filling of orders for dolls' house furniture, they began a correspondence about their mutual interest. "Do tell me about the *people* in your house," the old lady asked in one of her letters. My acquaintance had no "people" in his house; but, not wanting to disappoint the old lady, he imagined whom he might have as residents. He wrote that there was a military gentleman, who lived with his housekeeper, and that they had a "love child." When no letter came for several months, my acquaintance realized that perhaps his romantic ideas had been too advanced for someone brought up in the Victorian era. Then one day a letter came asking if the "unfortunate situation" in my acquaintance's house had been resolved. He wrote back immediately: yes, the military gentleman had married his housekeeper, and she now resided as the lady of the house. The next letter included a request for a photograph of the happy family. This was when my acquaintance had dolls specially made for the house.

Dolls make a dolls' house come alive; without them the house seems a sad place. Looking at an uninhabited dolls' house in a museum, I have felt that the house itself was a museum. The grand piano is to be looked at and admired, not to be played; and the dainty tea set remains unused in the china cabinet. Here are all the comforts for a happy domestic life and no tenants to take advantage of them. I know I am supposed to *imagine* the Prince and Princess in Colleen Moore's famous Fairy Castle, but I long to *see* the Princess reclining on her golden, canopied bed (which once belonged to the Sleeping Beauty), and to *see* the Prince reading in the Royal Library.

I started this book with a family of dolls in mind, and then made the furniture to suit their needs. At first, I didn't know exactly what the dolls would look like except that they would be made from wood, and have movable joints. (The baby doll's body and limbs are made not of wood but of bound pipe cleaners, for I wanted to include a simpler method for making dolls.) As I made them, they took on their own distinctive characters. I had intended the baby doll to be a girl, but when I put a frilly bonnet on her head, it looked absurd, so despite my efforts, the baby doll insisted on being a boy.

My doll family is called the Beads, for the simple reason that two essential parts of their bodies, their heads and hair, are made from beads. They live in a suburb of a large city. John, the father, works in the art department of an advertising agency. His wife Sarah, an old-fashioned girl, is very domesticated. She loves to sew and cook. Their eldest child Jenny has a talent for music and is learning to play the piano. William (never called Bill) is a year younger than Jenny but tall for his age. He daydreams too much, draws lovely pictures, and is very serious. And Timmy, the baby, always manages to be the center of attention.

General Instructions for Wooden Jointed Dolls

All the dolls are made in the same way. The basic materials are natural-colored wooden beads for the heads, dowels for the bodies and limbs, and straight pins for hinging the joints.

Please note that the drawings with these general instructions are only diagrams. The actual patterns for each doll are exactly to scale.

Before starting to make the dolls, refer to the section on whittling (page 29).

1. Assemble the various sizes of dowel needed to make the limbs and body. In pencil, mark the dowels where they will be cut and *shaped*, and what parts they are—e.g., upper arm. Cut the pieces of dowel to size, and put them aside.

2. Select the correct-size wooden bead for the head. Glue the neck to the head. (You may need to enlarge the hole in the bead.) Fill the hole at the top of the head with plastic wood, or a paste made from sawdust and white glue. Draw the hair and features on the head. Draw a little oblong where the nose will be inserted. Very gently retrace the oblong shape, with the tip of the blade of an X-acto knife. Make a cut about 1/16 inch deep. Gouge out the wood to make a groove where the nose will be inserted.

Cut the nose from a flat toothpick and glue it into the groove. When the glue has dried, sand the nose to make it smaller or to refine the shape. Paint the hair and features using acrylic paints. Then paint the whole head and hair with a coat of gloss polymer medium. This will act as a sealer and also give the head and hair a slight shine.

3. Now work on the body section.

Retrace the pencil marks (which were made to indicate where the body was to be shaped) with the tip of an X-acto knife blade, making cuts about 1/16 inch deep. (These cuts will act like a brake for the knife and will help to retain the shape you are carving.)

Drill a hole in the center of the top of the body about 1/4 inch deep. Mark with a pencil and then cut lines to indicate the final shape of the top of the body.

Using an X-acto knife carve and whittle the body to the correct shape. Smooth the surfaces using files and sandpaper. (Do *not* make the hole which will hold the hinge for the legs yet.)

4. The next step is to make the legs.

Retrace the pencil marks on the legs with the end of the X-acto knife blade, making about 1/16-inch cuts.

On the *upper* section of the leg carve the top as shown in the diagram on page 41, and make a mortise at the bottom. (After the initial cuts, I find the easiest way to make a small mortise is by securing the dowel in a table vise, and then *filing* the dowel into shape.)

Now for the *lower* section of the leg. Whittle a little peg at the bottom and a tenon at the top.

Smooth and shape the rough surfaces with files and sandpaper.

Put the tenon inside the mortise, and make sure that it fits properly.

Please note that the holes for hinging are not centered. Always make the hole near the side where the joint will bend.

Using a pin vise, drill a hole through both the mortise and the tenon. The hole should be the right size for a pin to fit snugly.

Insert a pin, and then judge how much of the mortise and tenon you will need to round off, by sanding, so that the joints can move freely. Keep sanding, and testing by inserting the pin, until you are satisfied with the movement of the joint. Now insert the pin. Trim off the end of the pin (leaving just enough of it protruding to bend), and secure the leg sections together. Follow the same procedure for the other leg.

5. Now join the legs to the body.

Hold the legs in position on either side of the body. Then, through the three pieces of wood, make a hole for hinging. Put a pin through the hole, and see if more sanding is needed to make the joints move freely.

Trim and bend the pin at the end, and secure the legs to the body. At the ankles, pull the legs slightly out to make room for the shoes and to help balance the doll when it stands.

6. The arms are next.

Make the center arm joints in the same way as the legs, with mortises and tenons. Round off the tops of the *upper arms*.

Carve, file, and sand spoon-hands on the end of the *lower* parts of the arms. (They are called spoon-hands because in shape they look like wooden kitchen spoons.)

You may wish to practice making a hand on a spare piece of dowel, before carving one on the actual arm.

7. To attach an arm, hold it in position against the side of the body.

Make a hole through the arm and the body.

Put a small bead between the arm and the body, when inserting the hinging pin. (If the arm is flat against the side of the body, the doll is difficult to dress.) Trim the pin and bend it at the end, to secure the arm to the body.

8. Carve the shoes from small blocks of wood 1/4 inch thick. Use a dark wood like mahogany, and leave it in its natural color.

Draw the outline of the shoes on the tops of the blocks of wood.

Carve and sand them to shape.

Drill a hole in the top of each shoe, where the pegs at the bottom of the legs will fit.

Give the shoes a coat of varnish or shellac.

When the shoes are dry, glue them to the legs.

9. Make the doll's clothes, following the patterns given with each doll. If necessary, use the hem allowances, included with the patterns; but if possible use the selvage edge of the fabric and have no turned hem.

10. Do *not* glue the doll's head to the body until the clothes are completed. It is easier to fit the clothes on the doll if the head can be removed. Also it is better to determine the exact length of the neck *after* the doll is dressed. Note that the arm hinging pins are secured inside the neck hole. Therefore some of the neck dowels may have to be whittled away for the neck to fit properly.

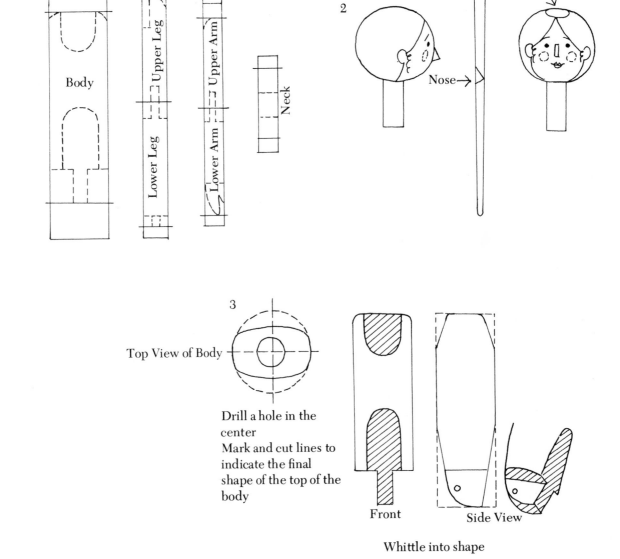

Top View of Body

Drill a hole in the center
Mark and cut lines to indicate the final shape of the top of the body

Whittle into shape

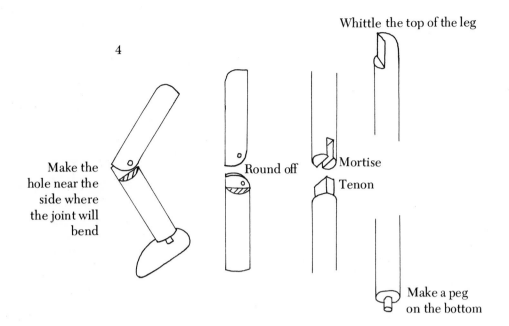

4

Make the hole near the side where the joint will bend

Round off

Whittle the top of the leg

Mortise

Tenon

Make a peg on the bottom

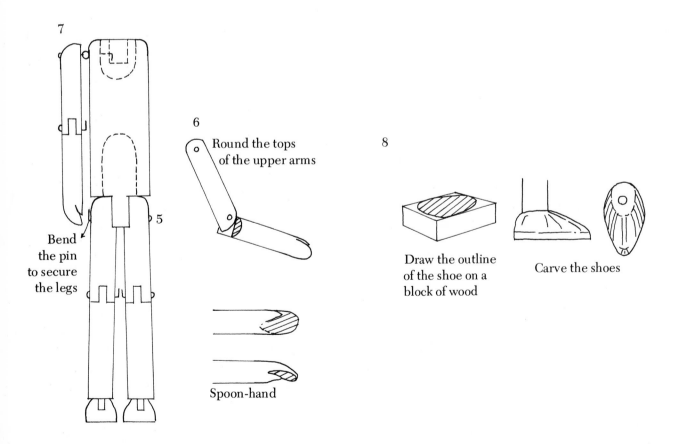

7

Bend the pin to secure the legs

5

6

Round the tops of the upper arms

Spoon-hand

8

Draw the outline of the shoe on a block of wood

Carve the shoes

Mother Doll

(Scale: 1 inch to 1 foot)

MATERIALS

    3/4-inch-diameter wooden bead for the head
    1/2-inch dowel for the body
    3/16-inch dowel for the neck and arms
    1/4-inch dowel for the legs
    1/4-inch-thick wood for feet
    A flat toothpick for the nose
    5/16-inch-diameter bead for the bun
    Seed beads for the arm joints, necklace, and shoe trim-
        mings
    Lightweight fabric for the dress
    Straight pins for the joints
    Tracing paper
    White glue
    Embroidery thread
    Acrylic paints
    Gloss polymer medium

Use the general instructions for making wooden dolls, with the following additions:

HAIR
Glue the bead bun to the head before painting the hair (A).

LEGS
Paint tights on the leg sections (a color to match the dress) *before* hinging them together.

DRESS
(The dress is put together on the doll's body.)
    1. Trace the pattern pieces (page 43) for the dress onto tracing paper, and cut them out.
    2. Pin the pattern pieces to a *double* thickness of fabric. Cut out two sleeves, the bodice back and front, and the skirt.
    3. Sew a row of running stitches along the top of the skirt and leave the thread loose. Sew the back seam of the skirt. Turn the skirt right side out. Put the skirt on the doll, and pull the thread to form gathers at the waist (B). Finish off the thread.
    4. Pin the back and front of the bodice together. Sew the side seams between the arrows, and sew the shoulder seams between the arrows. Turn the bodice right side out, and put it on the doll. Fold the bodice's seam allowances under, at the waist, armholes, and neck. Using tiny slip stitches, sew the bodice to the skirt.
    5. To make the sleeve, first sew a small row of running stitches along the top, leaving a loose thread (C). Then sew the side seam. Turn the sleeve right side out. Make a slight puff at the top of the sleeve by pulling the thread to form gathers. Finish off the thread.

    6. Attach the sleeve to the dress by tucking the seam allowance at the top of the sleeve *under* the edge of the bodice armhole. Ease and pin the sleeve into the armhole, and then sew it to the bodice with tiny slip stitches (D).
    Make the other sleeve in the same way.

SHOES
    1. Make two small bows, using embroidery thread. Sew a small bead on each bow. Glue the bows to the shoes (E).
    2. String small colored beads on a thread to make the necklace. Put the neck dowel through the necklace before gluing the neck and head to the body.
    3. Make a sash for the dress by twisting embroidery thread (using the same color as the shoe bows) into a cord, and then tying it around the waist, with a bow at the back.
    (To make a narrow cord from embroidery thread, proceed as follows. Take two or three 18-inch-long strands of thread. Wind one end of the threads several times around the pin on a thumbtack, then press the tack into a work table or drawing board to secure the ends of the threads. Hold the loose ends of the threads tautly between finger and thumb, and begin to twist the threads clockwise. Continue twisting until the threads feel tight and ready to twist back on themselves. Place the tip of a pencil in the center of the twisted threads, then loosen the tension and allow the threads to twist back from the center point, thus forming a 9-inch-long cord.)

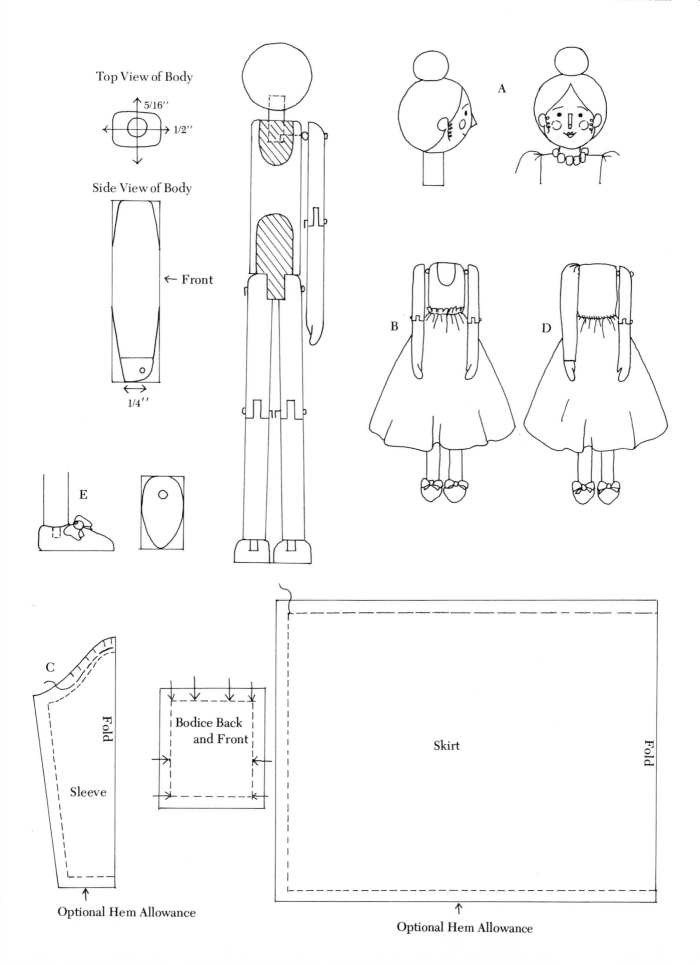

Top View of Body

5/16''

1/2''

Side View of Body

← Front

1/4''

E

A

B

D

C

Fold

Sleeve

Bodice Back
and Front

Skirt

Fold

Optional Hem Allowance

Optional Hem Allowance

Father Doll

(Scale: 1 inch to 1 foot)

MATERIALS

    3/4-inch-diameter wooden bead for the head

    5/8-inch dowel for the body

    3/16-inch dowel for the neck and arms

    1/4-inch dowel for the legs

    1/4-inch-thick dowel for the feet

    A flat toothpick for the nose and ears

    Seed beads for the hair, the cuff links, and the arm joints

    2 bugle beads for the mustache

    Lightweight fabric for the shirt

    Lightweight velvet for the pants

    Thin glove leather for the vest

    Narrow ribbon for the bow tie

    Typing paper for the collar stiffener

    Three small metallic beads or tiny brass nailheads for the vest buttons

    Straight pins for hinging

    Tracing paper

    Double-faced transparent tape

    White glue

    Fabric glue

    Acrylic paints

    Gloss polymer medium

Use the general instructions for making wooden dolls, with the following additions:

HEAD AND HAIR

1. Draw the features and the outline for the hair on the bead head.

Note: This doll has ears.

2. Make small grooves, 3/16 inch long, on each side of the head for the ears. Cut two small squares from a toothpick, and with sandpaper round off the squares to make semicircle shapes. Glue the ears in the grooves.

HAIR

1. Fill a small container, such as an eggcup, with seed beads. Evenly coat with glue the part of the head where the hair will be. Dip the glue-coated head into the container of beads to cover the hair area with a layer of beads. Glue on extra beads to make the hair a good shape and to give the effect of abundant curls (A).

2. Glue two bugle beads under the nose for the mustache. When the glue has dried, paint the hair, features, and mustache.

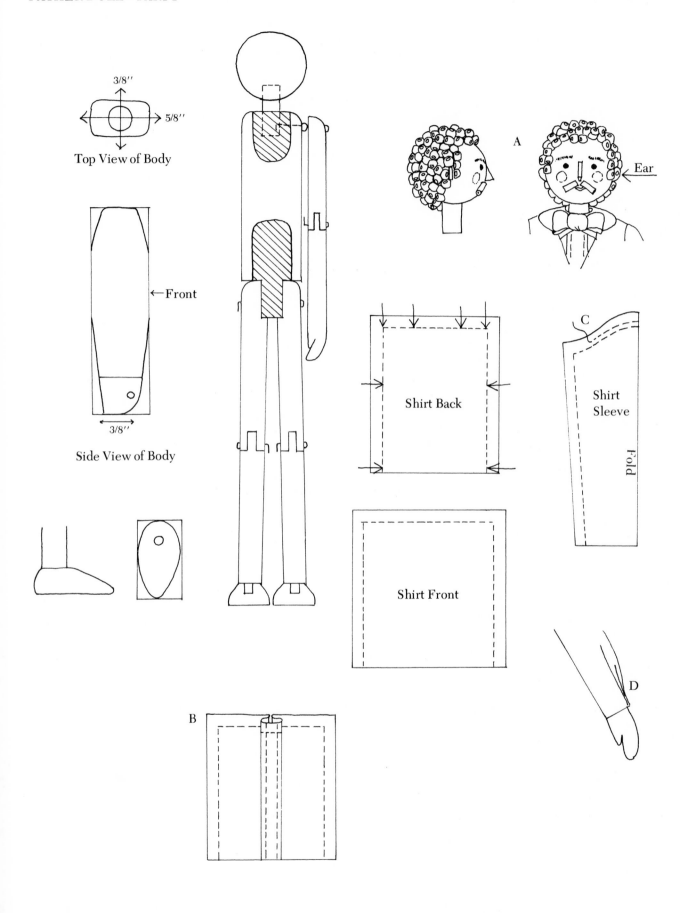

3/8''

5/8''

Top View of Body

Front

3/8''

Side View of Body

A

Ear

B

Shirt Back

Shirt Front

C

Shirt Sleeve

Fold

D

SHIRT, PANTS, AND VEST

Trace the pattern pieces onto tracing paper and cut them out.

SHIRT

1. Pin the patterns for the back and the front of the shirt on a *single* thickness of fabric, and cut them out.

2. Make a box pleat in the center front of the shirt, and back-stitch it down (B). *Note:* The back and front of the shirt should now be the same width.

3. Pin the back and front of the shirt together. Sew the side seams between the arrows, and sew the shoulder seams between the arrows. Turn the shirt right side out and put it on the doll. Tuck the seam allowance in, at the armholes and the neck.

4. Pin the sleeve pattern to a *double* thickness of fabric, and cut out two sleeves.

5. To make the sleeve, first sew a small row of running stitches along the top leaving the thread loose (C). Then sew the side seam. Turn the sleeve right side out. Slightly shape the sleeve at the top by pulling the thread. Finish off the thread.

6. Attach the sleeve to the shirt by tucking the sleeve allowance at the top *under* the edge of the shirt armhole. Ease and pin the sleeve into the armhole, and then sew it to the shirt with tiny slip stitches. Fold the fabric at the wrist into a small inverted pleat, and tack it with a couple of stitches (D).

Make the other sleeve in the same way.

PANTS

1. Pin the pattern for the pant leg to a *double* thickness of velvet. Cut out two pant legs.

2. Open up the pant legs, and sew the center seams in the back and front (E).

3. Sew the side seams of each pant leg together.

4. Turn the pant legs right side out and put them on the doll.

VEST

1. Using double-faced transparent tape to avoid making pin holes in the garment, stick the patterns for the vest onto a *double* thickness of leather. Pin the leather together making sure none of the pins goes through the pattern pieces. Cut a left and right side for the front of the vest, and a back.

2. Sew the side seams together, and sew the shoulder seams together.

3. Turn in the armhole and neck facings and the seam allowances, and stick them down with fabric glue.

4. Turn the vest right side out. Put it on the doll, slightly overlapping the left side of the front over the right side, and glue in place.

5. I made three small holes, in the front of the vest, and then glued tiny brass nailheads in the holes for buttons. If you use beads for buttons, sew them on before gluing the front of the vest in place.

COLLAR AND CUFFS

1. Pin the patterns for the collar and cuffs to a *single* thickness of fabric. Cut out the collar and two cuffs. (I used brown and white striped fabric for the shirt, and a solid brown fabric for the collar and cuffs.)

2. Trace the pattern for the collar stiffener (F) onto tracing paper. Then transfer the pattern to typing paper, and cut it out.

3. Place the paper collar on top of the fabric collar.

4. Turn the seam allowances in all around the fabric collar and glue them to the paper.

5. Attach the collar in place on the doll with a dab or two of glue.

6. Make a small ribbon bow tie. Glue it in place on top of the collar.

7. On each cuff turn in the seam allowances as shown in diagram G and press them flat. Fold the cuffs in half along the centerfold, and press them flat. Form the cuff shape and fasten the ends by attaching a couple of bead cuff links on either side of the cuff (H).

8. Slip a cuff on each of the doll's wrists.

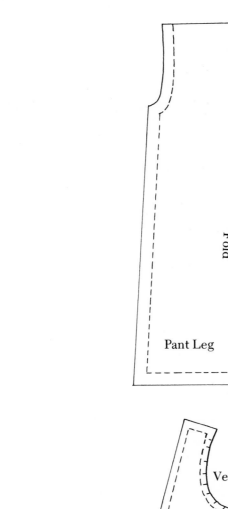

FATHER DOLL—PART II

Fold

Pant Leg

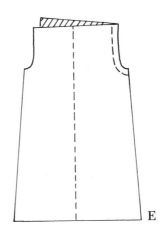

E

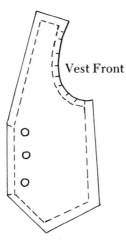

Vest Front

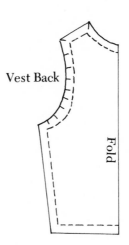

Vest Back

Fold

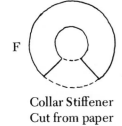

F

Collar Stiffener
Cut from paper

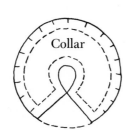

Collar

Cuff

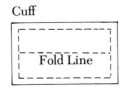

Fold Line

H

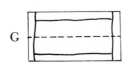

G

Girl Doll

(Scale: 1 inch to 1 foot)

MATERIALS

5/8-inch-diameter wooden bead for the head
1/2-inch dowel for the body
3/16-inch dowel for the neck and arms
1/4-inch dowel for the legs
1/4-inch-thick wood for the feet
A flat toothpick for the nose
2 seed beads for the arm joints
Seed beads and bugle beads for the hair
Straight pins for hinging
Lightweight fabric for the dress
Narrow ribbon for bows and sash
Tracing paper
White glue
Acrylic paints
Gloss polymer medium

Use the general instructions for making wooden dolls, with the following additions:

HEAD AND HAIR

1. Draw the features and hair on the head bead. Then drill a small hole through the head just above the ears (A).

2. To make a bunch of hair, string small beads on threads as shown in diagram B. Thread all four loose ends through the eye of a needle, then take them through the head and secure them with a knot (C). Follow the same procedure for the other bunch of hair.

3. Paint the hair, and make sure that the strings of beads don't stick together as they dry.

4. Make small bows from narrow ribbon and attach them on either side of the head covering the knots.

LEGS

Paint tights on the leg sections (a color to match the dress) *before* hinging them together.

DRESS

1. Trace the pattern pieces onto tracing paper and cut them out.

2. Pin the patterns to a *double* thickness of fabric. Cut two sleeves, a back, and a front. Note the 1/4-inch fold at the top of the dress and sleeves.

3. When the fabric pieces are unfolded the sleeves will look like diagram D, and the back and the front like diagram E. Join the sleeves to the back and front, along the dotted lines shown on diagrams D and E. Sew the sleeve seams, and the back and front side seams.

4. Turn the neck facing in, and sew it down with tiny running stitches leaving the end of the thread loose (later it will be pulled to form gathers). Do the same with the sleeve hems. The dress will now look like diagram F.

5. Turn the dress right side out. Fit it on the doll. Pull the threads to form gathers at the neck and wrists. Finish off the threads. (The dress can be worn loose or tied around the waist with a ribbon sash.)

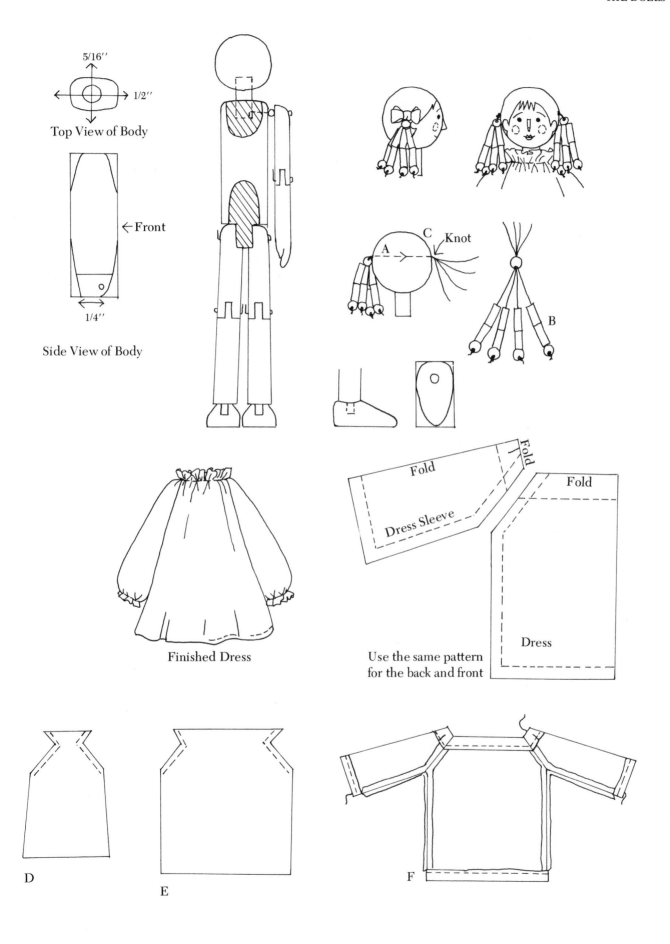

5/16″

1/2″

Top View of Body

← Front

1/4″

Side View of Body

C Knot

A →

B

Finished Dress

Fold

Fold

Fold

Dress Sleeve

Dress

Use the same pattern
for the back and front

D

E

F

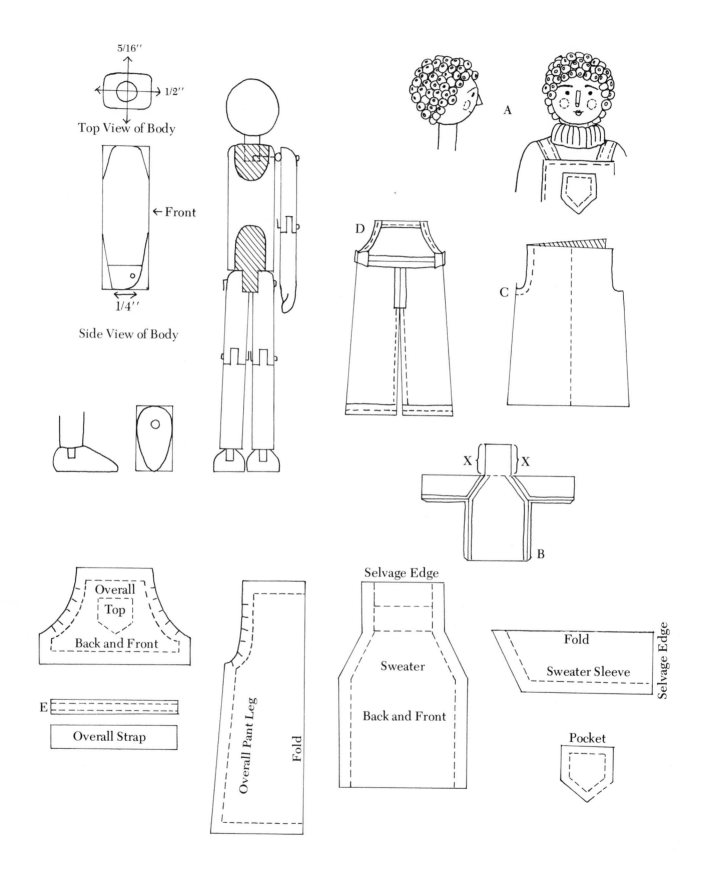

5/16″

1/2″

Top View of Body

← Front

1/4″

Side View of Body

A

D

C

X   X

B

Overall
Top

Back and Front

E

Overall Strap

Overall Pant Leg

Fold

Selvage Edge

Sweater

Back and Front

Fold

Sweater Sleeve

Selvage Edge

Pocket

Boy Doll

(Scale: 1 inch to 1 foot)

MATERIALS

 5/8-inch-diameter wooden bead for the head
 1/2-inch dowel for the body
 3/16-inch dowel for the neck and arms
 1/4-inch dowel for the legs
 1/4-inch-thick wood for the feet
 A flat toothpick for the nose
 Straight pins for hinging
 Seed beads for the hair and the arm joints
 Lightweight denim for the overalls
 An old lightweight stretch sock for the sweater
 White glue
 Tracing paper
 Acrylic paints
 Gloss polymer medium

*Use the general instructions for making wooden dolls,
with the following additions:*

HEAD AND HAIR

 1. Draw the features and the outline for the hair on
the bead head.

 2. Fill a small container, such as an eggcup, with seed
beads. Evenly coat with glue the part of the head where
the hair will be. Dip the glue-coated head into the container of beads. This will cover the hair area with a layer
of beads. Glue on extra beads to make the hair a good
shape and to give the effect of abundant curls (A).

 3. When the glue has dried, paint the hair.

SWEATER AND OVERALLS

Trace the patterns onto tracing paper and cut them out.

SWEATER

 1. Pin the patterns to a *double* thickness of stretch-
sock fabric. (Pin the cuff ends of the sleeves and the neck
parts of the sweater to the selvage edge at the top of the
sock.) Cut two sleeves and a back and front.

 2. Sew the side seams of the back and front together.
Sew the sleeve seams together. Sew the sleeves to the
sweater as shown in diagram B. Do *not* sew the neck
seams (X).

 3. Turn the sweater right side out. Sew the neck
seams together on the outside.

 4. Put the sweater on the doll, and roll down the neck
of the sweater.

OVERALLS

 1. Pin the patterns for the overall pant legs and top to
a *double* thickness of fabric. Cut two pant legs, and a
back and front for the overall top. Pin the other pattern
pieces to a *single* layer of fabric. Cut a pocket and two
straps.

 2. Open up the pant legs, and sew the center seams in
the back and front together as shown in diagram C.

 3. Sew the side seams of each leg together.

 4. Sew the side seams of the overall top together. Turn
the facings back on the armholes and top, and saddle
stitch them in place.

 5. Sew the top of the overalls to the pants (D).

 6. Turn the seam allowances back on the shoulder
straps and saddle stitch them down. Do the same with
the pocket.

 7. Turn the overalls right side out.

 8. Sew the pocket to the center of the top of the overalls.

 9. Put the overalls on the doll.

 10. Sew the straps (they are tucked inside the top)
attaching them at a slight angle.

 11. If you wish, put a little patch on one knee of the
overalls.

Baby Doll

(Scale: 1 inch to 1 foot)

MATERIALS

9/16-inch-diameter wooden bead for head
1/8-inch dowel for neck and for arms-legs support
A pipe cleaner for the arms and legs
2 small wooden beads for the hands
A flat toothpick for the nose
Old nylon stockings for binding the pipe cleaner
Lightweight stretch fabric for the jump suit and hat
Embroidery thread
Narrow ribbon for the bow
White glue
Acrylic paints
Gloss polymer medium

HEAD

Glue the bead head to the extended neck dowel. Follow the general instructions for making a wooden doll's head, except make a smaller snub nose (A).

ARMS, LEGS AND BODY

1. Drill holes through the dowel where indicated by the arrows in diagram B.
2. Cut the pipe cleaner to size and push the lengths through the holes in the dowel.
3. Glue the bead hands to the ends of the pipe cleaners (C).
4. Cut the stockings into long strips about 1/2-inch wide.
5. Bind the stocking strips around the pipe cleaners and dowel, as if you were putting on a bandage (D). Glue down any loose ends.

JUMP SUIT AND HAT

1. Trace the jump suit and hat patterns onto tracing paper and cut them out.
2. Pin the patterns to a *double* thickness of fabric. (I used lightweight stretch toweling.) Cut out the hat and *two* back and front pieces.

JUMP SUIT

1. Open up the two jump suit pieces, and stitch them together at the back center seam, as shown in diagram E.
2. Then fold the jump suit along the fold line, and stitch the arm and leg seams together. *Note:* The front center seam is left open.
3. Turn the jump suit right side out and put it on the doll.

4. To close the jump suit in the front, turn in the seam allowances and over stitch the center seam.
5. Turn in the seam allowances at the wrists and neck, and using embroidery thread (in a contrasting color to the jump suit) back-stitch them down.

HAT

1. Sew the hat together along the back seam.
2. Turn the hat right side out.
3. Turn in the front facing of the hat and back-stitch it down with embroidery thread.
4. Put the hat on the doll, tucking the seam allowance under at the neck. Secure the hat by joining it in front with a couple of stitches under the chin.
5. Make a small bow from narrow ribbon, and glue it under the chin.
6. Embroider French knots at the point of the hat, on each foot, and as "buttons" down the center of the jump suit.
7. Bend the feet forward at the dotted lines.

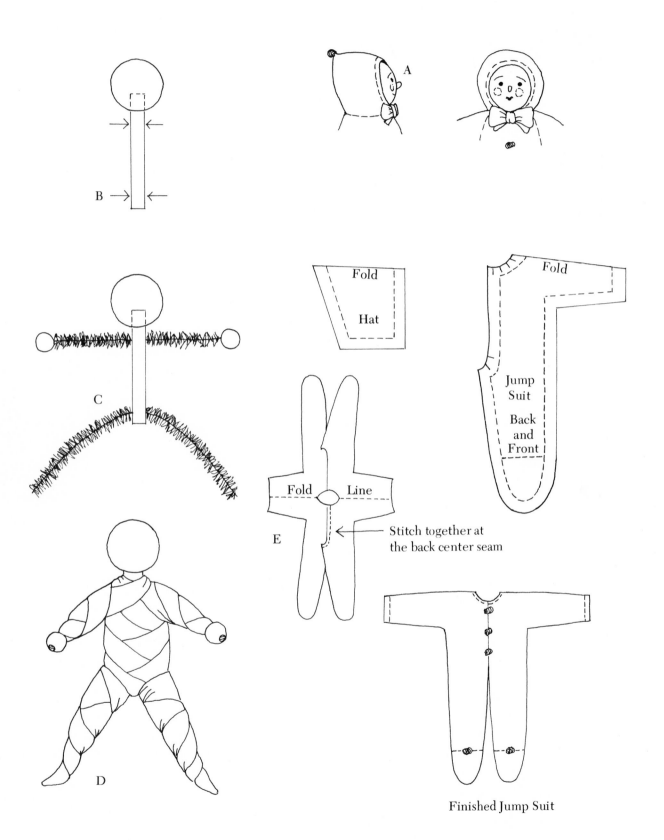

A

B

C

Fold

Hat

Fold

Jump
Suit

Back
and
Front

Fold   Line

E   ← Stitch together at
                        the back center seam

D

Finished Jump Suit

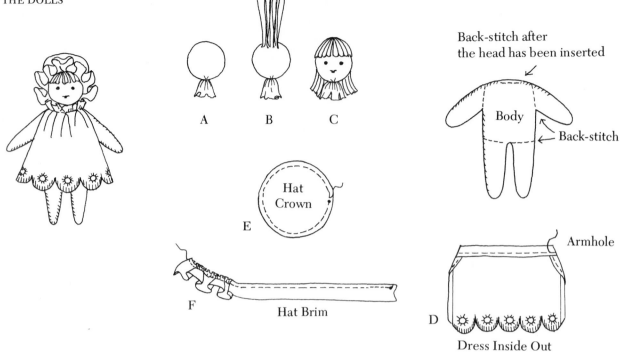

Doll's Doll No. 1

(Scale: 1 inch to 1 foot)

MATERIALS

    3/8-inch-diameter bead for the head
    A scrap of nylon stocking to cover the head
    Felt for the body
    Cotton for stuffing
    Darning yarn for the hair
    1-inch-wide embroidered edging for the dress and hat
        crown
    Narrow ribbon for the hat brim
    White glue
    Tracing paper
    Acrylic paints

HEAD

1. Cover the head with a scrap of nylon stocking, securing it at the base with several turns of thread (A).

2. Using darning yarn, sew loops at the top of the head to make the hair (B).

3. Paint the head the same color as the felt which will be used for the body. (Put a band around the yarn loops, to avoid getting paint on them.)

4. Cut the top of the loops of yarn. Trim and arrange the hair, sticking it in place with a little glue (C).

BODY

1. Trace the body pattern onto tracing paper and cut it out.

2. Pin the pattern onto a *double* thickness of felt, and cut out the body. Stitch the back and front of the body together with small whip stitches, leaving an opening at the top for the stuffing.

3. Stuff the legs and arms with cotton. Back-stitch through both thicknesses of felt at the tops of the arms and legs. Stuff the body.

4. Insert the head in the opening at the top of the body. Back-stitch through all the layers of the fabric to attach the head to the body.

DRESS

1. Make the doll's dress as shown in diagram D. Cut two small lengths of embroidered edging. Sew the side seams together, leaving spaces at the top for the armholes.

2. Turn back the armhole facings and hem them down. Turn down the neck facings, at the back and front of the dress, and make a row of running stitches, leaving the ends of the threads loose.

3. Turn the dress right side out and put it on the doll. Make gathers at the neck of the dress. Finish off the threads. Join the back to the front, at each shoulder, with a couple of stitches.

HAT

1. Cut a small circle from the same kind of edging as the dress, for the crown of the hat. Sew running stitches around the edge of the circle as shown in diagram E. Pull the thread to make gathers fit the crown of the hat to the doll's head.

2. To make the brim for the hat, sew running stitches along the edge of about four inches of narrow ribbon (F). When the thread is pulled to make gathers, the ribbon will form a circle. Join the two ends of the ribbon. Fit the brim over the edge of the crown to complete the hat.

Doll's Doll No. 2

(Scale: 1 inch to 1 foot)

MATERIALS

3/8-inch diameter wooden bead for the head
A flat toothpick for the nose
1/8-inch dowel for the neck
Knitting yarn for the hair
Felt for the body
A scrap of lightweight fabric for the dress
Embroidery thread for the hair ribbons
White glue
Tracing paper
Cotton for stuffing
Acrylic paints
Gloss polymer medium

HEAD

1. Cut the dowel for the neck and glue it inside the bead head.

2. Draw the features on the head with a pencil. Gouge out a small oblong groove where the nose will be inserted (A). Cut the nose from a flat toothpick and glue it into the groove.

3. Paint on the features. Give the head a coat of gloss polymer medium.

4. To make the hair, wind the knitting yarn around a book of matches about eight times. Back-stitch the yarn together, as shown in diagram B. Cut the yarn away from the book of matches. Glue the hair to the doll's head. Tie the hair in bunches using embroidery thread. Trim the hair to make it even (C).

BODY

1. Trace the patterns for the body, legs, and arms onto tracing paper, and cut them out.

2. Pin the patterns onto a *double* thickness of felt. Cut out the body, two arms, and two legs.

3. Using small whip stitches, sew the pieces of the legs together, and sew the pieces of the arms together. Stuff the arms and legs with cotton.

4. Pin the back and front pieces of the body together. Starting at point D, join the pieces of the body together using whip stitches; as you go around the body back stitch the arms and legs in place (sewing through all thicknesses of the fabric). Leave an opening at the top for the stuffing. Stuff the body with cotton.

5. Insert the neck into the opening at the top of the body. Secure the neck and head in place with a couple of whip stitches on either shoulder.

6. Paint the shoes on the doll.

DRESS

Make the dress for the doll, using the instructions on page 54 for the other little doll's dress.

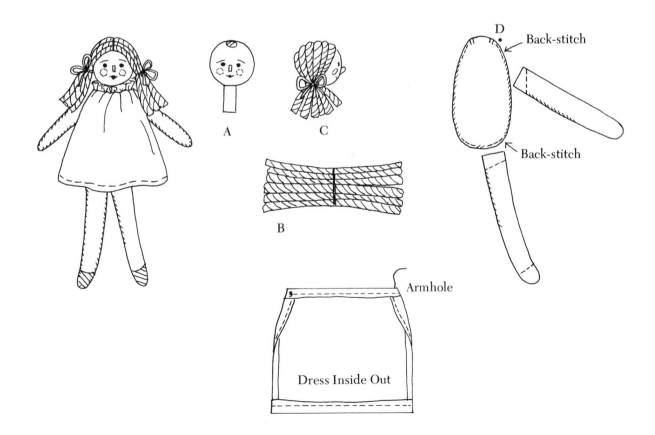

A

C

B

D

Back-stitch

Back-stitch

Armhole

Dress Inside Out

Furniture-
Wood and
Upholstered

Patterns and complete instructions for making a miniature blanket chest,
upholstered wing chair, chest of drawers, mirror
and three-drawer chest; a "scrap" screen, brass bed, trestle table,
bench, dresser; a kitchen sink and cupboard,
a stove and refrigerator; a rocking chair, highchair,
ladder-back chair; a dolls' house for the dolls, a sewing table (with lift-out tray),
a toy chest and bench, bunk beds, a child's table and chair,
a bookcase and closet, a crib, upholstered armchair, coffee table,
tilt-top table, grandfather clock, fireplace, upholstered sofa,
floor lamp; a piano and piano stool, a wash basin,
a bathtub and toilet, and a bathroom chair.

The dolls' house furniture I made can be divided into three categories: first, adaptations of furniture I own and love, such as the sofa, brass bed, tilt-top table, and ladder-back chair; second, furniture I wish I owned, like the screen, sewing table, arm chair, and kitchen dresser; third, furniture I thought would be appropriate to the rooms and to the Bead family—for example, the bathroom, the piano, and the crib.

The first step with each piece of furniture, whether an adaptation or an original design, was to make the necessary "scale" calculations. I did this by drawing a rough sketch of the piece of furniture and writing the "life-size" measurements on the sketch. I then translated these measurements so 1 inch equals 1 foot; this is a simple scale to adapt, even with my limited knowledge of arithmetic.

1/12 inch equals 1 inch
1/6 inch equals 2 inches
1/4 inch equals 3 inches
1/2 inch equals 6 inches
3/4 inch equals 9 inches
1 inch equals 1 foot

Therefore, if a chair is 3 feet, 9 inches high, it becomes, when reduced to 1-inch-to-1-foot scale, 3-3/4 inches high. A 6-foot sofa becomes 6 inches long.

You may find making a scale ruler useful. Cut a length of matte-board 1 inch wide by 12 inches long. Using a fine-nibbed pen, draw lines dividing the matte-board first into inches, and then into twelfths of an inch.

Next, I chose the wood or fabric, decided on the details and the finish for the piece of furniture. Since I wanted to test the possibilities of a number of woods, I worked with balsa, plywood, basswood, and mahogany. Using graph paper I worked out plans for the construction, and the pattern pieces for the furniture. I wrote notes as I made each piece of furniture. What follow in this chapter are drawings of the actual patterns I used, and descriptions of how I constructed the furniture—descriptions in the form of instructions.

GENERAL INSTRUCTIONS FOR
MAKING THE WOODEN FURNITURE

All the patterns are printed exactly to size; therefore, with a few exceptions I have omitted giving dimensional measurements. Read the instructions carefully before beginning a piece of furniture. You will then know exactly what materials and tools you will need. Assemble all the necessary materials and tools before starting to work on a project. And refer to the photographs and pattern drawings when making the pieces of furniture.

Trace and transfer the patterns to tracing paper following the method described on page 27. Draw all the straight lines using a ruler. Write the name of each piece, the thickness of wood, and the number of pieces to be cut from each single pattern on the tracing paper: e.g., cupboard door—1/8 inch—cut 2. The solid lines indicate where the patterns are to be cut. The dotted lines show either where one pattern piece comes in relation to another or where a piece of card has to be bent or a piece of fabric folded.

Consider the grain of the wood when laying out the patterns. Be consistent—the grain should run the same way on each drawer front. Write the name of each pattern piece on the wood before cutting it out. Unless you do this, you may not be able to distinguish between, say, a drawer front and a drawer side after they have been cut out.

When cutting the patterns from wood, cut just to the outside of your pencil line. (You cannot add to a piece of wood once it has been cut, but you can easily sand away any surplus wood.) *Careful sanding is probably the most important step in making a piece of furniture look finished and professional. Therefore, sand all the edges and surfaces of the wooden pieces smooth, before gluing them together.* Always sand with the grain of the wood. Also, lightly sand the completed piece of furniture before applying the finish. Check that a piece fits correctly before gluing it in place. However careful you have been, you may still make an error while tracing, cutting, or sanding.

I prefer to stain a piece of furniture after it has been assembled. Therefore, since glue will resist the stain, I take great care to wipe away any surplus glue when I am joining pieces together. If some glue nevertheless does get on the surface of the wood, scrape or sand it off before staining.

Allow the glue to dry thoroughly in between gluing the various parts of a piece of furniture together. Also let the glue dry thoroughly before applying any finish.

A pin-vise drill is an essential tool to have for drilling the small holes indicated in the patterns and instructions.

HINTS

Here are bits and pieces of useful information that I discovered (by trial and error) while making the furniture:

- If a whittled wooden peg should break off a leg or a spindle, the peg can be replaced with a length of steel cut from a straight pin. Drill a hole where the peg was attached, and glue the length of steel in place of the peg.
- When a hole has been drilled in the wrong place, or a crack has to be filled, use a mixture of sawdust and white glue. Mix the sawdust and glue so that it has a consistency similar to that of plastic wood.
- I find cutting a perfect circle or curve difficult, especially when using balsa wood. Therefore, I cut the shape roughly, leaving plenty of surplus wood between the cut and the pencil line, and then I sand the circle or curve to shape.
- Do not apply glue directly from the tube or bottle to

the wood, fabric, or card. Squeeze a small amount of glue onto a piece of paper, and then use a toothpick to apply the glue to the surface you wish to cover.

• In sanding a surface or straight edge, a "rocking" motion is unavoidable, and this will create an uneven surface or edge. To avoid getting an uneven surface, try the following method of sanding: Lay a piece of sand-paper flat on your work table. Place a block of wood on the sandpaper covering about half of it. Hold the block of wood firmly on top of the sandpaper with one hand. In the other hand take the section of wood that is to be sanded. Sand the section of wood that is to be smoothed, holding it firmly against the block as you sand back and forth. The block of wood acts as a brace. By sanding in this way, you can control the rocking motion.

Blanket Chest

(Scale: 1 inch to 1 foot)

MATERIALS

  1/8-inch-thick wood for all the parts of the chest
  Two small hinges
  Two tiny brass pins and epoxy glue for attaching the
    hinges
  White glue
  Shellac
  Butcher's wax
  Acrylic paints
  Gloss polymer medium
  Tracing paper

I used mahogany for the chest, leaving the wood in its natural color, and finishing the chest with shellac and Butcher's wax. See the Appendix for dealers who sell small hinges (page 216).

See the general instructions for making wooden furniture, page 59.

1. Trace and transfer the patterns to the wood (excluding the floral pattern designs). Cut a back, a lid, a base, a front, two ends, two end feet, the front feet, and a lower back.

2. Sand the front corners of the lid and the base, rounding them off.

3. Lay the back on a flat surface. Glue the ends to the back. Glue the front to the ends. (Note the correct positions for the pieces in the drawing.) Check that this completed section of the chest is squared, and then glue it to the top of the base. (The back edge of the base should be flush with the back. The ends and front of the base should extend 1/16 inch.)

4. Glue the lower back to the underneath side of the base (flush with the back). Glue the end feet to the underneath side of the base. Glue the front feet to the underneath side of the base. (Note the correct positions for the pieces in the drawing.)

5. Cut the recesses (A) in the back, for the hinges. (I cut the ends off a 1/2-inch-long hinge, to make it 1/4 inch long). Drill two holes (B) in the back for the brass pins. Attach the hinges to the back. Since the lid is only 1/8 inch thick, *glue* the free ends of the hinges to the underside of the lid. (The back edge of the lid should be flush with the back. The ends and front of the lid should extend 1/8 inch.)

6. Trace the designs for the floral panels onto tracing paper. Transfer only the outer borders of the panels (C) to the ends and front of the chest.

7. Finish the chest with shellac and Butcher's wax. (Apply the finish *around* the panels, taking care not to get any shellac or wax on the panel areas.)

8. Transfer the floral designs to the panels. Paint the designs with acrylic paints.

9. Finish the panel areas with gloss polymer medium.

BLANKET CHEST

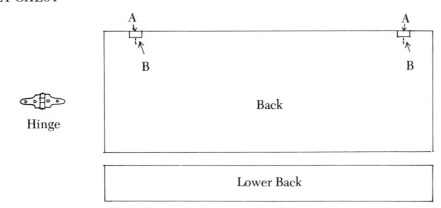

Hinge

Back

Lower Back

Front

Front Feet

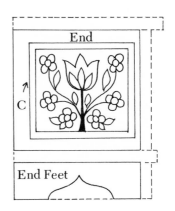

End

End Feet

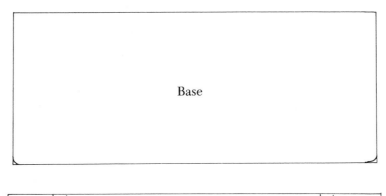

Base

Lid

Wing Chair

(Scale: 1 inch to 1 foot)

MATERIALS

1/8-inch-thick wood for the sides and bases
3/32-inch-thick wood for the back
3/8-inch-thick wood for the cushion
1/4-inch dowel for the armrests
3/16-inch-thick wood for the legs
1/4-inch-thick foam rubber for the padding
1/4 yard of cotton fabric for covering the chair
Card for the fabric backing
White glue
Fabric glue
Tracing paper

I used basswood for the back and sides of the chair, balsa wood for the cushion, and mahogany for the legs. (When I made this chair, I mistakenly made two *left* arms. Some men's suits have an extra pair of pants. This chair has an extra arm.) The patterns with floral designs are for fabric; the shaded patterns are for foam rubber; the solid patterns are for wood or card. An exception is the cushion pattern: the shaded area is for both the foam rubber *and* the wood.

See the general instructions for making wooden furniture, page 59.

1. Trace and transfer all the wood patterns. Cut a back, two sides, two bases, and a cushion. Cut four legs, each leg 1-1/6 inches long. Cut the two armrests, from dowel, each 1 inch long.

2. Sand each armrest so that it tapers off toward the end. Also sand each armrest so that it has a flat side (diagram 1).

3. Cut a strip 1 inch long diagonally off the outer edge of each side as shown in diagram 2.

4. Glue an armrest to each side as shown in diagram 3. (The flat side of the dowel should fit along the diagonal cut.)

5. Trace and transfer the patterns for the foam rubber. Cut a back, two sides, and the cushion padding.

6. Take a side and its padding. Glue the padding to the inside surface of the side, but bring the flap (A) over the armrest, and glue the end just under the dowel on the outside surface of the side.

7. Glue the back padding to the back of the chair.

8. Trace the fabric patterns onto tracing paper and cut them out.

(continued)

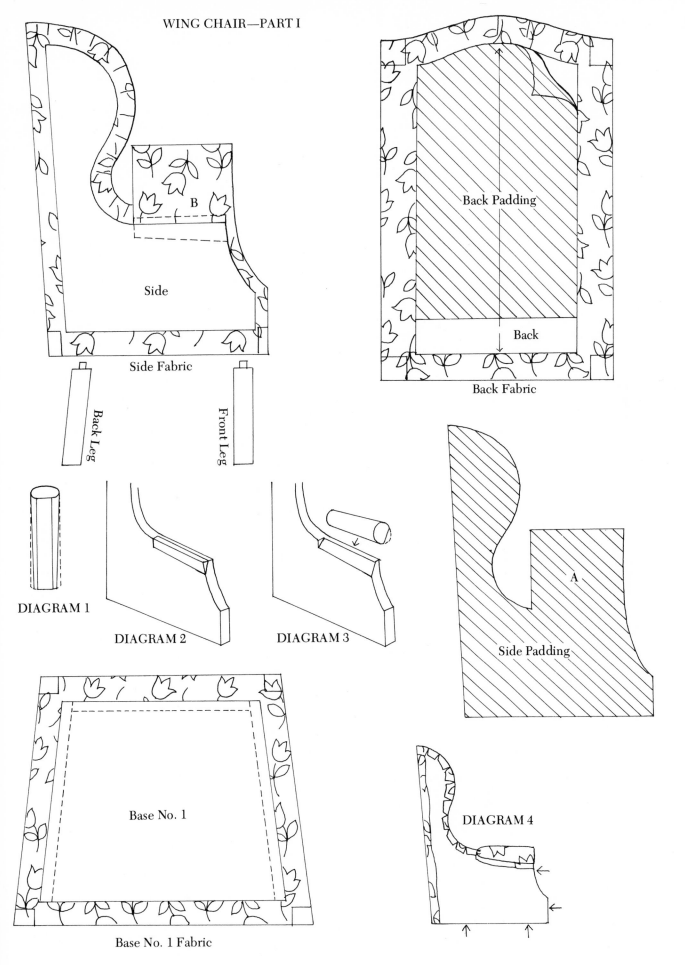

Side

Side Fabric

Back Leg

Front Leg

Back Padding

Back

Back Fabric

B

A

Side Padding

DIAGRAM 1

DIAGRAM 2

DIAGRAM 3

DIAGRAM 4

Base No. 1

Base No. 1 Fabric

9. Pin the patterns to the fabric. (The fabric for the wooden parts of the sides should be cut on the bias.) Cut the fabric for the wooden back and the card back; the wooden sides and the two card sides. Cut the fabric for the cushion, base no. 1, and the two arm fronts. Cut a strip of fabric 13-1/8 inches long by 1-1/4 inches wide for the skirt. (This measurement includes 1/8 inch at each end for the back seam selvages.) *Note:* The squares I have drawn at the corners of some of the fabric patterns are only rough guides as to how much fabric to cut away to decrease the bulkiness at the corners. Don't cut the corners until you are actually covering the section of furniture, and can judge the exact amount of surplus fabric.

10. Take the fabric for the wooden part of a side. Place the fabric wrong side up on a flat surface. Take the wooden part of a side and place it, padding down, on the fabric. Gently pull and glue the edges of the fabric to the side as shown in diagram 4. The flap (B) goes over and around the dowel armrest. Cover the other side in the same way.

11. Take the fabric for the back. Place the fabric wrong side up on a flat surface. Take the wooden part of the back, and place it, padding down, on the fabric. Gently pull the fabric over the edges of the back, and glue them to the outside surface of the back.

12. Take the fabric for base no. 1 and place it wrong side up on a flat surface. Take the base and place it on the fabric. Pull the fabric over the edges of the base. Glue the edges of the fabric to the top surface.

13. Take base no. 1 and place it on a flat surface, fabric side up. Glue the sides to the base, and then glue the back to the base. (Note the angle shown in the diagram.) Refer to the drawing for the correct positions.

14. Trace and transfer the patterns for the card sections of the chair. Cut a back, two sides, and two arm fronts.

15. Place each card pattern, as shown in the drawings, on top of the wrong side of its fabric cover. (Note that each side and each arm front should face in the opposite

way to its counterpart.) Fold the edges of the fabric over the card, and glue them in place, clipping the edges of the fabric on the curves so it will lie flat.

16. Glue the card back to the outside surface of the wooden back. Glue the card sides to the outside surfaces of the wooden sides. Glue the arm fronts to the fronts of the armrests and to the front edges of the sides.

17. Whittle a peg, 1/16 inch long and 3/32 inch in diameter, at the top of each leg.

18. Drill a hole, 1/16 inch deep and 3/32 inch in diameter, into each corner of base no. 2 as shown in the drawing. (The holes for the back legs should be drilled at a slight angle.)

19. Glue the pegs in the legs into the holes in the base.

20. Take the strip of fabric for the skirt. Sew the two ends together making the back seam. Turn the hem 1/4 inch, and sew it in place. The top 1/8 inch of the skirt is glued to the top of base no. 2 as shown in diagram 5. But first make an inverted pleat (each pleat should take up 1 inch of fabric) for each corner of the base. Fit the skirt on the base to make sure that the pleats are in the right places. Catch the top of each pleat with one or two stitches. Iron the pleats. Glue the skirt to base no. 2.

21. Glue the underneath side of base no. 1 to the top side of base no. 2—and the chair is complete, except for the cushion.

22. Coat with glue the top and front wooden sections of the cushion. Place the foam rubber pad on top of the wood. Pull the foam rubber over the edge of the top, so that it covers the front area too. Using a razor blade, shave off the sharp edge of the foam rubber at the front of the cushion (see diagram 6 in the sofa patterns on page 121). When the glue is dry, place the cushion—with the foam rubber down—on top of the wrong side of its fabric cover. Gently pull the fabric over the sides of the cushion and glue the edges of the fabric to the wooden underneath side of the cushion. (See "Covering a Cushion," page 33.) Put the cushion on the chair.

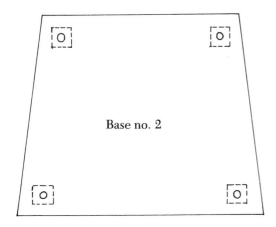

Base no. 2

Cushion (Padding and Wood)

Cushion Fabric

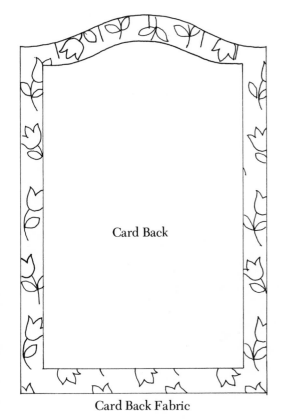

Card Back

Card Back Fabric

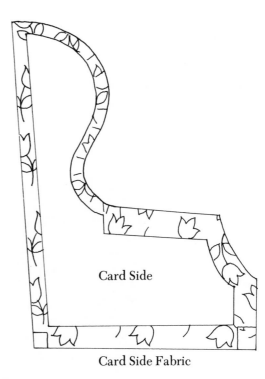

Card Side

Card Side Fabric

Arm Front

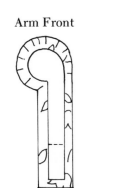

Arm Front Fabric

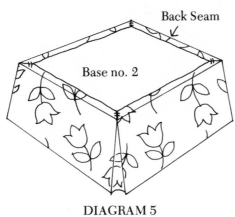

Back Seam

Base no. 2

DIAGRAM 5

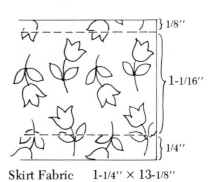

1/8''

1-1/16''

1/4''

Skirt Fabric   1-1/4'' × 13-1/8''

Chest of Drawers

(Scale: 1 inch to 1 foot)

MATERIALS

    1/8-inch-thick wood for all the parts of the chest except
        the feet
    1/4-inch dowel for the feet
    White glue
    Six crystal rondelle beads, six small bell-caps (for descrip-
        tion see page 24), and six small brass nails (or six map
        pins) for the drawer knobs
    Tracing paper
    Stain
    Shellac
    Butcher's wax

I used plywood for the chest. The Appendix (page 216) lists the names of dealers who supply small brass nails and bell-caps.

See the general instructions for making wooden furniture, page 59.

1. Trace and transfer the patterns to the wood. Cut a top, a base, a back, two ends, two drawer shelves, three drawer fronts, three drawer backs, three drawer bottoms, and six drawer sides.

2. Sand the front corners of the top and base, rounding them off.

3. Lay the back on a flat surface. Glue the ends to the back. Glue the base to the back and the ends. Glue the top to the back and the ends. Refer to the drawings for the correct positions of the various parts. (Note that the back edges of the ends, base, and top are flush with the back.)

4. Glue the drawer shelves in position to the back and sides.

5. Drill two holes (the correct diameter to fit either the brass nails or the map pins) in each drawer front, as indicated in the drawing.

6. Construct the three drawers, following the instructions for the basic drawer (page 31).

7. Cut four feet from dowel. Glue the feet (1/8 inch in from the outer edges) to the base.

8. Stain the chest.

9. Finish the chest with shellac and Butcher's wax.

10. Glue the "drawer knobs" into the holes in the front of the drawers.

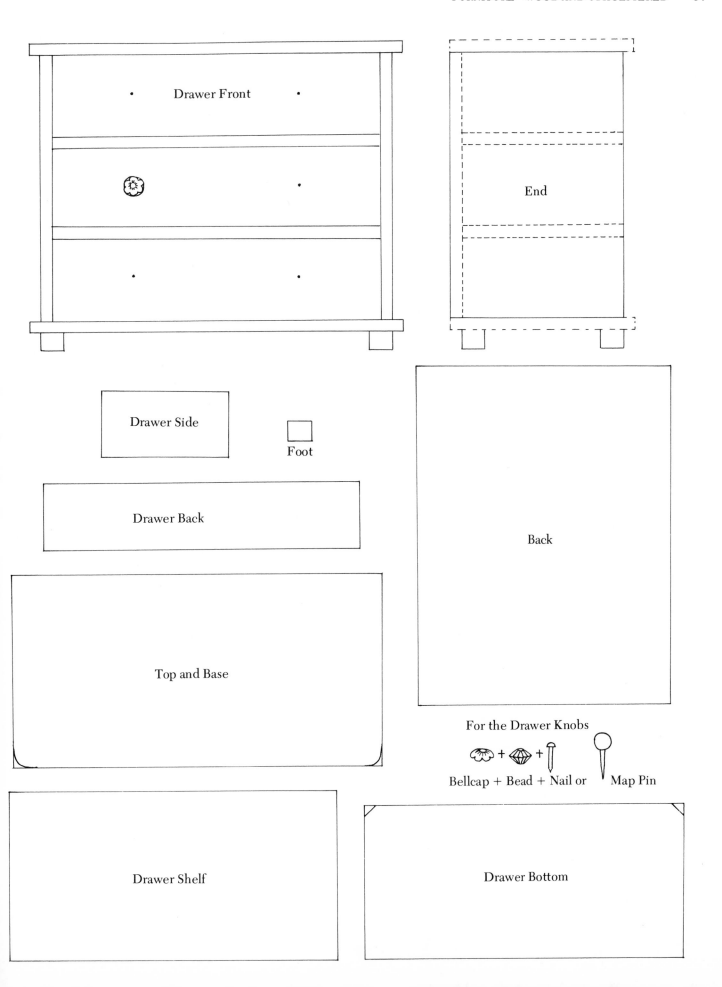

Drawer Front

End

Drawer Side

Foot

Drawer Back

Back

Top and Base

For the Drawer Knobs

Bellcap + Bead + Nail or   Map Pin

Drawer Shelf

Drawer Bottom

Mirror and Three-Drawer Chest

(Scale: 1 inch to 1 foot)

MATERIALS

　　1/16-inch-thick wood for the chest of drawers
　　1/8-inch-thick wood for the mirror frame and mirror supports
　　1/16-inch-thick balsa wood for the mirror backing
　　1/8-inch dowel for the drawer knobs and the feet
　　Straight pins for hinging and attaching the supports
　　Shiny silver paper for the mirror
　　White glue
　　Tracing paper
　　Stain
　　Shellac
　　Butcher's wax

I used basswood for all the parts of the chest except the mirror backing, which is balsa wood. After many futile attempts at trying to cut a mirror, and jinxing myself with at least forty-nine years of bad luck, I gave up and settled for shiny silver paper. In the photograph the mirror and chest are shown on top of the chest of drawers.

See the general instructions for making wooden furniture, page 59.

1. Trace and transfer the patterns for the chest to the wood. Cut the top, the base, the back, two ends, three drawer fronts, three drawer bottoms, three drawer backs, six drawer sides, and two drawer dividers.

2. Sand the two front corners of the top, rounding them off.

3. Lay the back on a flat surface. Glue the ends in place. Glue the base in place. Glue the top in place. (Refer to the drawings for the correct placement of the pieces. The top extends over the ends, 1/16 inch at the sides and 1/8 inch in the front. The ends of all the pieces are flush with the back.)

4. Glue the two drawer dividers in place.

5. Drill a 1/16-inch-diameter hole in the center of each drawer front.

6. Construct the drawers following the instructions for the basic drawer (page 31).

7. Cut three 1/4-inch lengths of dowel for the drawer knobs. Carve the knobs to shape. (If you wish, instead of wooden drawer knobs, you can use small beads fixed to the drawers with pins.) Glue the drawer knobs into the holes in the fronts of the drawers.

8. Cut four 1/8-inch lengths of dowel for the feet. Glue the feet to the base.

9. Trace and transfer the patterns for the frame and backing to wood, and the pattern for the mirror to silver paper. Cut the four parts of the frame. Cut the two supports. Cut the mirror backing from balsa wood. Cut the mirror.

10. Sand the front edges of each of the supports, rounding them off. Carve the curlicues on each support using a narrow, V-shaped gouge. (You may wish to practice carving curlicues on a spare piece of wood before attempting to carve them on the supports.)

11. Take the four parts of the frame. Sand the front edges of each part, rounding them off. Cut a 1/16-inch-wide and 1/16-inch-deep rabbet in the backs of each frame part, as shown in the shaded areas in diagram 1. (These recesses will allow the back of the "mirror" to fit flush with the back of the frame.) Glue the frame parts together.

12. Glue the silver paper to the mirror backing.

13. Fit and glue the "mirror" into the back of the frame.

14. Stain the various parts of the chest and mirror.

15. Finish the chest and mirror with shellac and Butcher's wax.

16. Drill pin-sized holes, 1/16 inch deep, in each support at points A and B.

17. Drill a pin-sized hole, 1/16 inch deep, on each side of the mirror frame (C).

18. Drill two pin-sized holes each 1/16 inch deep in the top of the chest (D).

19. Cut four 1/8-inch lengths from straight pins. Glue the lengths of pin into the holes in the supports.

20. Glue a support into the left-hand side of the top [fitting the pin in the support (B) into the hole (D)]. Take the mirror, and fit the pin in the support (A) into the hole in the mirror frame (C). Hold the mirror in position (with your left hand): take the second support, and glue the pin in the support (B) into the hole in the top of the chest (D), and fit the pin in the support (A) into the hole in the frame (C). The mirror hangs between the two supports, and may be tilted.

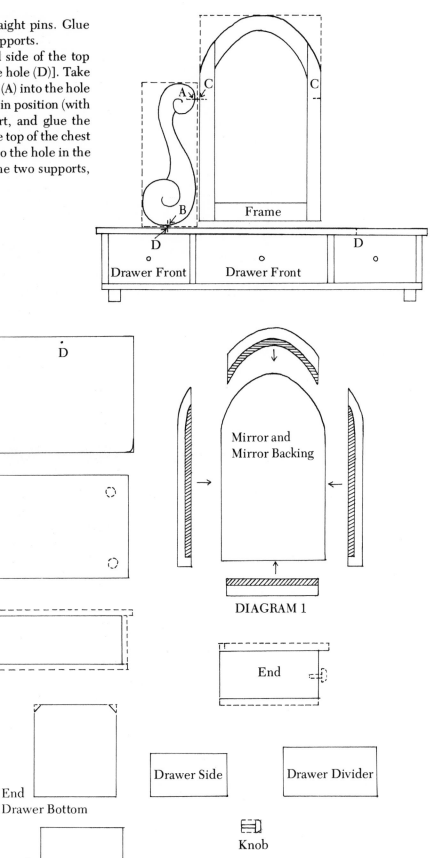

Frame

Drawer Front   Drawer Front

D   D

Top

Base

Back

Mirror and
Mirror Backing

DIAGRAM 1

End

Center Drawer Bottom

End
Drawer Bottom

Drawer Side

Drawer Divider

Center Drawer Back

End
Drawer Back

Knob

"Scrap" Screen

(Scale: 1 inch to 1 foot)

MATERIALS

1/8-inch-thick wood for the legs, upper rails, and lower rails
1/16-inch-thick wood for the panels
Plastic-coated fabric tape for the hinges
Colored paper for lining the panels
Paper "scraps" for decorating the panels
White glue
Gesso
Acrylic paints
Gloss polymer medium
Orange shellac
Six map pins for the feet
Tracing paper

I used plywood for the legs and rails of the screen, and balsa wood for the panels. See the Appendix (page 216) for dealers who sell sheets of scrap pictures, and sheets of decorative stamps and seals.
See the general instructions for making wooden furniture, page 59.

1. Trace and transfer the patterns to the wood. Cut three upper rails, three lower rails, and six legs. Cut three panels.

2. Line the front of each of the panels with colored paper. (I used marbled paper.)

3. Glue cutout pictures or decorative "scraps" to each panel.

4. Give each screen panel a coat of orange shellac. When the shellac is dry, sand each panel very gently with extra-fine sandpaper. Repeat this process three or four times.

5. Give the backs of the panels, the legs, and the upper and lower rails a coat of gesso.

6. Paint the various parts of the screen, and finish them with a coat of gloss polymer medium.

7. Take a panel and put it, picture side up, on a flat surface. Glue the top and bottom rails to the panel. Then glue the legs in place. Note that the back of the panel and the backs of the legs and rails are flush; and therefore the panel is recessed 1/16 inch in the front. Make the other two panels in the same way.

8. Cut four lengths of tape (1/2 inch long by 1/4 inch wide) for the hinges. Stick the hinges to the backs of the panels, allowing a space of 1/16 inch between each panel. Paint the tape hinges the same color as the screen.

9. Drill a pin-sized hole in the bottom end of each leg. For the feet, glue a map pin in each hole.

"SCRAP" SCREEN

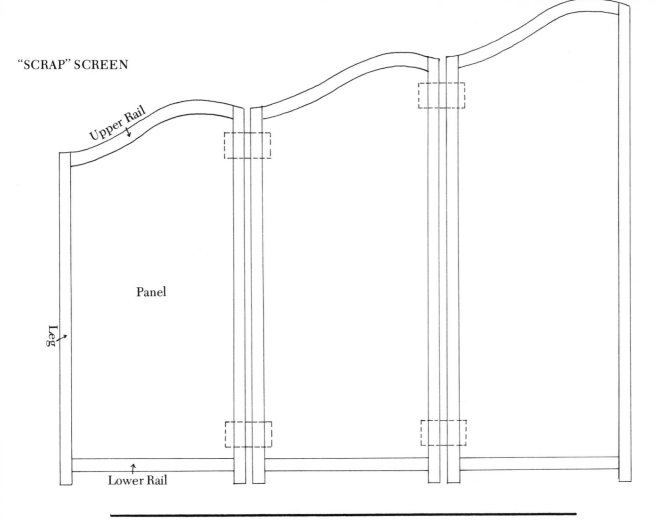

Upper Rail

Panel

Leg

Lower Rail

Sewing Table

(Scale: 1 inch to 1 foot)

MATERIALS

> 1/8-inch-thick wood for the table top and table sides
> 3/16-inch-thick wood for the legs
> 1/16-inch-thick wood for the table base
> 1/20-inch-thick wood for the sewing box
> 1/8 yard lightweight cotton fabric for the sewing bag and the sewing box lining
> A scrap of thin glove leather or felt for lining the base
> Card for the sewing bag base
> Narrow ribbon for the sewing box handles
> Fabric glue
> White glue
> Stain
> Shellac
> Butcher's wax
> Tracing paper
> 2 small hinges
> Quick-drying epoxy glue for fixing the hinges

I used basswood for all the wooden parts of the sewing table. The small balls of yarn to put in the sewing bag were made from crewel wool. For the sewing box I made skeins of embroidery floss using one thread of floss for the skeins and small strips of shiny paper for the labels; the spools of thread were cut from 1/8-inch dowel, and the darning yarn from crewel wool wound around cards. The knitting needles are bead-headed pins. The buttons are from discarded Barbie dolls' clothes. I also put some narrow lace and ribbon in the sewing box. See the Appendix (page 216) for dealers who supply small hinges.

See the general instructions for making wooden furniture, page 59.

1. Trace and transfer the patterns for the sewing table. Cut a top, a base, and four sides. Cut four legs.

2. Sand the corners of the top, rounding them off.

3. Cut a rabbet 3/16 inch deep and 1/16 inch wide in each of the back legs (A). (This will allow the top to open to a vertical position.) Mark the turnings on the legs; hand-turn and whittle the legs to shape. Note that from point B to point C the legs are round and taper toward the floor. See the general directions for whittling on page 29.

4. Take the side that will be at the back of the sewing table. Cut two grooves, 3/16 inch wide and 1/16 inch deep, in the top edge of the side (D) for the hinges.

5. Take the base and cut out the circle in the center. (Cut the hole as follows: Drill a hole in the center of the base. Release one end of the blade in a coping saw. Thread the free end of the blade through the hole in the base. Replace the free end of the blade in the coping saw. Then cut the circle.)

6. Arrange the sides, as shown in diagram 1, top edges down on a flat surface. Glue the legs to the sides, as shown in diagram 1. Glue the base to the sides. (The base should be flush with the bottom edges of the sides.) Turn the table right side up, and check that it is squared.

7. Cut the hinges so that each one measures about 1/4 inch in length. Glue the hinges in the grooves in the top edge of the side. Glue the free ends of the hinges to the table top.

8. Stain the sewing table.

9. Finish the table with shellac and Butcher's wax.

10. Draw a circle 4 inches in diameter on the fabric for the sewing bag. Cut the circle. Draw a circle 3/4 inch in diameter on the card. Cut the card circle and glue it to the center of the wrong side of the fabric circle. Sew a line of running stitches 3/8 inch in from the edge of the fabric circle, leaving the thread loose. Pull the thread so that the opening at the top of the bag is the same size as the hole in the table base. Finish off the loose thread. Back-stitch, a fraction in from the edge, around the circumference of the base of the sewing bag. Sew through two thicknesses of fabric and the card (see diagram 2). Glue the top of the sewing bag to the top of the base as shown in diagram 1. Cut away any surplus fabric.

11. Using the same pattern as for the base, cut the base lining from thin leather or felt. Glue the lining to the base, as shown in diagram 1.

12. Now make the sewing box. Trace and transfer the patterns to wood. Cut a base, a back, a front, two sides, and two of each of the lengths of partitions. Cut a square of fabric, 1/2 inch larger all around than the sewing box base. Glue the fabric to the base as shown in diagram 3. Cut two lengths of narrow ribbon, each about 3/4 inch long. Fold each length of ribbon in half and glue a "handle" to each side of the base. Cut the sewing box lining, making it, when the raw edges are folded in, 1/20 inch smaller than the sewing box base, as shown in diagram 3. Glue the lining to the base. Cut strips of fabric, about 1/4 inch wide and the correct length to cover the back and front of each partition. Glue the partitions into the sewing box, as shown in diagram 4. Fit the sewing box onto the sewing table.

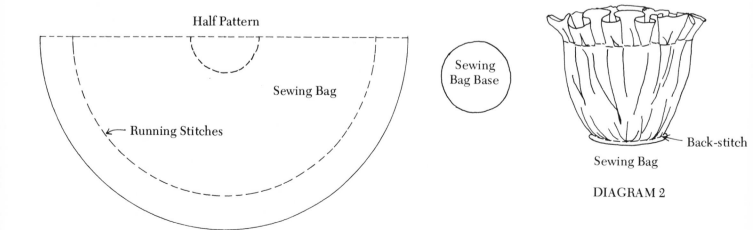

Half Pattern

Sewing Bag

← Running Stitches

Sewing Bag Base

Back-stitch

Sewing Bag

DIAGRAM 2

SEWING TABLE

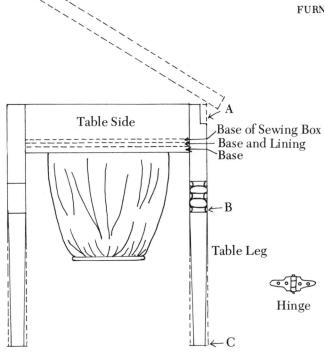

Table Side

A

Base of Sewing Box
Base and Lining
Base

B

Table Leg

Hinge

C

Back Leg

Hinge

Table Top

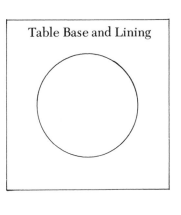

Table Base and Lining

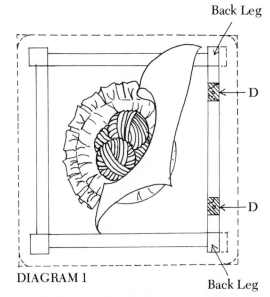

D

D

Back Leg

DIAGRAM 1

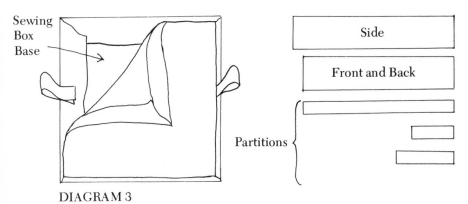

Sewing
Box
Base

Side

Front and Back

Partitions {

DIAGRAM 3

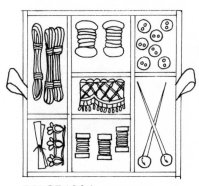

DIAGRAM 4

Brass Bed

(Scale: 1 inch to 1 foot)

MATERIALS

5/32-inch-diameter brass tubing for the legs
1/8-inch dowel for filling the legs
1/8-inch-diameter brass tubing for the cross bars
1/8-inch dowel for filling the cross bars (the dowel will have to be whittled and sanded down to fit the tubing)
3/32-inch-diameter brass tubing for the vertical bars
Round toothpicks for filling the vertical bars
4 brass beads about 1/4 inch in diameter
14 brass beads about 3/16 inch in diameter
8 brass jump-rings (for description see page 24)
4 map pins for the feet
1/8-inch square strips of wood for the sides
44 straight pins
Quick-drying epoxy glue
Gold paint
Carpet thread
White glue

Brass tubing can be bought at shops that sell supplies for model-ship building. (See the list of mail-order dealers in the Appendix on page 216.) The following instructions are for those who, like me, have not been able to master the skill of soldering metal. (This bed can also be made from three different thicknesses of dowel and wooden beads, rather than brass. When completed, the wooden bed can be sprayed with old gold paint.)

1. Cut all the lengths of tubing to size. Either use a jig saw to cut the tubing, or put the tubing in a table vise and cut it with a fine jeweler's blade in a coping saw. Cut two back legs, two front legs, seven back vertical bars, seven front vertical bars, and four cross bars. Sand the cut edges smooth.

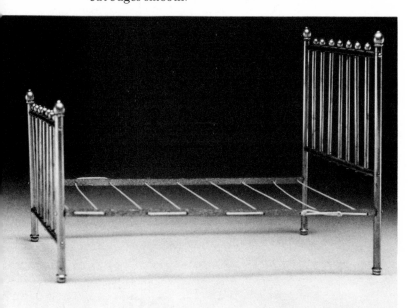

2. Cut two lengths of dowel the same length as the back legs and two lengths of dowel the same length as the front legs. Cut four lengths of dowel the same length as the cross bars.

3. Trickle one or two drops of white glue into a length of tubing, and then push a length of dowel into the tube. (You may have to whittle and sand the dowel so that it will fit the brass tube properly.) Fill all the legs and cross bars with dowels.

4. Take a vertical bar. Dip one end of a round toothpick into white glue, and then push about 1/2 inch of toothpick into one end of the tubing. Cut away the surplus part of the toothpick. Fill all the vertical bars, in this way, at both ends of each tube.

5. Take the legs, cross bars, and vertical bars for the back of the bed. Drill a pin-sized hole in each end of the vertical bars, the cross bars, and the legs. (All these holes are drilled into the wood dowel.)

Now pin-sized holes have to be drilled through both the metal and the wood. Using a fine-tipped felt marker, carefully mark the positions for the holes (taking the positions from the drawing) on each length of brass tubing. To drill the holes, proceed as follows: Place a length of tubing in a table vise. Remove the chuck from a pin vise. Fit the chuck with a pin-sized bit. Put the end of the pin vise chuck into the chuck jaws of an electric drill. Drill the holes right through the wood-filled brass tubing. Drill gently, as the thin bits break easily. The holes marked A are for attaching the sides.

6. When all the holes have been drilled, lay the legs on a flat surface. Pin and glue the top cross bar between the two legs. (Use epoxy glue for joining all the metal pieces.) Pin and glue the 3/16-inch-diameter beads through the top cross bar and into one end of the vertical bars. Pin and glue the bottom cross bar to the legs. Pin and glue the free ends of the vertical bars onto the bottom cross bar.

7. Glue a jump-ring to each end of each leg. Pin and glue a 1/4-inch bead to the top of each leg.

8. Make the other end of the bed in the same way.

9. Cut the two sides.

10. Take the four map pins, and sand the top of each map pin flat.

11. Paint the map pins and the sides gold.

12. Pin and glue a map pin into the bottom end of each leg.

13. Drill holes 1/16 inch in diameter through the sides as shown in the drawing. Drill a pin-sized hole into each end of the sides.

14. Pin and glue the sides to the back and front of the bed. Check that the bed stands firmly.

15. Make a knot in a long length of carpet thread. Weave the thread through the holes in the sides, as shown in the photograph. Pull the thread firmly, but take care not to distort the shape of the bed.

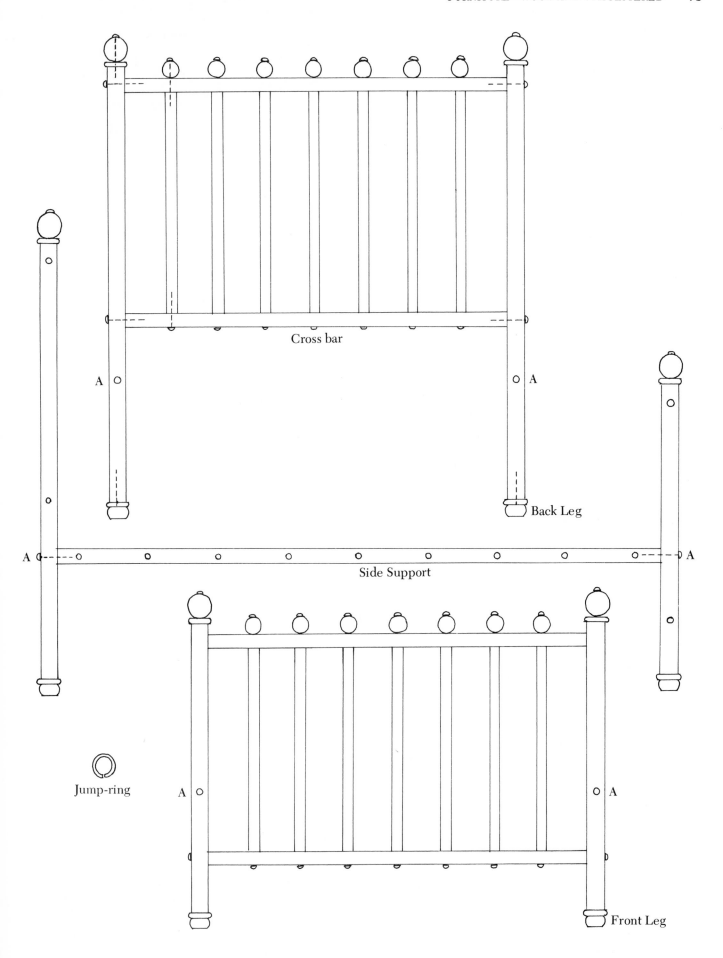

Cross bar

A   A

Back Leg

A   Side Support   A

Jump-ring   A   A

Front Leg

Trestle Table

(Scale: 1 inch to 1 foot)

MATERIALS

1/8-inch-thick wood for the table top, legs, cleats, and feet
An ice-cream stick for the stretcher
1/8-inch dowel for the pegs
Straight pins
White glue
Tracing paper
Shellac
Butcher's wax

I used a piece of old, seasoned plywood for the table. I left the wood in its natural color, using only shellac and Butcher's wax as a finish.

See the general instructions for making wooden furniture, page 59.

1. Trace and transfer the pattern pieces to the wood. (Mark off two 1/2-inch lengths on the dowel.) Cut one table top, two legs, two cleats, two feet, and two pegs. Cut the mortise in each leg, as follows: Put the leg in a table vise. Drill a hole 3/32 inch in diameter in the center of the leg (A). Remove *one* end of the blade in a coping saw. Thread the blade through the hole in the leg. Fix the loose end of the blade back into the coping saw, and cut the mortise. Smooth the edges of the mortise with a needle file.

2. Drill two pin-sized holes 1/16 inch deep in the top and the bottom of each leg, as indicated in the drawing.

Drill two pin-sized holes 1/16 inch deep, in the top and the bottom of each cleat, as indicated in the drawing. Drill two holes in the top of each foot, as indicated in the drawing. Cut twelve 1/8-inch lengths of steel from straight pins. Glue a length in each hole in the feet and cleats. Pin and glue a cleat to the top of each leg, and pin and glue a foot to the bottom of each leg.

3. Drill four pin-sized holes 1/16 inch deep in the underside of the table top, as indicated in the drawing.

4. Pin and glue the completed legs to the table top.

5. Drill a hole (B) at each end of the stretcher. Put the stretcher through the mortises in the legs of the table. Sand the ends of the pegs, rounding them off. Fix a peg in each hole at the ends of the stretcher.

6. Finish the table with shellac and Butcher's wax.

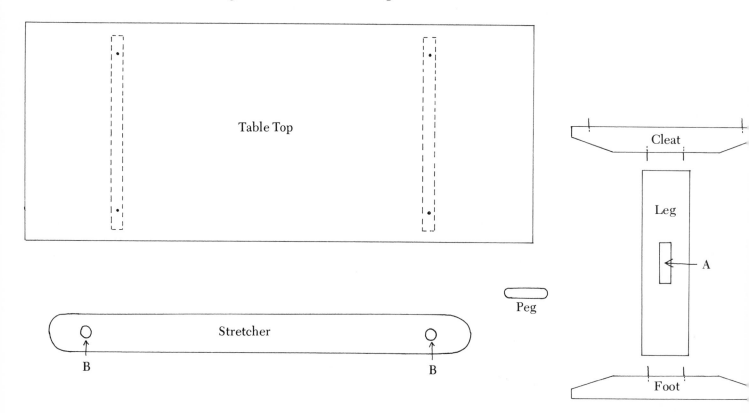

Table Top

Cleat

Leg

A

Peg

Stretcher

B   B

Foot

Bench

(Scale: 1 inch to 1 foot)

MATERIALS

1/8-inch-thick wood
White glue
Straight pins
Tracing paper
Shellac
Butcher's wax

I used a piece of old, seasoned plywood for the bench, leaving the wood in its natural color and using only shellac and Butcher's wax as a finish.

See the general instructions for making wooden furniture, page 59.

1. Trace and transfer the pattern pieces to wood. Cut one bench seat and two legs.

2. For the pins, drill two pin-sized holes, each 1/8 inch deep, in the top of each leg (A). Cut four 1/4-inch lengths of steel from the straight pins, and glue them in the holes in the legs.

3. Drill four pin-sized holes, each 1/8 inch deep, on the underside of the bench seat, as indicated by the arrows.

4. Glue the legs to the bench seat. Check that the legs are squared.

5. Finish the bench with shellac and Butcher's wax.

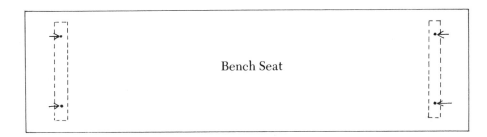

Bench Seat

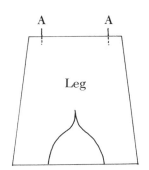

Leg

Dresser

(Scale: 1 inch to 1 foot)

MATERIALS

1/8-inch-thick wood for all the parts of the dresser *except* the door panels and the sides, backs, and bottoms of the drawers

1/16-inch-thick wood for the door panels and the sides, backs, and bottoms of the drawers

6 small brass beads for the drawer and cupboard knobs

4 small brass hinges

14-1/4-inch-long brass pins

6 small brass hooks

White glue

Tracing paper

A straight pin

Shellac

Butcher's wax

I made the dresser from old, seasoned plywood. For the door panels, I sanded down the plywood to 1/16 inch, and used basswood for the sides, backs, and bottoms of the drawers. I did not stain the wood, but finished it with shellac and Butcher's wax. (See the Appendix, page 216, for where to buy small hinges, hooks, and pins.)

See the general instructions for making wooden furniture, page 59.

1. Trace and transfer the pattern pieces to wood. Cut a back, two ends, a base, a top, a pediment, a counter, two drawer shelves, a center divider, two shelves, two drawer fronts, four stiles, two upper rails, and two lower rails. From 1/16-inch-thick wood cut two door panels, two drawer bottoms, four drawer sides, and two drawer backs.

2. Take the back and put it on a flat surface. Glue the sides to the back.

3. Bevel, by sanding, the top front edge of the counter from point A to point B, and round the corners. Glue the counter to the back and ends. (Refer to the drawings for the correct placement of the various pieces of the dresser.)

4. Glue the base in position.

5. Glue the top to the dresser. *Note:* The back edge of the top must come flush with the back. The top protrudes over the sides 1/8 inch in the front and 1/16 inch at each side.

6. Glue the pediment to the top in the position indicated by the shaded area.

7. Glue the dresser shelves in place. (They are recessed 1/16 inch.)

8. Drill a pin-sized hole at point C in the front lower end of the center divider. Cut a 3/8-inch length of steel from a straight pin. Glue the length of steel in hole (C),

1/8 inch protruding each side of the wood. (These protrusions will act as doorstops.)

9. Glue the center divider in place.

10. Glue the two drawer shelves in place. Check that all the pieces are squared.

11. Drill two pin-sized holes in each of the drawer fronts, as indicated on drawing. Make the drawers. (See the section on basic drawer construction, page 31). Glue the drawer knobs to the drawers (each knob: a brass bead and a brass pin). Put the drawers in the dresser.

12. Now make the cupboard doors. (For an alternative method of hinging, see the directions for the kitchen sink, page 82.) To make a cupboard door proceed as follows: Put the panel on a flat surface. Glue the upper and lower rails to the panel. Then glue the stiles to the panel. (*Note:* The panel is recessed 1/16 inch.) Let the glue dry.

Cut two 1/8-inch-long slots (D) in the side of the stile that will be attached to the dresser. (These slots are to allow the hinges to lie flat.)

Drill the holes for the hinges and for the doorknob. (The hinges I used were 1/2 inch long, and I trimmed each end to reduce the hinge to 1/4 inch in length.) Attach the hinges to the stile with brass pins.

Place the door in the dresser. Mark the end of the side of the dresser where the hinges will be attached by making marks with a pin through the holes in the unattached sides of the door hinges. Drill pin-sized holes in the end of the side of the dresser for the hinges.

DRESSER—PART I

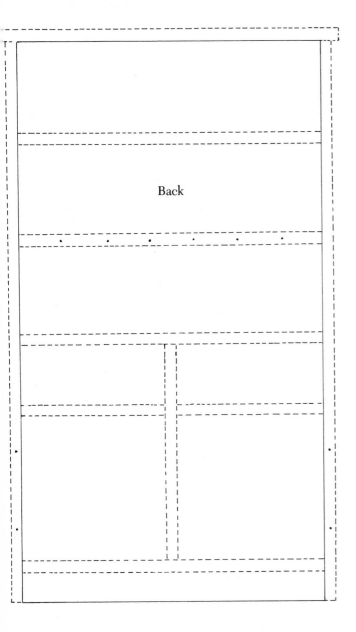

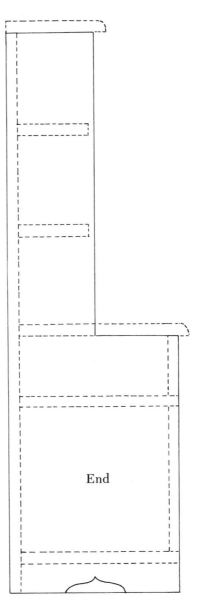

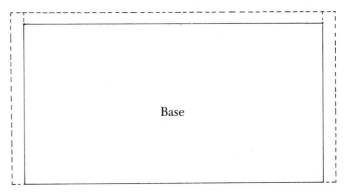

Before attaching the door to the side, hold the door in place to see if it swings smoothly. If the door does not open and close smoothly, sand the inside edge (behind the hinges) and round it off. Attach the door to the dresser.

If you wish, rather than drilling holes and using pins, you can attach the hinges with epoxy glue. Make the second door in the same way.

For the doorknobs, glue beads on pins into the small holes in the doors.

13. Drill six evenly spaced, pin-sized holes in the end of the lower dresser shelf. Glue small hooks in the holes.

14. Finish the dresser with shellac and Butcher's wax.

DRESSER—PART II

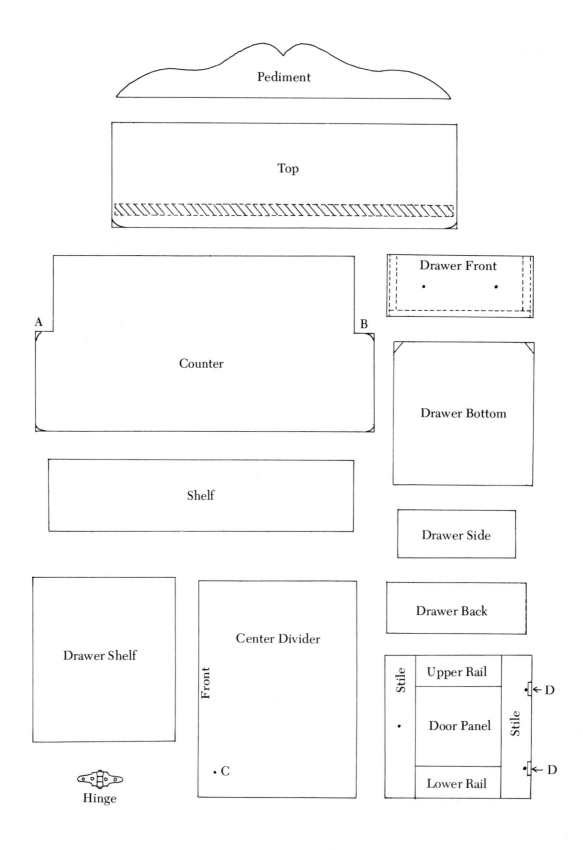

The living room. The painting on the wall is a framed British postage stamp (one of a series of stamps reproducing famous paintings). The paperweight on the left-hand side of the mantlepiece is a button, mounted on a snap. (This type of button is actually called a "paperweight button.") The tilt-top table to the right of the armchair is hinged at the top of the pedestal so that the tabletop does in fact "tilt."

A corner of the living room. The piano lid is hinged to the ends of the piano and opens and closes. The bowl on top of the piano is made from half a Ping-Pong ball (decorated with paper cutouts and then painted), mounted on a button. In the bowl are real dried flowers. The candles are lengths cut from toothpicks and then painted white. The candle flames are shapes cut from red sequins.

The bathroom. The fixtures are carved from blocks of balsa wood, except for the toilet seat cover, which is made from mahogany. The floor covering and the wall molding (the patterned part) are cut from printed paper table mats. The father doll's bathrobe on the door was made by my friend Robert Tynes.

A corner of the bathroom. The medicine cabinet above the wash basin is made from a small metal aspirin box. The mirror and its wooden frame are glued to the top of the box lid. The laundry basket next to the toilet was originally a plastic candy box, which is transformed by a cover made from string, wound and glued around the box, and then painted.

The A to Z of furnishings. These are some of the small objects described in pages 135–63. The candlesticks on the top shelf are push pins, with the pins removed. The labels on the coffee can and paper towel (on the third shelf) are cut from printed advertisements in magazines. The white cooking pot (second on the left at the bottom) is made from a plastic coaster — the type meant to be used on the bottom of metal chair legs, as a protection against scratched floors. The pot lid is made from the base of another coaster.

Rugs. From left to right, top line: braided rug, woven felt rug, and appliqué felt rug. Bottom line: spool-knitted rug, woven rug made on a simple homemade loom, and fur rug. (Consult the section on rugs, pages 168–73, for instructions on how to make all of these rugs.)

Wallpapers. From left to right, top line: the stenciled wallpaper which is in the children's room; potato-block printed wallpaper (the same design as shown in the kitchen but in different colors); and a potato-block printed wallpaper. Bot-

tom line: stenciled wallpaper (the molding is a combination of wooden molding and embossed paper), potato-block printed wallpaper, and a stenciled wallpaper. (Consult the section on wallpaper, pages 173–75, for instructions on potato-block and stencil cutting and printing.) The tiles: flowers and diamonds drawn on small white china tiles with felt markers and black ink; the blue and white tiles are alternating squares of white paper and motifs cut from the printed design inside an envelope. These tiles are glued to a card backing and then varnished.

Kitchen Sink and Cupboard

(Scale: 1 inch to 1 foot)

MATERIALS

1/8-inch-thick wood for all the wooden parts of the sink
    and cupboard, except the actual sink unit and the
    cupboard latch

1/16-inch-thick wood for the sink unit

1/8-inch dowel for the latch

Soldering wire for the towel rail, taps, and faucet

A half of a small snap for the drain cover

Straight pins for hinging

Silver paint

Two map pins for the doorknobs

Shellac

Butcher's wax

White glue

Tracing paper

Epoxy glue

I used aged plywood for the cupboard and sink and balsa wood for the sink unit. I painted the sink unit silver, but left the rest of the wood in its natural state.

See the general instructions for making wooden furniture, page 59.

1. Trace and transfer all the wooden pattern pieces to the wood. Cut the back, the top, the base, the pedestal, the upper rail, the lower rail, the stile, two doors, and two ends. Cut the sink base, front and back, and two ends.

2. Sand the top corners of the back, rounding them off. Drill three holes, 1/16 inch deep and 1/16 inch in diameter, in the back, for the taps and faucet.

3. Drill two holes, 1/16 inch deep and 1/16 inch in diameter, in *one* end for the towel rail.

4. Take the top. Sand all four corners, rounding them off. Cut the hole in the top for the sink unit. Do this by first drilling a hole in the center of the rectangle that is to be cut away. Remove the blade from one end of a coping saw and thread it through the hole in the rectangle. Replace the loose end of the blade in the saw, and cut out the rectangle.

5. Glue the pieces of the sink unit together. Refer to the drawing for the correct positions of the pieces.

6. Glue the sink unit into the rectangular hole in the top.

(continued)

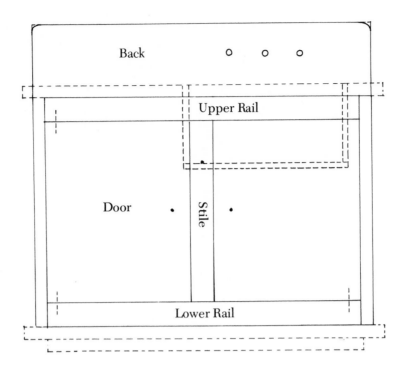

7. Sand the front corners of the base, rounding them off.

8. Take the upper and lower rails. Drill pin-sized holes, 1/8 inch deep, in the upper and lower rails, as indicated in the drawing.

9. Take the doors. Drill pin-sized holes (for hinging), 1/8 inch deep in the top and bottom of each door as indicated in the drawing.

10. Cut four 1/4-inch lengths of steel from straight pins.

11. Lay the back on a flat surface and glue the two ends in place.

12. Glue the lower rail between the ends. Glue a length of steel into each hole in the lower rail.

13. Glue a length of steel into the top holes in each cupboard door.

14. Fit the hole in the bottom of each cupboard door into the protruding lengths of steel in the lower rail.

15. Place the holes in the upper rail into the lengths of steel protruding from the tops of the cupboard doors, and glue the upper rail between the ends.

16. Glue the stile to the upper and lower rails.

17. Glue the top in place.

18. Glue the base in place.

19. Glue the pedestal to the base.

20. Drill pin-sized holes in the cupboard doors for the knobs.

21. Drill a pin-sized hole in the stile of the latch.

22. Paint the sink unit silver.

23. Finish the sink and cupboard with shellac and Butcher's wax.

24. Cut a length of solder wire for the faucet. Glue the faucet, using epoxy glue, in the center hole in the back.

25. Make the taps from solder wire, as shown in the drawing, gluing the parts together with epoxy glue. Glue the taps to the back, one on either side of the faucet.

26. Cut a length of solder wire, about 1-1/2 inches long, for the towel rail. Bend each end of the length of wire into a curve. Glue the ends of the towel rail into the holes in the end of the sink and cupboard.

27. Cut the length of dowel for the latch. Sand the latch so that it has a flat side. Then sand the latch to shape, as shown in the drawing. Drill a pin-sized hole through the center of the latch. Fix the latch to the stile with a pin.

28. Drill a small hole in the sink unit base. Glue the half snap (the "drain cover") in the hole.

29. Pin and glue the map-pin doorknobs to the cupboard doors.

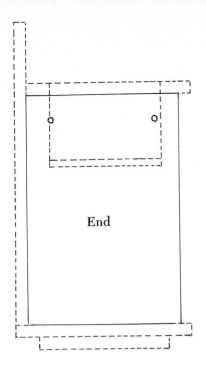

End

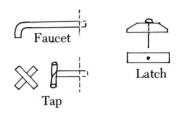

Faucet

Tap

Latch

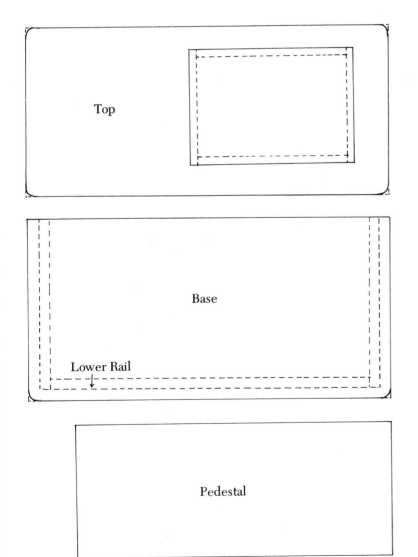

Top

Base

Lower Rail

Pedestal

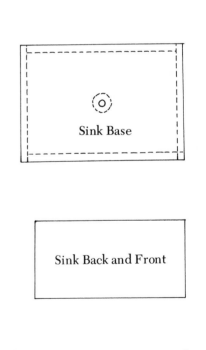

Sink Base

Sink Back and Front

Sink End

Stove

(Scale: 1 inch to 1 foot)

MATERIALS

1/8-inch-thick wood for all the exterior wooden parts of the stove

1/8-inch-thick strip of wood for the rack supports

1/16-inch-thick wood for the oven shelves, for the broiler back, bottom, and sides, and for the broiler shelf

Five map pins and a silver sequin for the oven controls

Four halves of large snaps for the top burners

Two pull-openers from the tops of soda or beer cans for the oven and broiler handles

A section of plastic from a berry or tomato box, for the oven rack

Straight pins for hinging the oven door

Gesso

Silver paint

Acrylic paints

Gloss polymer medium

White glue

Tracing paper

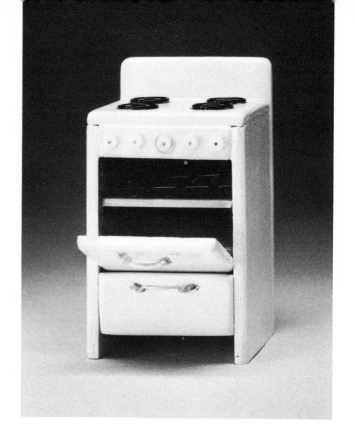

I made the exterior parts of the stove from plywood and the interior parts from balsa wood.

See the general instructions for making wooden furniture, page 59.

1. Trace and transfer the patterns to the wood. Cut the back, two sides, the control panel, the oven door, the broiler front, and the top. Cut the broiler bottom, back, two sides, and the broiler pan. Cut two oven shelves. Cut two rack supports. For the oven rack, cut a section of plastic from a berry box.

2. Sand the top corners of the back, rounding them off. Sand the top edges on the sides and front of the top, rounding them off. Sand the outside front edges of each of the sides, rounding them off. Sand all the front edges of the control panel, oven door, and broiler front, rounding them off.

3. Lay the back on a flat surface. Glue the sides to the back.

4. Glue the control panel between the two sides. (Note that it extends beyond the sides.)

5. Glue the top in place.

6. Glue a rack support to each side.

7. Glue the oven shelves in place.

8. For the handles, cut slits in the oven door and broiler front as shown in the drawing.

9. Place the oven door in position in the oven. Drill pin-sized holes (A) through each side and into the oven door as shown in the drawing. Remove the door.

10. Using a narrow U-shaped gouge blade, cut grooves in the broiler pan.

11. Glue the various pieces of the broiler together. Refer to the drawing for the correct positions of the pieces.

12. Paint all the parts of the stove, including the oven rack, with gesso.

13. Paint the outside and inside of the stove. (I used off-white for the exterior parts of the stove, and dark blue mottled with white for the interior parts of the stove.)

14. Paint the oven rack silver.

15. Finish the stove with a coat of gloss polymer medium.

16. Cut the sections from two can pull-openers as shown in the drawing. Glue a "handle" into the slits in the oven door and in the broiler front.

17. Drill four holes, each about 3/32 inch in diameter, in the top of the stove for the "burners." Glue half of a snap into each hole.

18. Drill five pin-sized holes in the control panel. Sand the tops of five map pins flat. Glue the silver sequin onto the center of the control panel. Pin and glue the map-pin "oven controls" to the panel.

19. Cut two lengths of steel, 1/4 inch long, from straight pins.

20 Place the oven door in position. Push a length of steel through each side of the oven into the oven door, hinging the door in place.

21. Place the rack in the oven.

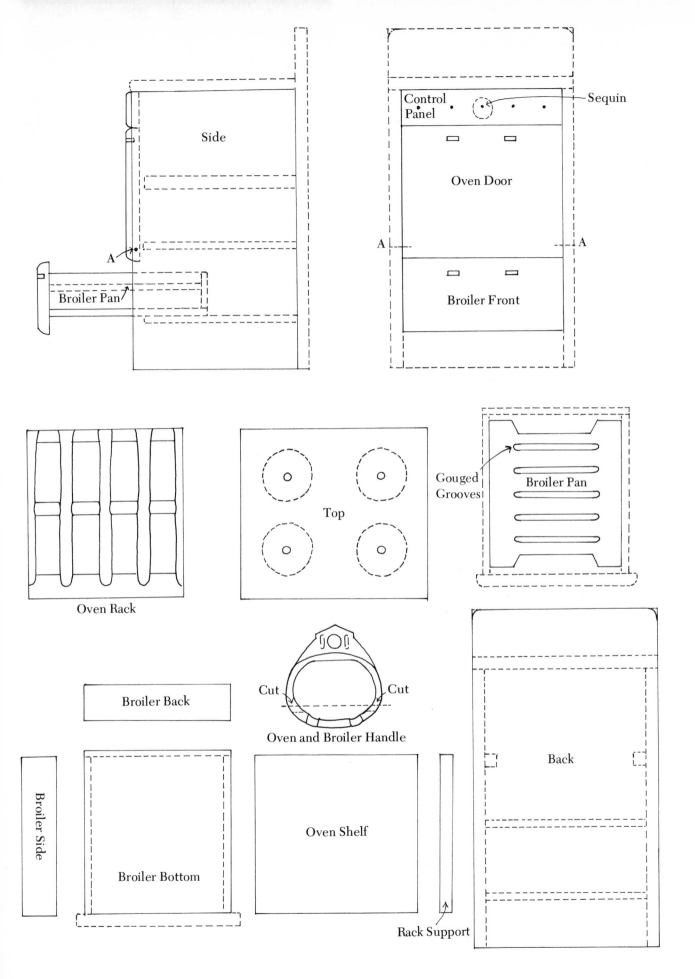

Side

Sequin

Control Panel

Oven Door

A — — A

Broiler Pan

Broiler Front

Oven Rack

Top

Gouged Grooves

Broiler Pan

Broiler Back

Cut   Cut

Oven and Broiler Handle

Broiler Side

Broiler Bottom

Oven Shelf

Rack Support

Back

Refrigerator

(Scale: 1 inch to 1 foot)

MATERIALS

1/8-inch-thick wood for the exterior parts of the refrigerator

1/16-inch-thick wood for the interior parts of the refrigerator, including the front strip

Two small hinges for the refrigerator door

Plastic-coated fabric tape for hinging the freezer door

A section of plastic from a berry or tomato box for the
racks

Solder wire for the refrigerator door handle

Rubber bands to use as "insulation"

A tiny magnet

A small strip of magnetic tape

White glue

Epoxy glue

Gesso

Silver paint

Acrylic paints

Gloss polymer medium

Tracing paper

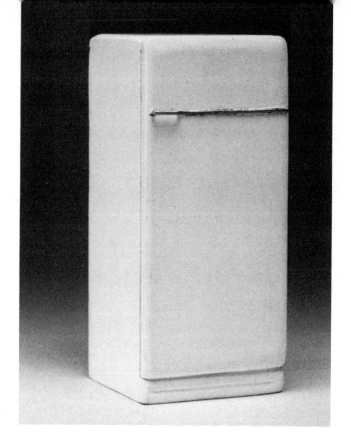

I used plywood for the exterior parts of the refrigerator,
and balsa wood for the interior parts. See the Appendix
(page 216) for mail-order dealers who supply small
hinges. *See the general instructions for making wooden*
See the general instructions for making wooden furni-
ture, page 59.

1. Trace and transfer the patterns to the wood. Cut the
door, the kickboard, two sides, the base, and the top.
Cut the freezer door, base, and two sides. Cut the support strips and the front strip. Cut a strip for the freezer
handle. Cut two racks from a section of a berry or tomato
box.

2. Take the door. Sand the top corners, rounding
them off. Sand all the front edges of the door, rounding
them off. Cut a groove, using a narrow U-shaped gouge
blade, from point A to point B in the front of the door.
Drill two holes, 1/16 inch deep and 1/16 inch in diameter,
in the front of the door, as shown in the drawing.

3. Take the kickboard. Cut a groove, using a U-shaped
gouge blade, along the center of the kickboard as indicated in the drawing. Sand the top and side edges of the
kickboard, rounding them off.

4. Take the top. Sand the top side edges of the top,
rounding them off.

5. Lay the back on a flat surface. Glue the sides to the
back.

6. Glue the top in place.

7. Glue the base in place.

8. Glue the kickboard to the base and sides.

9. Glue the front strip in place.

10. Glue the supports in position to the sides.

11. Glue the various parts of the freezer together as
shown in the drawing. Hinge the door to the base as
follows: Cut a length of tape about 1-1/2 inches long.
Stick half of the width of the tape to the inside of the
freezer door (refer to the drawing) and *glue* the other half
of the width of tape to the underneath side of the base.

12. Paint all the parts of the refrigerator, including the
racks, with a coat of gesso.

13. Paint the exterior and interior of the refrigerator
white or a color. Paint the racks silver.

14. Finish the refrigerator with a coat of gloss polymer
medium.

15. Cut lengths of rubber band, and glue them, using
epoxy glue, around the front ends of the sides, top, and
front strip, as shown in the drawing.

16. Cut the strip of magnetic tape and glue it in place,
as shown in the drawing.

17. Snip the ends of each hinge, so that it measures 1/4
inch across.

18. Glue the hinges, using epoxy glue, to the right-
hand side of the refrigerator, as shown in the drawing.

19. Cut an indentation, the correct size for your small
magnet, in the inside of the refrigerator door. (The magnet is used to keep the door closed, and therefore should
be placed directly opposite the strip of magnetic tape.)

20. Glue the free ends of the hinges to the inside of
the door.

21. Cut a length of solder wire about 1-7/8 inches long.
Bend one end of the wire into the shape of a handle,
about 3/8 inch long and 1/16 inch wide. Glue one end of
the handle into hole (C) in the door, and glue the rest of
the length of wire along the groove, pushing and gluing
the end of the wire into hole (B).

22. Place the racks in the refrigerator.

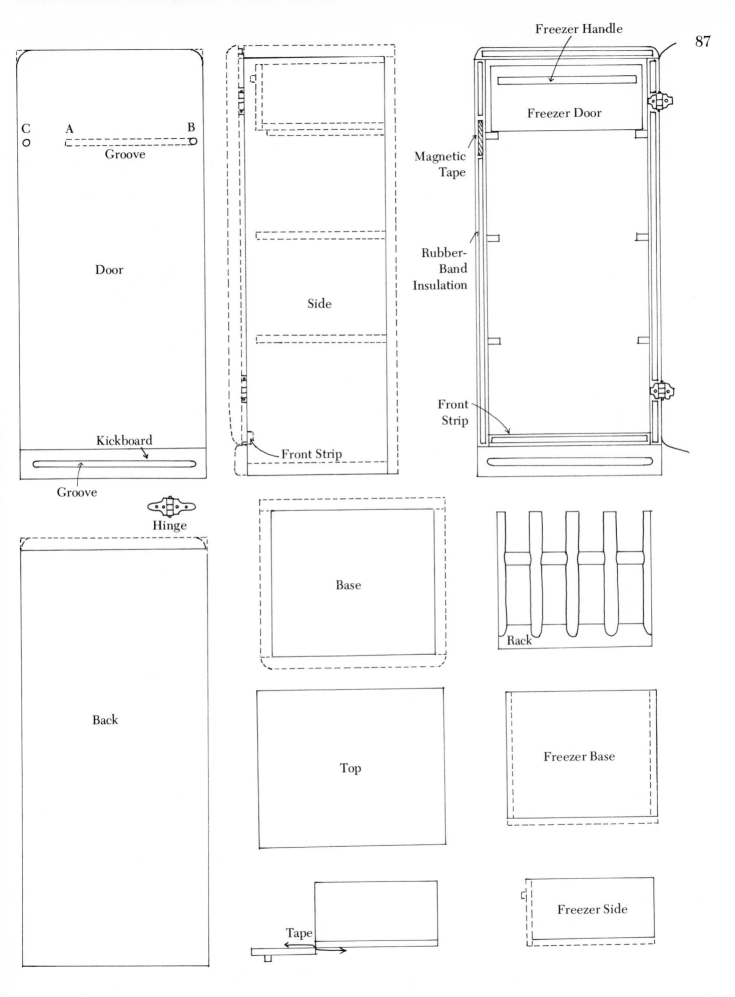

87

Freezer Handle

Freezer Door

Magnetic Tape

Rubber-Band Insulation

Front Strip

C   A   B
○   ○
Groove

Door

Kickboard

Groove

Hinge

Side

Front Strip

Back

Base

Rack

Top

Freezer Base

Tape

Freezer Side

Rocking Chair

(Scale: 1 inch to 1 foot)

MATERIALS

1//8-inch-thick wood for the seat, headrest, arms, and
   rockers
Round toothpicks for the spindles and stretchers
1/8-inch dowel for the legs
White glue
Tracing paper
Stain
Shellac
Butcher's wax

I used aged plywood for all the parts of the rocking chair
except the spindles and stretchers.
*See the general instructions for making wooden furni-
ture, page 59.*

1. Trace and transfer the patterns for the arms, seat,
headrest, and rockers, to wood. Cut two arms, the seat,
the headrest, and two rockers.

2. Cut the thirteen spindles from toothpicks. Each
spindle should include a 1/16-inch allowance at both ends
for the pegs. Carve a peg, 1/16 inch long and 1/16 inch in
diameter, at each end of the spindles.

3. Cut the two side stretchers, the back stretcher, and
the front stretcher from toothpicks. Each stretcher
should include a 1/16-inch allowance at both ends for the
pegs. Carve a peg, 1/16 inch long and 1/16 inch in diameter, at each end of the stretchers.

4. Cut the four legs from dowel. Each leg should include a 1/16-inch allowance at both ends for the pegs.
Carve a peg, 1/16 inch long and 1/16 inch in diameter, at
each end of the legs.

5. Take the chair seat. Sand the top front edge, rounding it off. And sand the back bottom edge rounding it off.
Drill four holes, 1/16 inch deep and 1/16 inch in diameter,
in the underneath side of the seat, for the legs. Drill
thirteen holes, 1/16 inch deep and 1/16 inch in diameter,
in the top side of the seat, for the spindles.

6. Take the two arms. Sand the top edges lightly,
rounding them off. Using a rounded needle file, sand a
shallow groove at the back end of each arm (A). Make the
groove conform to the shape of the spindle to which it
will be attached. Drill two holes, 1/16 inch deep and 1/16
inch in diameter, in the underside of each arm, for the
spindles, as shown in the drawing.

7. Drill the holes in the legs, 1/16 inch deep and 1/16
inch in diameter, for the stretchers. Refer to the drawings for the correct positions of the holes.

8. Take the rockers, and drill two holes, 1/16 inch deep
and 1/16 inch in diameter, in the top of each rocker for
the legs.

9. Take the headrest. Shape the headrest by sanding.
Sand the back so that it curves slightly, as shown in the
drawing of the bottom view of the headrest. Drill nine
holes, 1/16 inch deep and 1/16 inch in diameter, in the
bottom of the headrest for the spindles. Now all the parts
of the rocking chair are ready to assemble.

10. Take two legs, and join them together by gluing
the pegs in a side stretcher into the appropriate holes in
the legs. Glue the pegs in the bottom ends of the legs
into the holes in one of the rockers. Join the other two
legs in the same way.

11. Take a set of legs, and glue the pegs in the top
ends of the legs into the two left-hand side holes in the
bottom of the seat.

12. Glue a peg at the end of the front stretcher into the
hole in the side of the front leg that is attached to the
seat.

13. Glue a peg at the end of the back stretcher into the
hole in the side of the back leg that is attached to the
seat.

14. Take the other set of legs. Glue the pegs on the top
of the legs into the two right-hand side holes in the
bottom of the seat; and glue the pegs on the free ends of
the front and back stretchers into the appropriate holes
in the sides of the legs.

15. Glue the pegs on the bottom ends of the spindles
into the appropriate holes in the top of the seat.

16. Glue the pegs on the top ends of the nine back spindles into the holes in the bottom of the headrest. Note the angles of the spindles and the headrest.

17. Take the arms. Glue the pegs on the free ends of the arm spindles into the appropriate holes in the bottoms of the arms; and glue a back end of each arm to the last back spindle on either side of the chair.

18. Stain the rocking chair, and finish it with shellac and Butcher's wax.

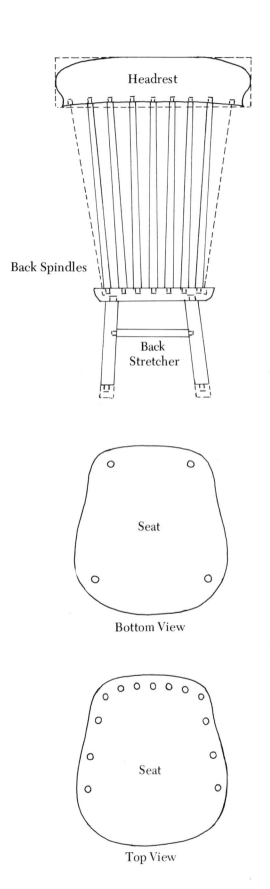

Headrest

Back Spindles

Back
Stretcher

Seat

Bottom View

Seat

Top View

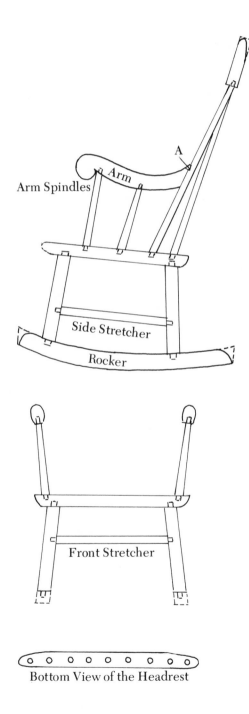

Arm Spindles

Arm

A

Side Stretcher

Rocker

Front Stretcher

Bottom View of the Headrest

Highchair

(Scale: 1 inch to 1 foot)

MATERIALS

    1/8-inch-thick wood for the stiles, arms, and seat

    3/32-inch-thick wood for the tray and the footrest

    1/16-inch-thick wood for the upper and lower rails and the back panel

    1/8-inch dowel for the legs

    Round toothpicks for the stretchers and spindles

    Straight pins

    White glue

    Gesso

    Acrylic paints

    Gloss polymer medium

    Tracing paper

I made the highchair (though not the legs or spindles) from basswood. The tray is not glued to the highchair, but has pins in its underside that fit into holes in the arms. Therefore the tray can be lifted on and off the highchair.

See the general instructions for making wooden furniture, page 59.

1. Trace and transfer to wood the patterns for the seat, stiles, and arms. Cut a seat, two arms, and two stiles. Sand the top corners of each stile, rounding them off.

Sand the corners of the seat, rounding them off. Bevel the front of the seat as indicated in the drawing. Drill six holes, 1/20 inch in diameter and 1/16 inch deep, in the top side of the seat, for the spindle pegs, as indicated in the drawing. Drill four holes, 1/16 inch in diameter and 1/16 inch deep, in the underside of the seat as shown in diagram 1. The legs are not set in straight, but cant outward; therefore, drill the holes at the correct angles for the leg pegs.

2. Take an arm. Carve and sand the top of the arm to shape as shown in the drawing. Drill three holes, 1/20 inch in diameter and 1/16 inch deep, in the underside of the arm for the spindle pegs, as shown in the drawing. Drill a pin-sized hole 3/32 inch deep in the top side of the arm, as shown in diagram 2. Follow the same instructions for the other arm.

3. Trace and transfer the patterns for the tray and footrest to the wood. Cut the tray and footrest.

4. Take the tray. Retrace the dotted lines on the tray with the tip of the blade in an X-acto knife, making a cut only about 1/32 inch deep. The rim of the tray, from the dotted line to the outer edge, is 1/32 inch higher than the center area. Therefore, using a chisel blade, gently gouge out the center area of the tray, taking care not to cut deeper than 1/32 inch. Sand the top of the tray so that the surface is smooth.

5. Take the footrest. Sand the surface of the underneath side, so that the front of the footrest is narrower than the back (A).

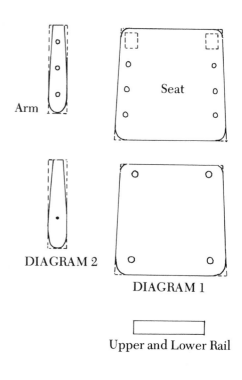

Arm

Seat

DIAGRAM 2

DIAGRAM 1

Upper and Lower Rail

6. Cut the four legs from dowel. Each leg length should include a 1/16-inch allowance for the pegs.

7. Whittle pegs, 1/16 inch long, at the top end of each leg. Drill holes, 1/16 inch in diameter and 1/16 inch deep, in the legs for the stretchers. (Refer to the drawings for the positions of the holes.)

8. Cut the back and front stretchers and the two side stretchers from round toothpicks. Each stretcher length should include a 1/8-inch allowance for the pegs. Whittle a peg 1/16 inch long at the end of each stretcher.

9. Glue the pegs in the front stretcher into the holes in the front legs. Glue the pegs in the back stretcher into the holes in the back legs. Glue the pegs at one end of the side stretchers into the holes in the back legs. Glue the pegs at the other end of the side stretchers into the holes in the front legs. Glue the pegs at the top of the legs into the holes in the underneath side of the seat. Check that the chair stands firmly.

10. Trace and transfer the patterns for the panel and the rails to the wood. Cut the panel and an upper and lower rail.

11. Glue the panel between the two stiles in the position shown in the drawings.

12. Glue the upper and lower rails in place.

13. Glue the bottom ends of the stiles to the seat.

14. Cut six spindles from round toothpicks. Each spindle length should include a 1/8-inch allowance for the pegs. Whittle a peg, 1/16 inch long, at both ends of each spindle.

15. Glue the pegs on the bottom ends of the spindles into the holes in the top of the seat.

16. Take and arm. Glue the back end of the arm to a stile, and the pegs at the top of the spindles into the holes in the underneath side of the arm. Glue the other arm in position in the same way.

17. Drill a pin-sized hole, 1/16 inch deep, into each of the front legs (where the footrest will be attached). Take the footrest and hold it in position against the front legs. Check the correct positions for the holes in the back end of the footrest (B). (They should be aligned with the holes in the legs.) Drill two pin-sized holes, 1/16 inch deep, in the end of the footrest. Cut two 1/8-inch lengths from a straight pin..Glue the lengths of pin into the holes in the back end of the footrest. Glue the pins in the footrest into the holes in the front of the legs.

18. Take the tray. Mark the position for the holes on the underneath side of the tray, as shown in diagram 3. Hold the tray in position on the top of the arms, and check the correct position for the holes. (They should be aligned with the holes in the top of the arms.) Drill two pin-sized holes, 1/20 inch deep, in the underneath side of the tray.

19. Cut two 1/8-inch lengths from a straight pin. Glue the lengths of pin into the holes in the tray.

20. Give the highchair and tray a coat of gesso.

21. Paint the highchair and tray.

22. Trace and transfer the flower design to the panel. Paint the flower.

23. Finish the highchair and tray with a coat of gloss polymer medium.

24. When the highchair is dry, place the tray in position.

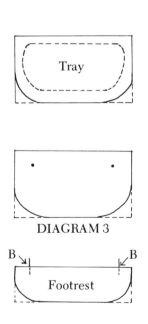

DIAGRAM 3

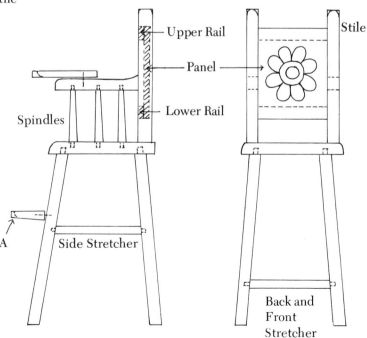

Ladder-Back Chair

(Scale: 1 inch to 1 foot)

MATERIALS

 1/16-inch-thick wood for the slats

 3/16-inch dowel for the legs

 1/8-inch dowel for the seat stretchers and the turned front stretcher

 Round toothpicks for the plain front stretcher, the back stretcher, and the side stretchers

 Upholstery thread or carpet thread for the "rush" seat

 White glue

 Plastic-coated fabric tape

 A jar or can approximately 12 inches in diameter

 Stain

 Shellac

 Butcher's wax

I used basswood for the slats. I stained the wooden parts of the chair a light golden oak color. I used upholstery thread for the rush seat (the slightly waxed kind of twine that is used to sew buttons onto tufted sofas and chairs). After the seat was completed, I painted it with watercolors—a straw color.

See the general instructions for making wooden furniture, page 59.

1. Trace the pattern for the slats. Cut out four slats.

2. The slats have to be bent into a slight curve (diagram 1). Use the following procedure to bend the slats: Soak the slats in hot water for about twenty minutes. While the slats are still warm, tape them firmly, at each end, to the jar or can (diagram 2). Allow the slats to dry overnight.

3. Cut the back and front legs from dowel, adding 1/4 inch or more to each length, as shown by the dotted lines. (The extra wood makes it easier to hold the dowel when you are turning and whittling it to shape.)

4. Take a back leg. Mark the turning on the top of the leg. Hand-turn and whittle the leg to shape. (See the general directions for whittling on page 29.) Turn and shape the other back leg.

5. Take a front leg. Sand the top edge of the leg, rounding it off. Mark the turning on the bottom of the leg for the foot. Hand-turn and whittle the foot to shape. Turn and shape the other front leg.

6. Take the slats. By sanding, reduce the thickness of each end of the slats (A) to 1/32 inch.

7. Cut the four seat stretchers from dowel. (Each stretcher length should include 1/10-inch allowance for the pegs. Note that the seat stretchers are not all the same length.)

8. Whittle a peg, 1/20 inch long, at each end of the stretchers.

9. Cut the turned front leg stretcher from dowel. (The stretcher length should include 1/10-inch allowance for the pegs.)

10. Mark the turnings on the front stretcher. Hand-turn and whittle the stretcher to shape. Whittle a peg 1/20 inch long on each end of the stretcher.

11. Cut one back and one front and four side stretchers from toothpicks. (Each stretcher length should include 1/10-inch allowance for the pegs.)

12. Whittle a peg, 1/20 inch long, at each end of the stretchers.

13. Take the back legs. Cut oblong grooves, 1/8 inch long by 1/32 inch wide by 1/16 inch deep in the legs, for the slats to fit into. Refer to the drawings for the correct positions of the grooves. Drill the holes in the back legs, 1/16 inch in diameter and 1/20 inch deep, for the seat stretchers and the back and side stretchers.

14. Take the front legs. Drill holes, 1/16 inch in diameter and 1/20 inch deep, for the seat stretchers and the front and side stretchers.

15. Next, construct the chair as follows: Lay a back leg on a flat surface (slat grooves facing to your right). Glue the four slats into the grooves (concave side up). Glue a peg on the end of the back seat stretcher into its hole in the leg. Glue a peg on the end of the back stretcher into its hole in the leg. Take the other back leg (slat grooves facing your left). Glue the free ends of the slats and the free pegs on the ends of the stretchers into the appropriate grooves and holes in the back leg. Take a front leg and lay it on a flat surface (front stretcher holes facing your right). Glue a peg on the end of the front seat

stretcher into its hole in the leg. Glue a peg on the ends of each front stretcher into their holes in the leg. Take the other front leg, and glue the free pegs on the ends of the stretchers into the appropriate holes in the legs. Turn the front legs over, so that the holes for the side stretchers are facing you. Glue the pegs on the ends of the seat side stretchers and the side stretchers into the appropriate holes in the front legs. Glue the pegs on the free ends of the side stretchers into the appropriate holes in the back legs. (During the construction of the chair, refer to the drawings for the correct positions of the various pieces.) Check that the chair stands firmly.

16. Stain the chair.

17. Finish the chair with shellac and Butcher's wax.

18. When the finish is dry, you can weave the "rush" seat. The seat is wider at the front than at the back. Therefore, since the threads must always cross the seat stretchers at right angles to avoid a gap when you come to the center, the front corners have to be filled in first. Start by squaring off the seat (to do this use an L-shaped square) as shown in diagram 3. The measurement between B and C should be the same as the back seat stretcher. Make pencil marks at points B and C.

19. Cut three or four lengths of thread each about 10 inches long. (I find it easier to weave the thread using a short embroidery needle, which has a large eye.)

Take a length of thread and glue one end to point D, clamping it in place with a spring-type clothespin. Begin to weave the thread in the directions shown by the arrows in diagram 4. (Bring the thread under and then over the front stretcher; then under and over the left-hand side stretcher; across the seat and under and then over the right-hand side stretcher; finally under and then over the front stretcher.) At point E glue and clamp

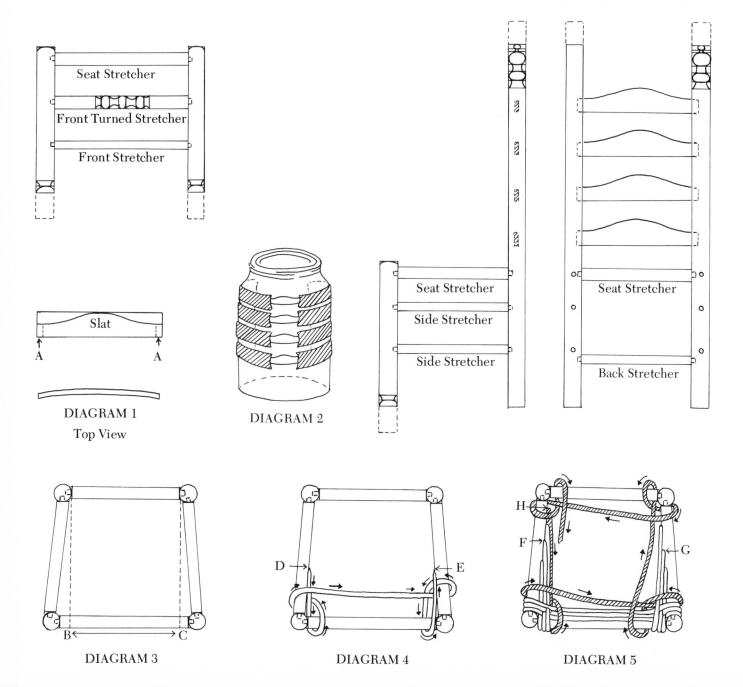

DIAGRAM 1
Top View

DIAGRAM 2

DIAGRAM 3

DIAGRAM 4

DIAGRAM 5

the end of the thread (cutting off any surplus thread) to the side stretcher, exactly parallel with point D. Note when weaving the "rush" seat, the thread should be pulled firmly and pushed into the corners as you weave. Take care not to pull too firmly, as the shape of the seat will get distorted or the chair might even fall apart.

Glue and clamp another length of thread to point F. Weave the thread over and under the stretchers in the same way as with the first piece of thread, but gluing and clamping it at point G parallel to F.

Continue in the same way with one or two more pieces of thread, until the two front corners are filled.

20. Now start weaving full bouts, going around the *entire* chair seat. Glue and clamp a long length of thread to point H. Weave the thread following the directions of the arrows in diagram 5. Continue weaving the thread until the seat stretchers are filled. If your length of thread is not long enough to complete "rushing" the seat, join extra thread with a knot under the seat. (*Note:* Even though you have squared off the seat, you may find that the back and front stretchers are filled before the side stretchers, or vice versa. Should this be so, simply weave the thread back and forth—or from side to side—making figure eights, between the cross thread in the center, until all the stretchers are filled.) Finish off by weaving the end into the underside of the seat.

Dolls' House (for the dolls)

(Scale: 1 inch to 1 foot)

MATERIALS

　　1/16-inch-thick balsa wood for the front, sides, and back of the house
　　1/8-inch-thick balsa wood for the front and back of the roof, and for the base
　　3/8-inch-square block of balsa wood for the chimneys
　　1/32-inch-thick balsa wood for the door and window casings, the window sills, and the pediments
　　Clear, stiff plastic (from wrappings) for the window glass
　　A scrap of lightweight fabric for the curtains
　　A small bead and a pin for the doorknob
　　White glue
　　Gesso
　　Acrylic paints
　　Gloss polymer medium
　　Plastic-coated fabric tape to hinge the door
　　Tracing paper

See the general instructions for making wooden furniture, page 59.

1. Trace and transfer the pattern pieces to the various thicknesses of wood that are indicated above. Cut a front, a back, and two sides. (Using an X-acto knife and steel ruler, cut spaces for the door and windows in the front section, and save the "door" piece of wood.) Cut a base, and the front and back of the roof. For the door, cut two side casings and a top casing. Miter the corners as shown in the drawing. Cut the pediment to go above the door.

For the windows, cut eight side casings and four top casings. Miter the corners as shown in the drawing. Cut four pediments to go above the windows. Cut four window sills. Make two chimneys in the following way: Cut the blocks of wood. Draw an X from corner to corner, on both sides of each block. Cut out the triangle-shaded area in each block, as shown in drawing 1.

2. For the curtains, cut four small strips of fabric. Sew running stitches along the top of each length. Pull the threads on each "curtain" to form gathers. Finish off the threads. Glue the edges of a curtain to the top and side edges of a window frame. (The curtains are glued to the inside of the front of the house.)

3. For the glass window panes, cut four rectangles from stiff, clear plastic, each a fraction larger than the window frames. Working on the front of the house, glue the edges of a piece of "glass" over a window.

4. Put the door back in position. Hinge one side with a strip of tape (on the inside).

5. Glue the door and window casings in place. Glue an edge of each sill (so that it protrudes) to the bottom of each window frame.

6. Glue the pediments in place.

7. Put the back of the house on a flat surface. Glue the sides to the back, and then glue the front to the sides. Check that the house is squared.

8. Bevel the length of the sides of each piece of the

roof as shown in drawing 2. Glue the front and back of the roof to the house.

9. Glue the chimneys to the roof.

10. Glue the house to the base.

11. Paint the house with gesso.

12. Paint the house with acrylic paints. Paint a + on each piece of window "glass." If you wish, paint flowers on one side of the house, as shown in drawing 2, and a tree on the other side as shown in drawing 3. Finish the house with a coat of gloss polymer medium. Should you decide to make a dolls' house for the dolls' dolls' house, you may be in trouble!

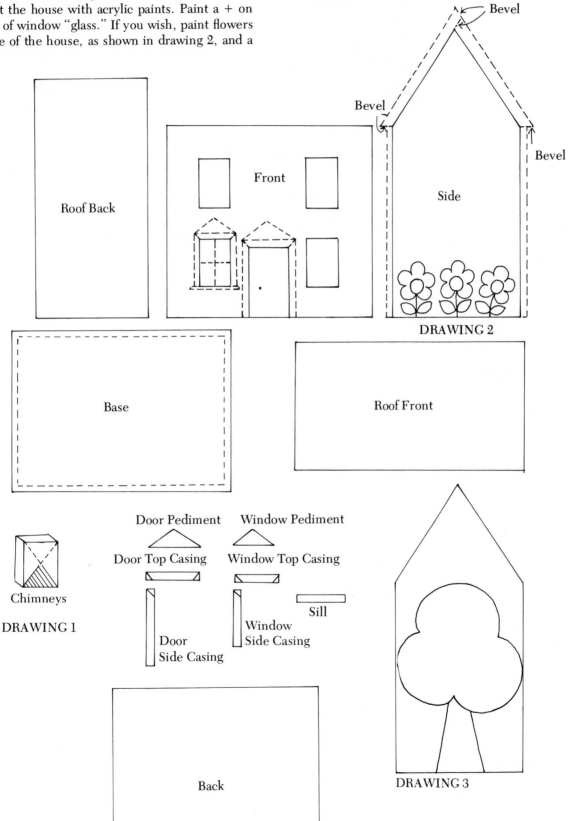

DRAWING 2

DRAWING 1

DRAWING 3

Toy Chest and Bench

(Scale: 1 inch to 1 foot)

MATERIALS

    1/8-inch-thick wood for all the parts of the chest
    Two small hinges
    White glue
    Quick-drying epoxy glue for attaching the hinges
    Gesso
    Acrylic paints
    Gloss polymer medium
    Tracing paper

I used 1/8-inch-thick plywood for the chest. The Appendix (page 216) lists dealers who sell small hinges.
See the general instructions for making wooden furniture, page 59.

1. Trace and transfer the patterns to the wood (excluding the toy train designs). Cut a back, a base, a lid, a front, and two ends.

2. Sand the corners of the feet and the two extended parts on the back, rounding them off. Sand the front corners of the lid, rounding them off.

3. Lay the back on a flat surface. Glue the ends to the back. Glue the base (between the ends) to the back. Glue the front to the ends. (Note the correct positions for the pieces in the drawing.)

4. Cut the recesses (A) in the top of the lid for the hinges. Glue the hinges to the lid. Glue the free ends of the hinges to the back. (The lid should extend 1/8 inch over the front of the chest.)

5. Give the chest a coat of gesso.

6. Paint the chest.

7. Trace and transfer the patterns for the toy train design to the front and ends of the chest. Paint the designs.

8. Finish the entire chest with a coat of gloss polymer medium.

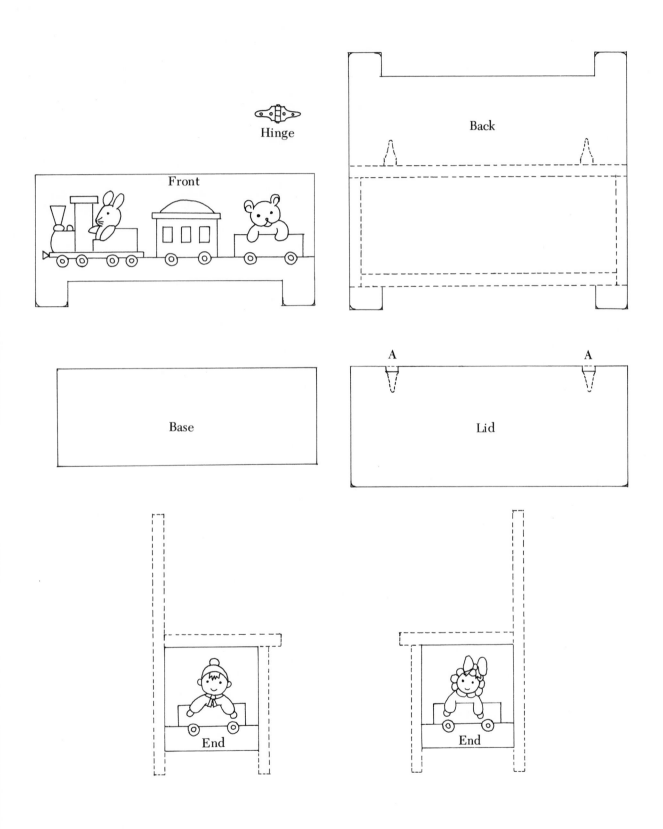

Hinge

Front

Back

Base

Lid

A   A

End

End

Bunk Beds

(Scale: 1 inch to 1 foot)

MATERIALS

    1/8-inch-thick wood for the headboards, guard rails, sides,
        ends, and bases, and for the rungs of the ladder
    1/4-inch-thick wood for the legs
    3/16-inch-thick wood for the side supports of the ladder
    Straight pins
    White glue
    Tracing paper
    Shellac
    Butcher's wax

I used basswood for the bunk beds and the ladder. I did
not stain the wood, but finished it with shellac and
Butcher's wax.

Note: To make a single bed using these patterns, cut
the legs from point A to point B. I have drawn two extra
headboard designs; either shape could be used in place
of the rectangular headboard.

*See the general instructions for making wooden furni-
ture, page 59.*

1. Trace and transfer the pattern pieces to the wood.
Cut four headboards, four legs, four ends, four sides,
two guard rails, two bases, five ladder rungs, and two
side supports for the ladder.

2. Sand each of the top corners of the four legs, rounding them off.

3. Take two of the legs, and put them on a flat surface.
Glue two ends and two headboards to the legs as shown
in drawing 1. (The backs of the ends and the headboard
must be flush with the backs of the legs.) Construct the
other end of the bunk bed in the same way.

4. Glue an end of each base to each of the four end
pieces. (Make the joints so that the bottom of each base
is flush with the bottom of each end piece.)

5. Glue the sides to the bases and legs as shown in
drawing 2. (The bottom edges of the sides must be flush
with the bottoms of the bases.)

6. Glue the guard rails to the legs.

7. Next make the ladder. Take the two side supports
and sand each of the top corners to round them off. Draw
a center line along the length of one side of each side
support. Drill five pin-sized holes, 1/16 inch deep, along
the lines on each of the side supports, spacing them as
indicated in the drawing of the ladder.

8. Drill a pin-sized hole, 1/16 inch deep, in the center
of the ends of each rung.

9. Cut ten 1/8-inch lengths of steel from straight pins.
Glue a length of steel in each hole in the side supports.

10. Put one of the side supports on a flat surface (pins
pointing to your right). Pin and glue an end of each rung
to the side support. Take the other side support (pins
pointing to your left) and pin and glue the support to the
free ends of the rungs. Let the glue dry.

11. Drill a pin-sized hole, 1/8 inch deep, in the center
of the top of each side support. Cut two lengths of steel,
each 3/4 inch long, from straight pins. Bend them into
shape (C). Glue the short end of each bent pin into the
top of each side support (D). Hook the ladder to a guard
rail on one of the sides of the bunk beds.

12. Finish the ladder and the beds with shellac and
Butcher's wax.

BUNK BEDS—PART I

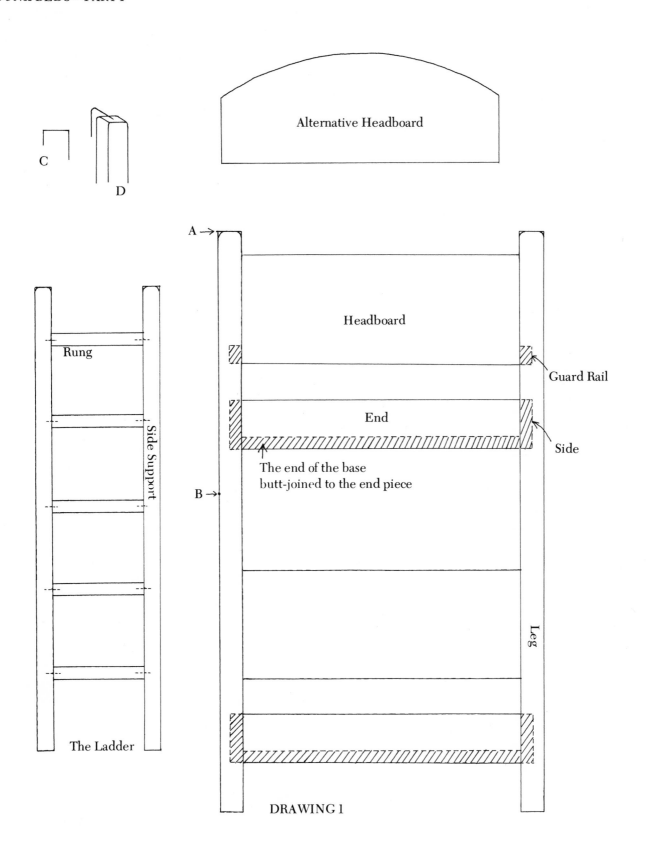

Alternative Headboard

C

D

A →

Headboard

Guard Rail

End

Side

The end of the base
butt-joined to the end piece

B →

Rung

Side Support

The Ladder

Leg

DRAWING 1

BUNK BEDS—PART II

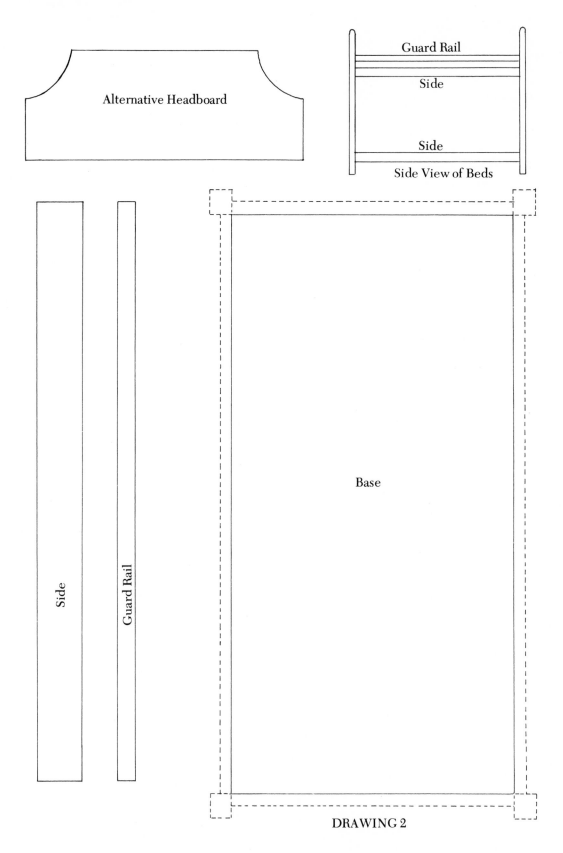

Alternative Headboard

Guard Rail

Side

Side

Side View of Beds

Side

Guard Rail

Base

DRAWING 2

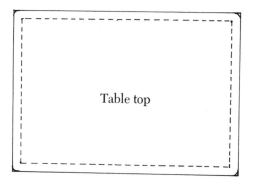

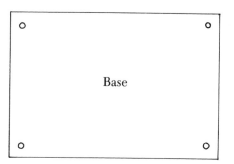

Child's Table

(Scale: 1 inch to 1 foot)

MATERIALS

    1/8-inch-thick wood for the table top and base
    1/8-inch dowel for the legs
    White glue
    Gesso
    Acrylic paints
    Gloss polymer medium
    Tracing paper

I used plywood for the table top and base.
See the general instructions for making wooden furniture, page 59.

1. Trace and transfer the patterns to the wood. Cut a table top and a base. Sand each corner of the table top to round it off. Cut four legs from the dowel.

2. Whittle a peg 1/16 inch long on one end of each leg. Sand the length of each leg, so that it tapers toward the bottom.

3. Glue the base to the table top.

4. Drill a hole 1/16 inch deep in each corner on the underside of the base. (Note that the legs are not set in at right angles to the base, but are canted slightly outward.)

5. Glue a leg in each corner hole.

6. Give the table a coat of gesso.

7. Paint the table, and finish it with gloss polymer medium.

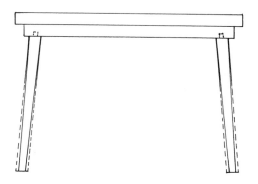

Bookcase and Closet

(Scale: 1 inch to 1 foot)

MATERIALS

> 1/8-inch-thick wood for all the parts of the bookcase and closet, except the interior parts of the drawer
>
> 1/16-inch-thick wood for the drawer bottom, back, and sides
>
> Seven map pins for the feet, the door, and the drawer knobs
>
> Straight pins for hinging, for the doorstop, and for the hanger rail
>
> White glue
>
> Gesso
>
> Acrylic paints
>
> Gloss polymer medium
>
> Tracing paper

I used plywood for the bookcase and shelves, except for the inside parts of the drawer; for that I used balsa wood. I painted the map pins the same color as the shelves.

See the general instructions for making wooden furniture, page 59.

1. Trace and transfer all the patterns to the wood. Cut the base, closet back, closet top, closet end, bookcase top, two bookcase ends, three bookcase shelves, drawer front, and drawer shelf.

Cut the drawer bottom, drawer back, and two sides.

2. Glue the two bookcase ends and the closet end to the base.

3. Glue the three bookcase shelves to the bookcase ends.

4. Glue the closet shelf in place.

5. Put the closet door in position. Drill a pin-sized hole (A) through the base and into the door. Drill a pin-sized hole (B) through the closet shelf and into the door.

6. Drill a pin-sized hole (C) in the closet end, for the doorstop.

7. Cut three 1/4-inch lengths of steel from straight pins.

8. Push a length of steel through the hole in the base and into the door. Push another length of steel through the closet shelf and into the door. (The door is now hinged in place, and should swing freely back and forth.)

9. Push and glue the remaining length of steel into hole (C) in the closet end, leaving one end of the steel protruding about 1/8 inch.

10. Glue the top of the closet in place.

11. Glue the top of the bookcase in place.

12. Glue the closet back in place.

13. Drill a pin-sized hole (D) in the back of the closet. Bend the head end of a straight pin into a hook shape. Pin and glue the "hanger rail" into the hole in the back of the closet, as indicated in the diagram.

14. Glue the various parts of the drawer together, following the instructions for basic drawer construction, page 31.

15. Give the piece of furniture a coat of gesso.

16. Paint the bookcase and cupboard.

17. Use gloss polymer medium as a finish.

18. Drill pin-sized holes in the base for the feet. Sand four map pins flat on top. Pin and glue the map pins to the base in the positions indicated.

19. Drill two pin-sized holes in the drawer front. Drill a pin-sized hole in the closet door. (See diagram for positions.) Pin and glue the drawer knobs and the doorknob in place.

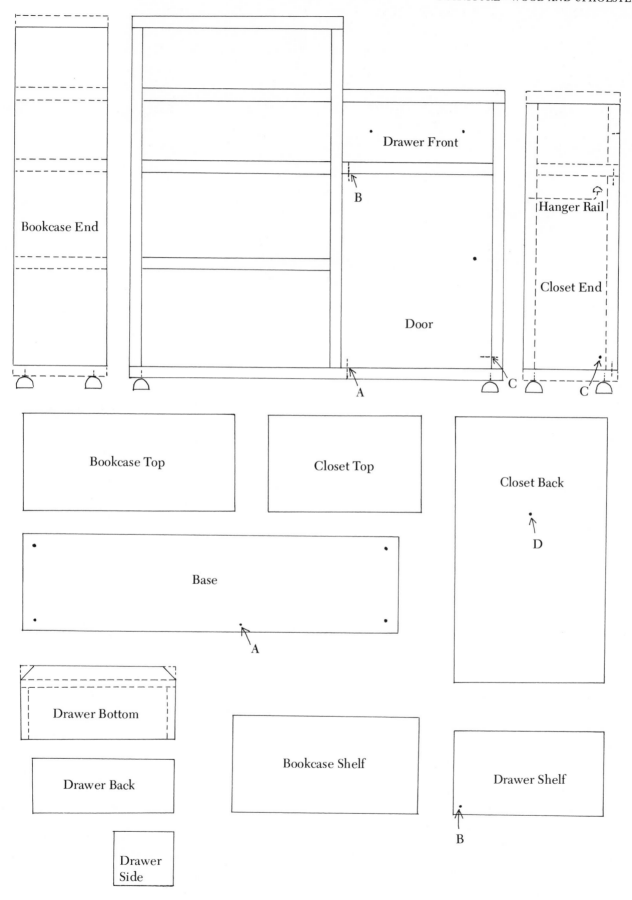

Bookcase End

Drawer Front

B

Hanger Rail

Closet End

Door

A

C

C

Bookcase Top

Closet Top

Closet Back

D

Base

A

Drawer Bottom

Drawer Back

Bookcase Shelf

Drawer Shelf

B

Drawer
Side

Crib

(Scale: 1 inch to 1 foot)

MATERIALS

1/8-inch-thick wood for the legs, rails, cross bars, and base
1/16-inch-thick wood for the panels
24 round toothpicks for the bars
16 beads
Thin wire for the beads
4 map pins for the feet
White glue
Epoxy glue
Gesso
Acrylic paints
Gloss polymer medium
Tracing paper

I used plywood for the legs, base, cross bars, and rails. And balsa wood for the panels.

See the general instructions for making wooden furniture, page 59.

1. Trace and transfer the patterns to wood.

2. Cut the base, four legs, four cross bars, six rails. Cut two panels. Cut twenty-four bars. Each bar should include a 1/16-inch allowance at each end for the pegs.

3. Sand the tops of the legs, rounding them off.

4. Lay two of the legs on a flat surface. Glue a panel in position between the legs. Note that the panel should be flush with the back of the legs.

5. Glue the lower and center rails in place.

6. Drill a pin-sized hole (A) in the side of each leg for the bead wire.

7. Glue the upper rail in place.

8. Make the other end of the crib in the same way.

9. Glue the base to the two ends of the crib.

10. Carve a peg, 1/16 inch long and 1/16 inch in diameter, at both ends of each bar.

11. Drill twelve holes, 1/16 inch deep and 1/16 inch in diameter, in the appropriate places in each cross bar.

12. Lay a cross bar on a flat surface, holes facing to your right. Glue the pegs on one end of each of twelve bars into the holes in the cross bar. Take a second cross bar, and glue the free pegs on the ends of the bars into the holes in the cross bar.

Make the other side of the crib in the same way.

13. Give all the parts of the crib a coat of gesso.

14. Paint the crib.

15. Finish the crib with gloss polymer medium.

16. Glue the sides of the crib to the ends.

17. If you wish, paint the heart design on the end panels.

18. Cut two lengths of wire, each about 2-5/16 inches long. Lay the crib on its side. Using epoxy glue, fix a length of wire in each of the holes in the upper legs that are furthest away from you. Allow the glue to dry. Thread eight beads on each wire, and then glue the free ends of the wire into the holes in the legs nearest to you.

19. Make pin-sized holes in the bottom of each leg. Sand the tops of the map pins to flatten them. Pin and glue a map pin into each leg for the feet.

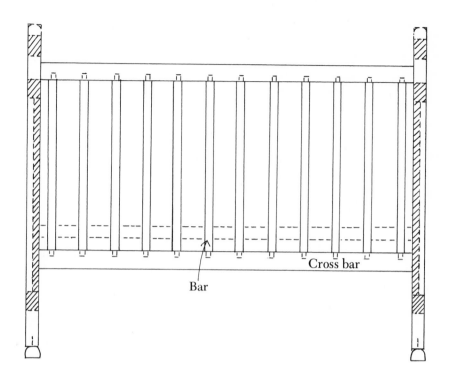

Bar

Cross bar

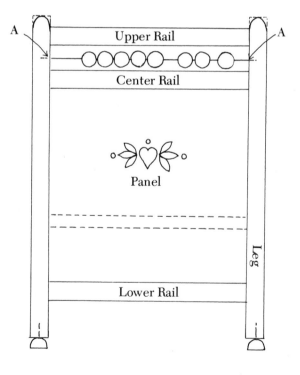

A   A

Upper Rail

Center Rail

Panel

Leg

Lower Rail

Base

Turn the seat top-side up, and drill five holes, each 1/16 inch in diameter and 1/16 inch deep, for the bottom pegs on the spindles. (Note that the holes are not in a straight line.)

2. Take the back rail and sand the front top edge to shape (A). Drill five holes, 1/16 inch in diameter and 1/16 inch deep, in the base of the rail as shown in diagram 2. (Note that the holes are not in a straight line.)

3. Cut four legs from dowel. Each leg length should include the 1/16-inch allowance for the peg. Whittle a 1/16-inch-long peg at the top of each leg.

4. Cut a back, a front, and a center stretcher from round toothpicks. Each stretcher length should include 1/8-inch allowance for the pegs. Whittle a 1/16-inch-long peg on each end of each stretcher.

5. Drill a hole, 1/16 inch in diameter and 1/16 inch deep, in each leg for the back and front stretchers. (Refer to the drawings for the correct positions.) Drill a hole, 1/16 inch in diameter and 1/16 inch deep, in the center of the back stretcher and in the center of the front stretcher.

6. Glue the pegs on the ends of the back stretcher into the holes in the back legs. Glue the pegs on the ends of

Child's Chair

(Scale: 1 inch to 1 foot)

MATERIALS

    1/8-inch-thick wood for the seat and back rail
    1/8-inch dowel for the legs
    Round toothpicks for the stretchers and spindles
    White glue
    Gesso
    Acrylic paints
    Gloss polymer medium
    Tracing paper

I used plywood for the seat and back rail of the chair.
See the general instructions for making wooden furniture, page 59.

1. Trace and transfer the patterns for the seat and the back rail to the wood, and cut them out. Sand the corners of the seat, rounding them off. Working on the underneath side of the seat, bevel the edges as shown in the drawings.

Drill four holes, each 1/16 inch in diameter and 1/16 inch deep, in the underside of the seat for the leg pegs, as shown in diagram 1. (The holes should be drilled at an angle, as the legs are not set in straight, but cant outward.)

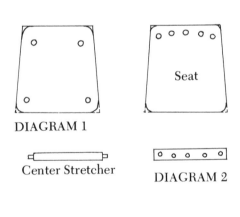

DIAGRAM 1

Seat

Center Stretcher

DIAGRAM 2

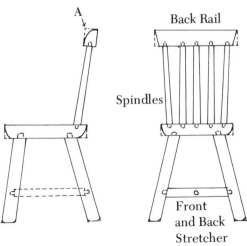

A

Back Rail

Spindles

Front and Back Stretcher

the front stretcher into the holes in the front legs. Glue the peg on one end of the center stretcher into the center hole in the back stretcher. Glue the peg on the other end of the center stretcher into the center hole in the front stretcher.

7. Glue the pegs at the top of the legs into the holes on the underneath side of the seat. (Check that the chair stands firmly.)

8. Cut five spindles from round toothpicks. Each spindle length should include 1/8-inch allowance for the pegs. Whittle a peg, 1/16 inch long, on the end of each spindle.

9. Glue the pegs on the bottom ends of the spindles into the holes in the seat.

10. Glue the pegs at the top ends of the spindle into the holes at the base of the back rail. (Note the angle of the back of the chair.)

11. Give the chair a coat of gesso.

12. Paint the chair, and finish it with gloss polymer medium.

Armchair

(Scale: 1 inch to 1 foot)

MATERIALS

    3/8-inch-thick balsa wood for the arms
    1/8-inch-thick balsa wood for the back
    3/4-inch-thick balsa wood for the base
    1/4-inch-thick balsa wood for the cushion
    A square of 1/2-inch-thick foam rubber, approximately 8 inches by 8 inches for the padding
    1/4 yard of fabric for covering the armchair
    Thin card
    White glue
    Fabric glue
    Two 1/2-inch diameter wooden beads for the feet (the beads are cut in half to make four feet)
    Tracing paper

I used fabric from an old paisley shawl to cover the armchair, but any fabric that is not too heavy would be suitable. The patterns with floral designs are for fabric; the shaded patterns are for foam rubber; the solid patterns are for wood or card. An exception is the cushion pattern; the shaded area is for both the foam rubber *and* the wood.

See the general instructions for making wooden furniture, page 59.

1. Trace and transfer all the wood patterns. Cut a back, two arms, a base, and a cushion. Note that the back of the arm is cut at a slight angle.

2. Sand the top edges of the arms, rounding them off as shown in diagram 1. Cut a 1/8-inch wedge-shape diagonally off the back of each arm, from top to bottom, as indicated in diagram 1. (Because the backs of the arms are cut at an angle, when they are glued to the back of the armchair they will cant out slightly.)

3. Trace and transfer the patterns for the foam rubber. Cut the padding for the back, the cushion, and the two arms.

4. Trace the patterns for the fabric, and cut them out. Pin the patterns to a single layer of fabric. Pin the arm patterns on the bias. Cut out the fabric pieces. *Note:* The squares shown at the corners of some of the fabric patterns are only rough guides as to how much fabric to cut away to decrease the bulkiness at the corners. Don't cut the corners until you are actually covering the section of furniture, and you can therefore judge the exact amount of surplus fabric.

5. Take the wooden back of the armchair and its foam rubber padding. Glue the foam rubber to the back. Put some glue on the 1/8-inch-wide top edge of the back. Gently pull the top of the foam rubber and fix it to the top edge of the back. Using a razor blade, shave off some of the foam rubber, toward the bottom end of the back, so that it tapers into the wood.

6. Place the back—with the foam rubber surface down—on top of the wrong side of its fabric cover. Gently pull the fabric over the bottom edge of the back, and glue the edge of the fabric in place with fabric glue.

Pull the fabric over the top edge of the back, and glue the fabric in place, clipping the fabric edge so it will lie flat. Then glue the sides of the fabric to the back. (See diagram 2.)

7. Use the following directions to make each arm: Take the foam rubber padding for the arm. Roll one end of the foam rubber, and glue the length of foam rubber to the arm. Using a razor blade, shave off some of the foam rubber (the unrolled end) so that it tapers into the wood. (See diagram 3.) Take the fabric cover for the arm. Sew running stitches from point C to point D on each side of the fabric. Leave the threads loose.

Place the fabric over the arm and padding. Pull the threads to form gathers. The gathers will make the fabric fit firmly over each end of the arm.

Glue the bottom end of the fabric to the bottom of the arm. Glue the top end of the fabric to the side of the arm just below the padding. Fasten off the loose threads. (See diagram 4.)

8. With white glue fix the arms to the back. (See diagram 5.)

9. Take the wooden base of the armchair and its fabric cover. Place the wooden base on top of the wrong side of the fabric. Using fabric glue, first fold the fabric over one side and glue it to the bottom of the base. Then fold over and glue the other side to the bottom of the base. Then fold over and glue each end to the bottom of the base, trimming off excess fabric at corners.

10. Using white glue fix the base in position to the back and arms of the armchair.

11. Trace and transfer the pattern for the back-and-sides to card. Cut out the shape from the card.

12. Place the card, as shown in the pattern drawing, on top of the wrong side of its fabric cover. Fold the top of the fabric over the card, clipping the fabric edge so it will lie flat, and glue it in place. Fold each side over the card and glue them in place. Fold the bottom of the fabric over the card and glue it in place. Let the glue dry.

13. Glue the length of fabric-covered card, right side out, to the outer sides of the back and arms of the armchair. (See the side view of the chair—diagram 6.)

14. Cut two arm-fronts from card. Place the card, as shown in the pattern drawing, on top of the wrong side of its fabric cover. Fold the fabric over the edges of the card and glue in place.

Make the other arm-front in the same way. (*Note:* The curve must go in the opposite direction to the first arm front.)

15. Glue the arm-fronts to the arms.

16. Now make the cushion: Glue the foam rubber pad to the top of the wooden section of the cushion. Put some glue on the front area of the wood. Pull the foam rubber over the edge of the top, so that it covers the front area too. Using a razor blade, shave off the sharp edge of the foam rubber at the front of the cushion. (See diagram 6 for the sofa pattern, page 121.)

17. Take the fabric cushion cover. Center the cushion with the foam rubber surface down—on top of the wrong side of the fabric. Gently pull the fabric over each side of the cushion, and glue the edges of the fabric to the wooden bottom part of the cushion (see "Covering a Cushion," page 33). *Note:* Make sure the fabric is stretched tightly across the cushion, so that it is firm. Put the cushion on the chair.

18. For the feet, saw each wooden bead in half. Glue each foot in position to the underneath side of the base. (See diagram 7.) *Note:* You may wish to stain or paint the feet before gluing them to the armchair.

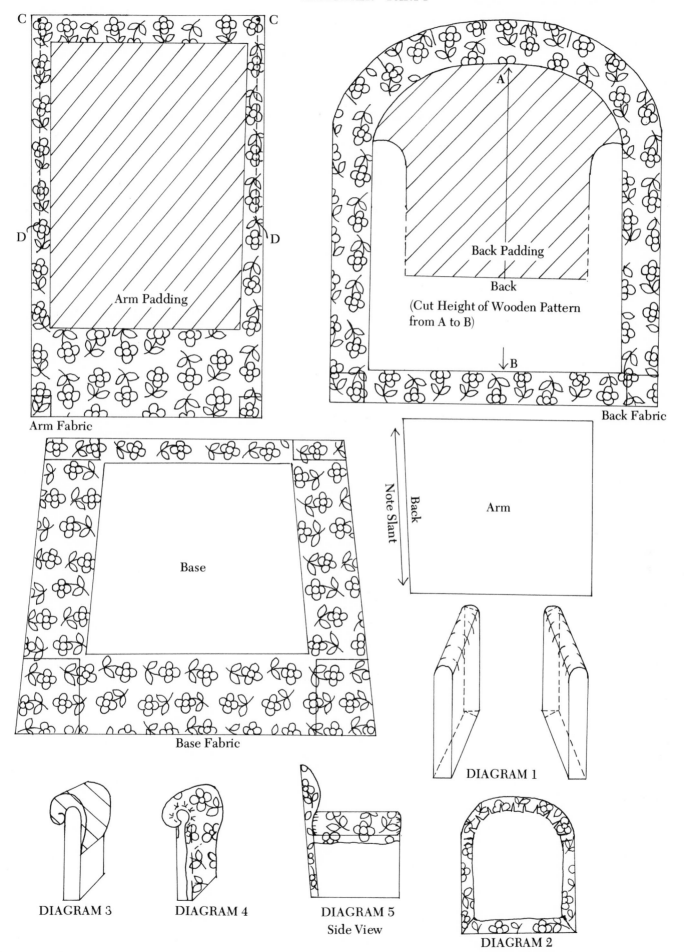

C   C

D   D

Arm Padding

Arm Fabric

A

Back Padding

Back

(Cut Height of Wooden Pattern
from A to B)

B

Back Fabric

Base

Base Fabric

Note Slant

Back

Arm

DIAGRAM 1

DIAGRAM 3

DIAGRAM 4

DIAGRAM 5
Side View

DIAGRAM 2

ARMCHAIR—PART II

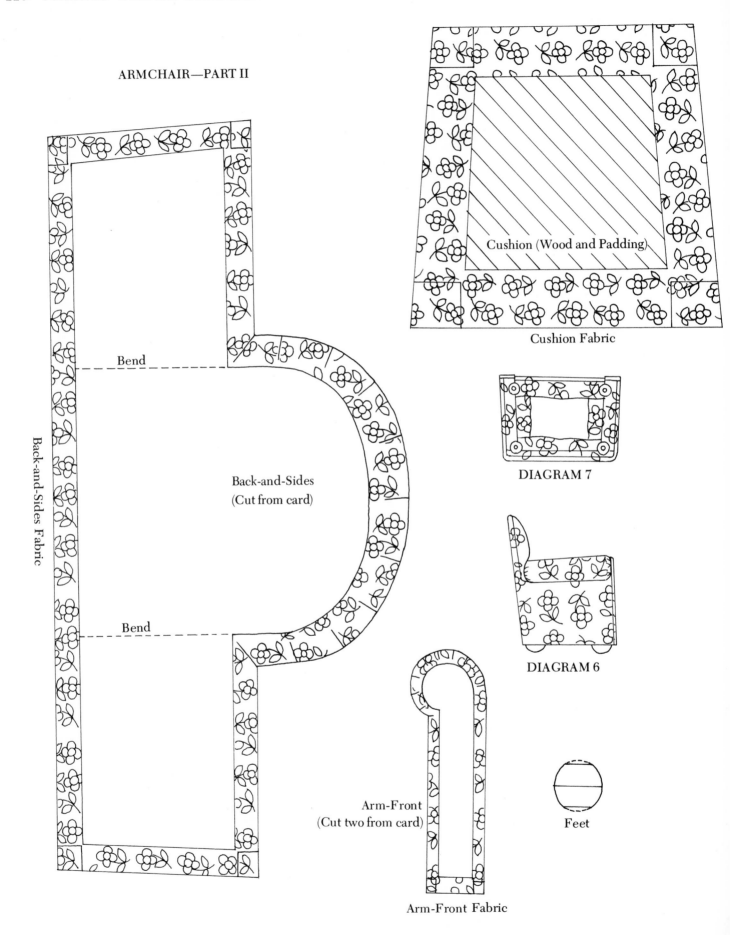

Cushion (Wood and Padding)

Cushion Fabric

DIAGRAM 7

DIAGRAM 6

Bend

Bend

Back-and-Sides Fabric

Back-and-Sides
(Cut from card)

Arm-Front
(Cut two from card)

Arm-Front Fabric

Feet

Coffee Table

(Scale: 1 inch to 1 foot)

MATERIALS

    1/4-inch-thick wood for the table top and legs
    White glue
    A straight pin
    Gesso
    Acrylic paints
    Gloss polymer medium
    Tracing paper

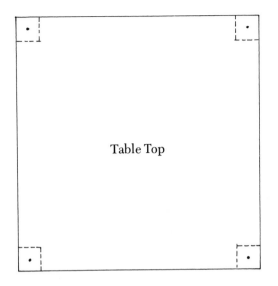

Table Top

Leg

I used cigar-box wood to make the table.
See the general instructions for making wooden furniture, page 59.

    1. Trace and transfer the patterns to the wood. Cut a table top and four legs.

    2. Drill a pin-sized hole 1/16 inch deep in each corner of the underside of the table top, as shown in the drawing.

    3. Cut four 1/8-inch lengths of steel from a straight pin.

    4. Drill a pin-sized hole 1/16 inch deep in the top end of each leg. Glue a length of pin in each leg top.

    5. Glue a leg to each corner of the table. Check that the table stands square.

    6. Give the table a coat of gesso.

    7. Paint the table, and finish it with gloss polymer medium.

Grandfather Clock

(Scale: 1 inch to 1 foot)

MATERIALS

9/16-inch x 1-inch x 1-1/8-inch block of balsa wood for the clock

1/2-inch x 3/4-inch x 2-5/8-inch block of balsa wood for the cabinet

1/2-inch x 1-inch x 1-inch block of balsa wood for the pedestal

5/16-inch x 3/4-inch x 1-3/16-inch block of balsa wood for the base

1/8-inch x 3/4-inch x 1-3/16-inch block of balsa wood for the clock base, and the same for the pedestal top and the clock top

1/16-inch x 5/8-inch x 1-inch block of balsa wood for the cabinet top, and the same for the cabinet base

1/8-inch dowel for the pillars

1/16-inch-thick wood for the pediment

3/32-inch-thick balsa wood for the pediment facing, the door, and the pedestal facing

A small brass nail (or a pin and a bead) for the doorknob

Three small brass beads and three small brass nails (or wooden beads and pins) for the finials

A clock face

Card and pin for the clock hands

Two large jump-rings (for description see page 24) or brass wire for the rim of the "glass"

Stiff clear plastic for the "glass"

White glue

Gold paint

Stain

Shellac

Butcher's wax

Tracing paper

The door of the cabinet does not open. For the clock face either cut one from a magazine or catalogue, or draw a clock face on paper with black ink.

See the general instructions for making wooden furniture, page 59.

1. Measure and cut the blocks of balsa wood for the top, the clock, the clock base, the cabinet top, the cabinet, the cabinet base, the pedestal top, the pedestal, and the base.

2. Trace and transfer to wood the patterns for the door, the pediment, the pediment facing, and the pedestal facing. Cut the pieces out.

3. Bevel the edges of the pediment facing, the door, and the pedestal facing, as shown in the drawing.

4. Cut the two pillars from dowel. Mark the turnings on the pillars. Hand-turn and whittle the pillars to shape. (For general instructions on whittling see page 29.) Sand the pillars so that each has a flat side.

5. Glue the clock face to the clock.

6. Either use gold paper, or paint a small area of card gold. Cut the clock hands from the card. Pin the hands to the center of the clock face.

7. Take a large brass jump-ring (or bend a length of brass wire around a 5/8-inch dowel to form a circle) and glue it to the edge of the clock face.

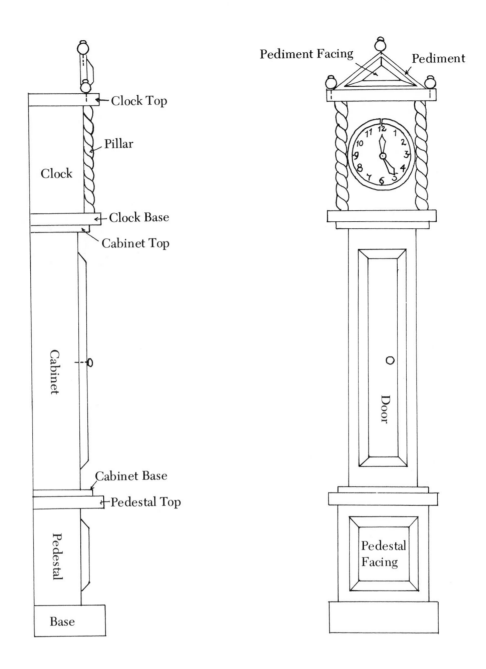

8. Cut a circle of clear plastic the same size as the jump-ring. Glue the plastic to the edges of the jump-ring.

9. Take the second jump-ring and glue it to the edges of the plastic circle. (The plastic stands away from the clock face and is sandwiched between the two jump-rings.)

10. Glue the pillars in position to the front of the clock.

11. Glue the pediment facing to the pediment.

12. Glue the door to the cabinet.

13. Glue the pedestal facing to the pedestal.

14. Glue the pediment to the top.

15. Working on a flat surface, glue the various pieces of the grandfather clock together, starting at the base.

16. Stain the grandfather clock, and finish it with shellac and Butcher's wax.

17. Drill pin-sized holes in the door, the top, and the top of the pediment.

18. Pin and glue the doorknob and finials in place.

Fireplace

(Scale: 1 inch to 1 foot)

MATERIALS

1/8-inch-thick and 1/16-inch-thick balsa wood for the two parts of the mantelpiece

3/4-inch x 3/4-inch x 4-1/2-inch balsa wood block for the upper beam

3/8-inch x 3/8-inch x 3-inch balsa wood block for the lower beam

3/4-inch x 3/4-inch x 2-9/16-inch balsa wood block for the outer side supports

3/8-inch x 3/8-inch x 2-3/16-inch balsa wood block for the inner side supports

1/16-inch x 1/16-inch balsa wood strips for the trim

1/16-inch-thick balsa wood for the "marble" hearth

Thin card for the "brick" hearth and fireplace back and for the grate

Round toothpicks and small brass beads for the finials

A small brass bead for the grate knob

A flat toothpick and a bead for the grate cross bar

Small tiles

Waterproof felt markers

Waterproof black ink and a fine-nibbed pen

White glue   Gloss polymer medium

Gesso   Tracing paper

Acrylic paints   Straight pins

I bought the small tiles at a hobby store; they are made in white and pastel colors, and are usually used to make decorative table tops.

See the general instructions for making wooden furniture, page 59.

1. Cut the top part of the mantelpiece 1 inch x 5-7/16 inches. Cut the bottom part of the mantelpiece 7/8 inch x 4-15/16 inches.

2. Working on a flat surface, glue the lower beam to the two inner side supports, as shown in the drawing.

3. Glue the outer side supports to the inner side supports.

4. Glue the upper beam in place, as shown in the drawing.

5. Glue the bottom of the mantelpiece to the top beam.

6. Glue the top of the mantelpiece to the bottom of the mantelpiece. (Note that all the pieces that have been glued together are flush at the back.)

7. Glue the top strip of trim onto the top beam, and the side strips of trim onto the outer side supports.

8. Paint the fireplace.

9. Trace and transfer the patterns for the brick hearth and the fireplace-back to card. Cut the hearth and fireplace-back. Give each card pattern piece a thick coat of paint (I used dark gray), and while the paint is still wet, draw the bricks, using the end of a toothpick. When the paint is dry, take the fireplace back, and bend along the dotted lines.

Glue flaps (B) to the front of the inner side supports (the flaps will be hidden by the tiles). And glue flap (A) to the back of the lower beam. Take the brick hearth, and glue it to the base of the fireplace. *Note:* The dotted line (C) should conform to the inner shape of the fireplace.

10. Draw the designs on the tiles with black ink, and color them in with markers. Glue the tiles to the inner side supports and the lower beam.

11. Trace and transfer the "marble" hearth to the wood. Cut out the hearth. Paint the hearth pale gray. When the paint has dried, use a fine paintbrush to "vein" the hearth to get a marbled effect. Use a lighter gray and a darker gray paint than the background to draw the veins. Glue the marble hearth to the base of the fireplace. (The marble hearth should extend 13/16 inch beyond the edge of the brick hearth.)

12. Now make the grate. Trace and transfer the patterns for the card parts of the grate. Cut the base and the front. Bend the sides and back of the grate-base down. Glue flaps (D) to the back.

Bend the front of the grate into a curve as shown in diagram 1. Cut the finials from round toothpicks, and the cross bar from a flat toothpick. Thread the bead onto the cross bar, and glue the cross bar to the finials. Glue the finials to the grate-front. Glue the grate-front to the base. Paint the entire grate black.

Cut three straight pins, so that each pin measures about 1/2 inch. Pin and glue a bead to each finial. Pin and glue a bead to the front of the grate. (I glued tiny pieces of real coal in the grate, and made "flames" from red sequins cut to shape and glued between the coals.)

13. Give the entire fireplace, including the tiles and hearth, a coat of gloss polymer medium.

14. Place the grate in the fireplace.

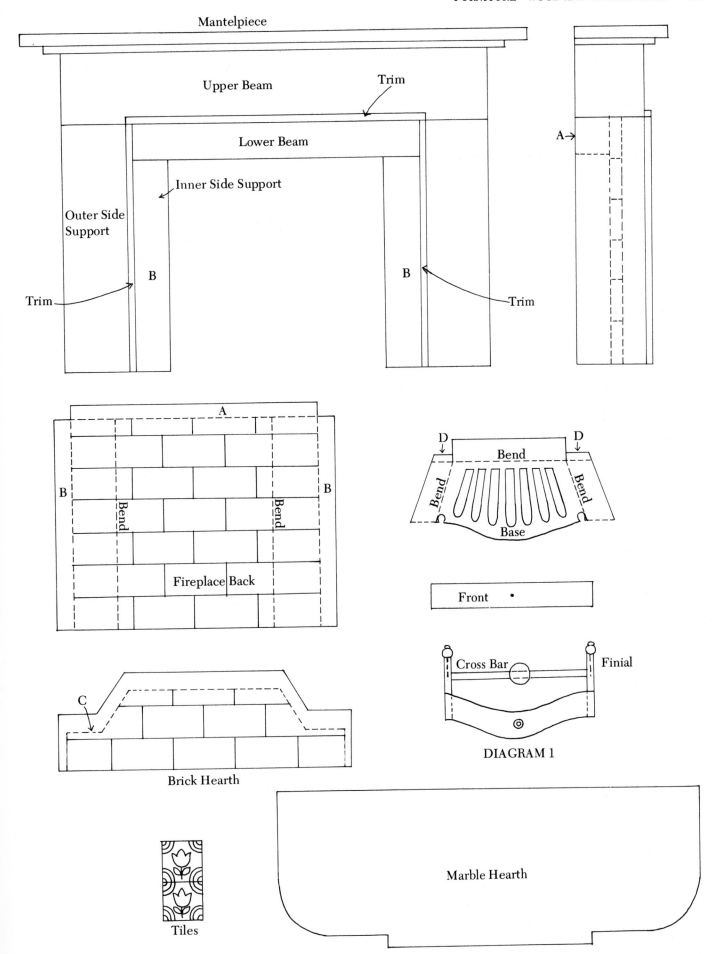

Mantelpiece

Upper Beam

Trim

Lower Beam

Inner Side Support

Outer Side Support

Trim

B

B

Trim

A→

A

B

B

Bend

Bend

Fireplace Back

D

D

Bend

Bend

Bend

Bend

Base

Front

Cross Bar

Finial

DIAGRAM 1

C

Brick Hearth

Tiles

Marble Hearth

Tilt-Top Table

(Scale: 1 inch to 1 foot)

MATERIALS

> 1/8-inch-thick wood for all the pattern pieces except the pedestal
>
> 3/16-inch dowel for the pedestal
>
> Straight pins
>
> White glue
>
> Tracing paper
>
> Stain
>
> Shellac
>
> Butcher's wax

I used basswood for the table. I stained the wood, and used shellac and Butcher's wax as a finish.

See the general instructions for making wooden furniture, page 59.

1. Trace and transfer the pattern pieces to the wood. Cut a table top, three legs, two cleats, and the pedestal top.

2. Cut the length of dowel 3/4 inch longer than the actual length of the pedestal. Mark the turnings on the dowel. Hand-turn and whittle the pedestal to shape. (For general instructions for whittling, see page 29.) Note the peg (A) on top of the pedestal.

3. Sand the top edges of each leg (B) to round them off. Sand a curved ridge at the top of each leg, so that when the legs are attached they will fit the round form of the pedestal. See diagram 1.

4. Also in the top of each leg drill two parallel pin-sized holes, 1/8 inch deep, at the positions indicated in the drawing. Drill three pairs of parallel pin-sized holes, 1/16 inch deep, spacing each pair evenly around the base of the pedestal.

5. Cut six 3/16-inch lengths of steel from straight pins. Glue a steel length in each leg hole. Fit the pins in the legs into the holes in the pedestal, and glue the legs in place.

6. Drill a pin-sized hole, 1/16 inch deep, on one side of each cleat (C). (Note the position of the hole shown in the drawing.)

7. Drill two pin-sized holes, each 1/16 inch deep, on opposite sides of the pedestal top (D). Drill each hole 1/16 inch from the nearest corner.

8. Drill a hole, 1/16 inch in diameter and 1/16 inch deep, in the center of the bottom of the pedestal top (E). Fix the pedestal to the pedestal top by gluing the peg (A) into the hole (E).

9. From a straight pin cut two 1/8-inch lengths of steel for hinging the pedestal to the table top. Glue a steel length into the hole in the side of each cleat.

10. Place the table top on a flat surface, underneath side up. Glue *one* cleat in position F, pin hole facing in, on the table top. Place, do *not* glue, the top of the pedestal, as indicated by the dotted lines, in the center of the table top. Fit the pin in the cleat into the hole in the pedestal top. Take the second cleat, pin hole facing in, and glue it in position G on the table top, fitting the pin in the cleat into the hole in the pedestal top.

11. Stand the table right side up. The table top can be in a horizontal position, or tilted back so that it is vertical.

12. Stain the table.

13. Finish the table with shellac and Butcher's wax.

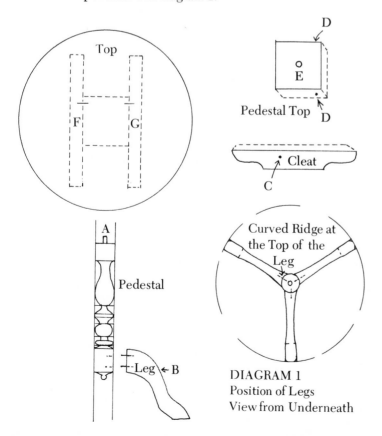

DIAGRAM 1
Position of Legs
View from Underneath

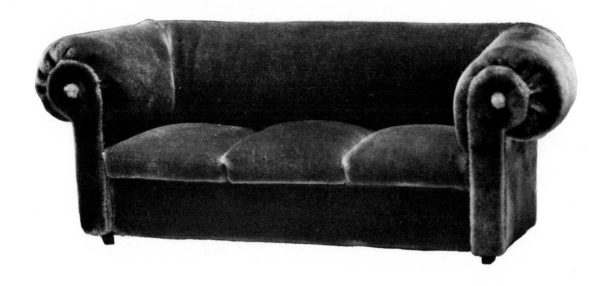

Sofa

(Scale: 1 inch to 1 foot)

MATERIALS

3/8-inch-thick balsa wood for the back and arms

7/8-inch-thick balsa wood for the base

1/4-inch-thick balsa wood for the cushions

Approximately a 1-foot square of 1-inch-thick foam rubber for the padding

Tracing paper

1/4 yard fabric for covering the sofa

Thin card

White glue

Fabric glue

Two small bead-headed pins for the arm buttons

1/2-inch dowel for the feet

I used lightweight velvet to cover the sofa, but any fabric that is not too heavy would be suitable. The patterns with floral designs are for fabric; the shaded patterns are for foam rubber; the solid patterns are for wood or card. An exception is the cushion pattern; the shaded area is for both the foam rubber *and* the wood.

See the general instructions for making wooden furniture, page 59.

1. Trace and transfer all the wood patterns. Cut a back, two arms, three cushions, and a base.

2. Glue the arms to the back. Let the glue dry.

Sand the top edges of the arms and back, rounding them off as indicated by the arrows in diagram 1.

3. Draw a horizontal line (1-1/8 inches from the bottom) around the inside of the arms and back (A). This line shows where the foam rubber will end on the inside of the sofa. Draw a horizontal line (1-5/8 inches from the bottom) around the outside of the arms and back (B). This line shows where the foam rubber will end on the outside of the sofa.

4. Cut off a 1/8-inch-thick strip of wood lengthways from each back corner—cut from the top of the sofa to line B. (The strip will be triangular shaped.) Sand the corners, rounding them off as indicated by the arrows in diagram 1. Note that there is now a small shelf on each back corner on line B.

5. Cut a length of foam rubber 12 inches long and 6 inches wide. (This length will be the padding for both the arms and the back.)

6. Roll and glue the top of the foam rubber as shown in diagram 2. Let the glue dry.

7. Put an ample amount of glue along the area of sofa above line A. Also put an ample amount of glue along the area of sofa above line B.

8. Form the length of foam rubber into a curve (the roll on the outside). Place and press the foam rubber in position on the glue-covered areas of the sofa as shown in diagram 3. *Note:* The foam rubber roll will "sit" on the small corner shelves on the back of the sofa. Also there will be a deep crease at each corner in the foam rubber at the front of the sofa. Let the glue dry.

9. Using a razor blade, shave off some of the foam

rubber, starting about 1/2 inch above line A, so that the foam rubber tapers toward the wood.

10. Trace the fabric patterns onto tracing paper and cut them out.

11. Pin the patterns to the fabric in the following way: Pin the back and arm patterns to a *double* thickness of fabric that has been folded on the bias. (Put the pattern fold line in the back, along the fold in the fabric.) Cut out the back and two arm covers. Pin the patterns for the arm fronts and the back-and-sides to a *double* thickness of fabric and cut them out. (Place the fold in the back-and-sides along the fold in the fabric.) Cut out the back-and-sides and two arm-front covers. Pin the patterns for the cushion covers and the base to a *single* layer of fabric. Cut out the base and three cushion covers.

Note: I have drawn squares at the corners of some of the fabric patterns. They are only rough guides as to how much fabric to cut away to decrease the bulkiness at the corners. Don't cut these corners until you are actually covering the section of furniture and can therefore judge the exact amount of surplus fabric.

12. Take the fabric to cover an arm. Sew a line of running stitches at the top, and along side C, as shown in the drawing. Leave the ends of the threads loose.

13. Make a 1/4-inch cut in the fabric (E). Fold the fabric in, along the dotted line from E to the top.

14. Place the fabric over the foam rubber on the arm of the sofa. The folded edge of the fabric (side D) should follow the corner crease in the foam rubber and then hang over the roll at the back of the sofa.

15. Pull the threads to form gathers along the top of the arm fabric, and along side C. (The gathers at the top will make the fabric fit the form of the roll on the outer side of the arm. The gathers along the side will fit over the foam rubber roll on the front of the arm.)

16. Using fabric glue, first glue the bottom of the fabric underneath the base of the wooden part of the arm. Let the glue dry. Gently pull the top of the fabric, making sure it fits firmly over the roll of foam rubber; then, using fabric glue, attach the top edge of the fabric just below line B on the outside section of the wooden part of the arm. Let the glue dry.

Using a toothpick as an applicator, run a small amount of glue along the inside edge of side D from the bottom to E and press the edge of the fabric in place. Run a small amount of glue along the inside edge of side C and press the edge of the fabric in place. Finish off the loose threads.

Cover the other arm following the same instructions.

17. Take the fabric to cover the back. Sew running stitches along the top of the fabric, where indicated by the dotted lines. Leave the ends of the threads loose.

18. Make a 1/4-inch cut on each side of the fabric (F). Fold the fabric in, on each side, along the dotted lines from F to the top.

19. Place the fabric over the foam rubber on the back of the sofa.

20. Pull the threads to form gathers. (The gathers will make the fabric fit the form of the foam rubber roll. See diagram 4.)

21. Using fabric glue, first glue the bottom of the fabric underneath the base of the wooden part of the back. Let the glue dry. Gently pull the top of the fabric, making sure that it fits firmly over the roll of foam rubber; then glue the top edge of the fabric just below line B on the outside section of the wooden part of the back. Let the glue dry.

Using a toothpick as an applicator, run a small amount of glue along the inside edges of each side of the fabric, from the bottom to F, and press the edges of the fabric in place. Finish off the loose threads.

22. Take the wooden base of the sofa and its fabric cover. Center the wooden base on top of the wrong side of the fabric, as shown in the pattern drawing. First fold the fabric over one side and glue it with fabric glue to the bottom of the base. Then fold over and glue the other side to the bottom of the base. Then fold over and glue each end to the bottom of the base. (See diagram 5.)

23. Glue the base in position to the back and arms of the sofa.

24. Cut a length of card (11-1/4 inches long by 1-5/8 inches wide) for the back-and-sides of the sofa.

25. Place the back-and-sides card on top of the wrong side of its fabric cover, as shown in the pattern drawing. Fold the top of the fabric over the card and glue it in place. Fold each side over the card and glue them in place. Do not glue the bottom of the fabric to the card. Let the glue dry.

26. Glue the length of fabric-covered card to the outer sides of the arms and back of the sofa. (The top of the strip of card will run along line B.)

27. Glue the loose fabric (at the bottom of the fabric-covered card) to the base of the arms and the base of the back. (See diagram 5.)

28. Cut two arm-fronts from card.

29. Place the card, as shown in the pattern drawing, on top of the wrong side of its fabric cover. Fold the fabric over the edges of the card and glue them in place. Clip the top edge of the fabric so it will lie flat.

Make the other arm-front in the same way. (*Note:* The curve must go in the opposite direction to the first arm front.)

30. Glue the arm-fronts to the arms.

31. Cut three foam rubber pads for the cushions.

Line B on the back of the wood

Line A on the front of the wood

Glue base here

Glue arm here

Glue arm here

Back

Line B

Arm

Line A

Top

Gather

Gather

Fold in

Side D

Side C

Arm Fabric

E →

Bottom

DIAGRAM 3

Line A

1-1/8''

Round
the edges

Line B

1-5/8''

DIAGRAM 2

DIAGRAM 1

Top

Back-and-Sides
Cut from card
(Half Pattern)

Fold

Bend

Bottom

Back-and-Sides Fabric

Top

Gather

Fold in

Sides

Fold

Back Fabric

← F

Bottom

Arm-Front
Cut 2 from
card

Arm-Front Fabric

DIAGRAM 4

32. Use the following directions to make each cushion: Coat with glue the top and front of the wooden section of the cushion. Place the foam rubber pad on the top of the wood. Pull the foam rubber over the edge of the top, so that it covers the front area too. Let the glue dry. Using a razor blade, shave off the sharp edges of the foam rubber at the front of the cushion (see diagram 6).

33. Take a fabric cushion cover. Center the cushion—with the foam rubber surface down—on top of the wrong side of the fabric. Gently pull the fabric over each side of the cushion, and glue the edges of the fabric to the wooden bottom part of the cushion. (See general instructions for covering a cushion, page 33.) *Note:* Make sure that the fabric is stretched tightly across the cushions, so that they are firm. Put the cushions on the sofa.

34. Cut two small fabric circles, each circle the correct size to cover the bead on a bead-headed pin. Glue each fabric circle over each bead head. Push each covered pin through the front of each arm as shown in the photograph.

35. Cut four 3/16-inch lengths from a 1/2-inch dowel for the feet. By whittling and sanding, shape the feet as shown in the drawing.

36. Stain and then shellac the feet.

37. Glue the feet in position on the base of the sofa, as shown in diagram 5.

SOFA—PART III

Cushion (Padding and Wood)

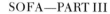

Cushion Fabric

DIAGRAM 5
Bottom View

Foot

Base

DIAGRAM 6
Side View of Cushion

Base Fabric

Floor Lamp

(Scale: 1 inch to 1 foot)

MATERIALS

An eraser-tipped pencil for the pedestal
A large button for the base
1/4-inch dowel for the pedestal extension
Thick card for the shade support
A bead and a round toothpick for the finial
Straight pins
A scrap of buckram for the shade
White glue
Dye or felt markers
Seed beads and bugle beads for the fringe
6 inches of narrow braid
Gesso
Acrylic paints
Gold paint
Gloss polymer medium
Tracing paper

1. Cut the pencil so that it measures 4-1/2 inches in length. Cut the eraser off the end of the pencil.

2. Cut the length of dowel and the length of toothpick.

3. Drill pin-sized holes in each end of the dowel, through the entire length of the toothpick, and in the top of the pencil, as shown in the drawing.

4. Cut two 1/2-inch lengths of steel from straight pins, keeping the head on one length.

5. Pin and glue the extension to the pedestal, and the "finial" to the extension.

6. Draw a circle 1 inch in diameter on the card. Draw a circle within the first circle, 1/4 inch in diameter. Cut the large circle out of the card and cut away the center circle. Glue the card circle to the pedestal extension as shown in the drawing.

7. Glue the bottom end of the pedestal to a large button.

8. Give the entire lamp stand a coat of gesso.

9. Paint the finial gold, and the lamp stand another color.

10. Finish the lamp stand with gloss polymer medium.

11. For the shade, dye or color with felt markers a scrap of buckram (color the braid trimming to match the shade).

12. Trace and transfer the pattern for the shade to tracing paper. Cut out the pattern.

13. Pin the pattern to the buckram, and cut out the shade.

14. Starting at point A, sew the seed and bugle beads to the shade, as shown in diagram 1, making the fringe.

15. When the fringe is completed, overlap and glue the ends of the shade together. Glue a length of trimming around the top and bottom of the shade.

16. Place the shade over the finial, and balance the shade on its support.

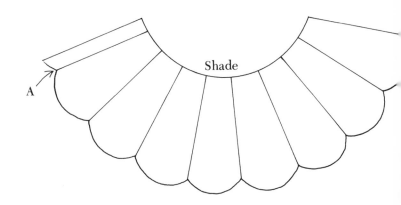

A

Shade

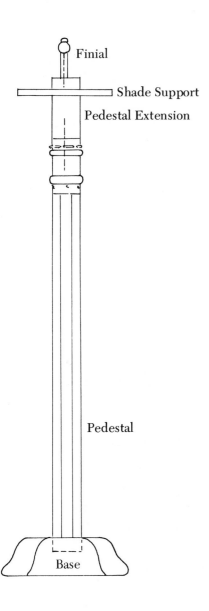

Finial

Shade Support

Pedestal Extension

Pedestal

Base

DIAGRAM 1

Piano

(Scale: 1 inch to 1 foot)

MATERIALS

> 1/8-inch-thick wood for all the parts of the piano except the base, the legs, the black keys, and the molding
> 3/8-inch-thick wood for the base
> 5/32-inch cove molding
> 1/4-inch dowel for the legs
> Flat toothpicks for the keys
> Waterproof black ink and a fine-nibbed pen
> Typing paper
> Card for the foot pedals
> Straight pins
> White glue
> Gold paint
> Tracing paper
> Stain
> Shellac
> Butcher's wax

I made the piano from basswood, but used balsa wood for the base, which does not show when the piano is completed. See the Appendix (page 216) for mail-order dealers who stock narrow moldings.

See the general instructions for making wooden furniture, page 59.

1. Trace and transfer all the wooden pattern pieces to wood. Cut the back and the front, two ends, two end extensions, the top, the base, the base front, the rail, the keyboard, the lid rim, the piano lid, and the molding. Cut two legs from dowel, and cut seventeen black piano keys from flat toothpicks.

2. Lay the back on a flat surface and glue the two ends in place (they come flush with the back).

3. Glue the front between the two ends. Note that the front is recessed 1/16 inch.

4. Glue the top in place. Note that the top is flush with the back but extends over the front and ends.

5. Glue the end extensions to the ends. (Diagram 1 shows a side view of the piano, without the end and end extension attached, so that the various pieces that make the front extension of the piano can be seen clearly.)

6. Glue the base to the back and between the two side extensions.

7. Glue the rail and the piano keyboard to the top of the base.

8. Glue the base front to the front of the base.

9. Take the piano lid and sand the front top edge, rounding it off.

10. Glue the rim to the underneath side of the lid.

11. Place the piano lid (with the rim resting on the

base front) in position between the two end extensions.

12. Drill a pin-sized hole (H) in each end extension, going through to the lid. (The lid will be hinged in place later.)

13. Take the lengths of dowel for the piano legs. Mark the turnings on the legs. Hand-turn and whittle the legs to shape. (See the general instructions for whittling, page 29.) Drill a pin-sized hole in the top of each leg. Drill pin-sized holes in the base (I).

14. Cut two lengths of steel, each about 1/4 inch long, from straight pins. Glue a length of steel into each leg top.

15. Pin and glue the legs to the base.

16. Stain the piano, including the lid and the molding.

17. Finish the piano with shellac and Butcher's wax.

18. Trace and transfer the piano keys to typing paper. Draw the lines for the piano keys in ink. Cut out the drawn oblong. Paint the black piano keys cut from toothpicks with ink, and when they are dry, glue them in place. Bend the paper down along the dotted line. Glue the piano keys to the top and front of the keyboard.

19. Cut two lengths of steel, each about 1/4-inch long, from straight pins. Put the piano lid in position, and push a length of steel through each end extension and into the holes in the ends of the lid. (The lid should move smoothly up and down on its hinges.)

20. Take the molding and glue it to the front of the piano. Note that the molding covers the gap between the front of the piano and the lid and also that the molding extends just a fraction over the lid.

21. Trace and transfer the pattern for the foot pedals to card. Cut two pedals. Paint the pedals gold. Cut two small slits (J) in the front of the piano. Push and glue the tags on the pedals into the slits.

22. Using a fine brush, give the piano keys a coat of shellac.

PIANO—PART I

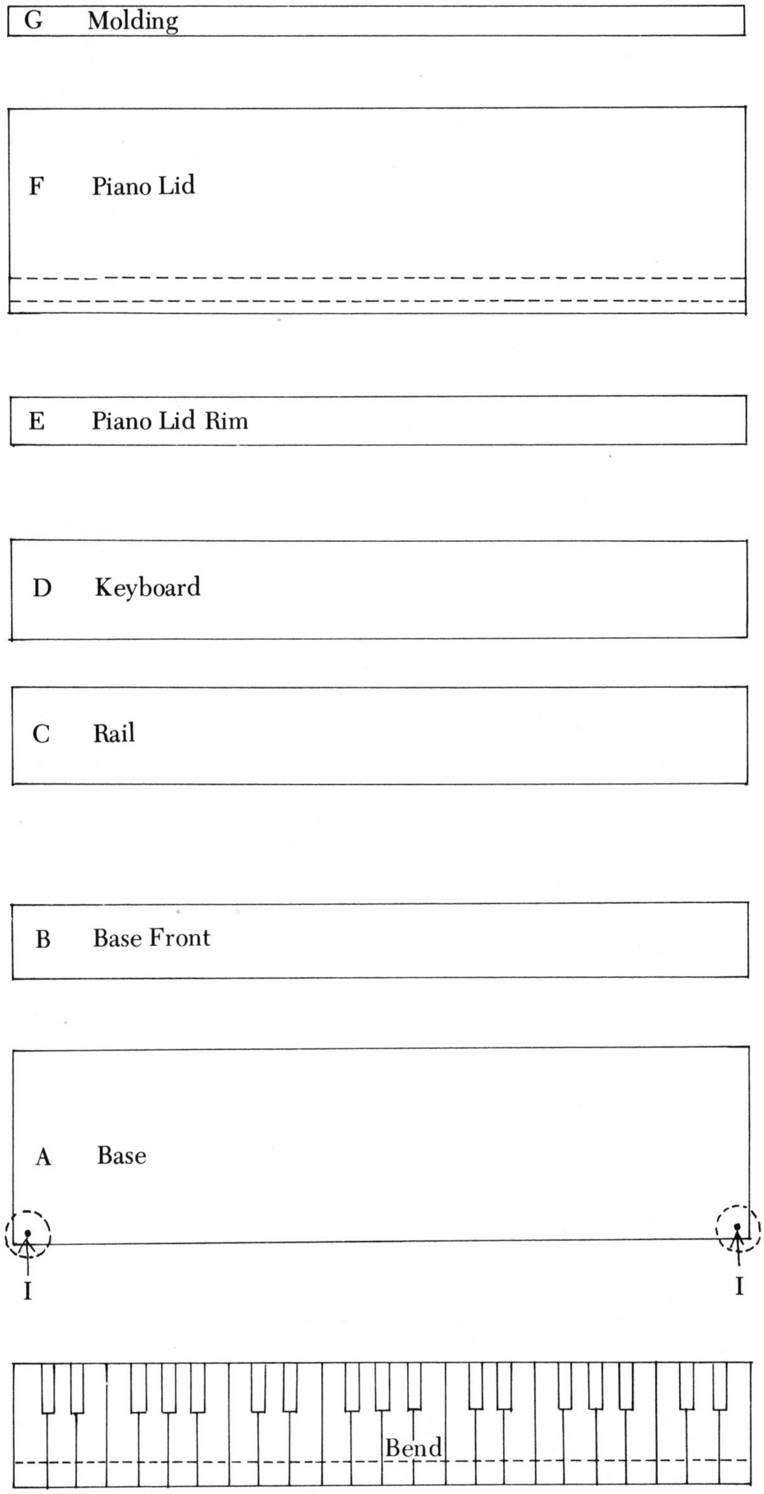

G   Molding

F   Piano Lid

E   Piano Lid Rim

D   Keyboard

C   Rail

B   Base Front

A   Base

I   I

DIAGRAM 1

Black Key   H   G
        F
E   D   C
B   A

Foot Pedal

Bend

Piano Keys (Draw on paper)

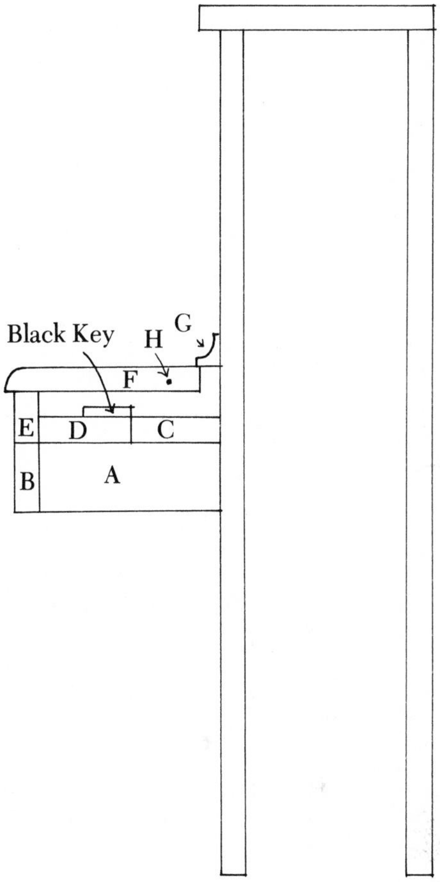

PIANO—PART II

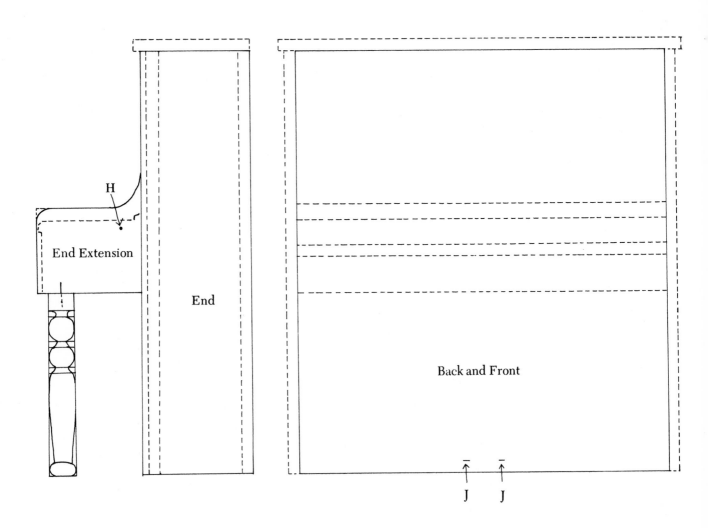

Piano Stool

(Scale: 1 inch to 1 foot)

MATERIALS

1/8-inch-thick wood for the sides, the ends, and the cushion

3/16-inch-thick wood for the legs

1/16-inch-thick wood for the top

1/2-inch-thick foam rubber for the cushion padding

A scrap of fabric for the cushion cover

White glue

Fabric glue

Tracing paper

Stain

Shellac

Butcher's wax

I made the wooden parts of the stool from basswood and used velvet for the cushion cover.

See the general instructions for making wooden furniture, page 59.

1. Trace and transfer the patterns for the wooden parts of the stool to the wood. Cut two sides, two ends, and the cushion. Cut the top. Cut four legs. Each leg length should include 1/16-inch allowance for the pegs.

2. Whittle a peg, 1/16 inch long and 1/16 inch in diameter, at the end of each leg.

3. Drill a hole, 1/16 inch deep and 1/16 inch in diameter, in each corner of the top as shown in the drawing.

4. Lay the top—holes side up—on a flat surface. Glue the pegs in the legs into the holes in the top. Glue the sides and the ends to the top. Turn the stool right side up and check that it stands firmly.

5. Stain the stool.

6. Finish the stool with shellac and Butcher's wax.

7. Cut a piece of foam rubber the same size as the wooden part of the cushion. Glue the foam rubber to the wood.

8. Cut the rectangle, for the cushion cover, from fabric. (*Note:* I have drawn squares at the corners of the pattern. They are only rough guides as to how much fabric to cut away to decrease the bulkiness at the corners. Don't cut these corners until you are actually covering the cushion.) Place the cushion, foam side down, in the center of its fabric cover. Glue the edges of the fabric to the bottom of the wooden part of the cushion. (See the general instructions for covering a cushion, page 33.) Glue the completed cushion to the top of the stool.

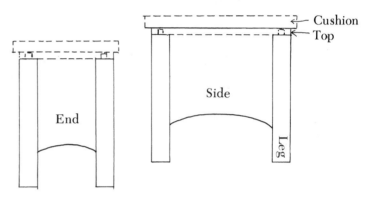

End

Cushion
Top

Side

Leg

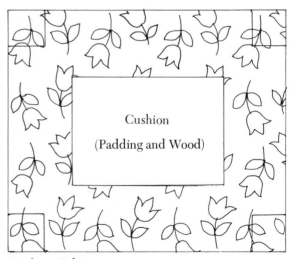

Cushion

(Padding and Wood)

Cushion Fabric

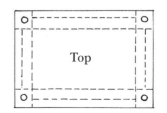

Top

Wash Basin

(Scale: 1 inch to 1 foot)

MATERIALS

A block of balsa wood 2-1/4 inches long x 1/2 inch high x 1-1/4 inches wide for the basin

A block of balsa wood 2 inches long x 1 inch high x 1 inch wide for the pedestal

1/8-inch dowel for the plug

Half a small snap for the drain cover

3/4-inch length of thin, gold-colored chain

A small length of thin wire

Two faucets

White glue

Gesso

Acrylic paints

Gold paint

Gloss polymer medium

Tracing paper

In the Appendix (page 216) I give the names of dealers who supply small faucets.

See the general instructions for making wooden furniture, page 59.

1. Trace and transfer the pattern for the pedestal onto each of the four sides of the block of wood. Trace and transfer the square at the top of the pedestal (A).

2. Retrace line B with the blade of an X-acto knife, making a cut about 1/16 inch deep. Retrace square A at the top of the pedestal with the blade, making a cut about 1/16 inch deep. Carve the rough shape of the pedestal, working from the top to line B at the bottom. Cut the corners off the pedestal as shown in diagram 1. Dilute white glue with water (two-thirds glue and one-third water). Paint the pedestal with the diluted glue. (This will improve and harden the surface of the balsa wood for sanding.)

3. When the pedestal is dry, sand it to shape.

4. Trace and transfer the pattern for the basin top to the block of wood.

5. Retrace line C, around the rim of the bowl, with the blade of an X-acto knife. Then, using gouges to cut from the rim toward the base, hollow out the rough shape of the bowl. Cut the corners and edges of the wash basin top to form the shape shown in diagram 2. Paint the wash basin top with diluted glue.

6. When the glue is dry, sand the wash basin top to shape.

7. Glue the top to the pedestal.

8. Give the wash basin a coat of gesso.

9. Paint the wash basin, and finish it with a coat of gloss polymer medium.

10. Drill a hole in the base of the bowl (D) for the drain cover.

11. Drill two holes in the rim of the wash basin for the faucets (E).

12. Paint the faucets and drain cover gold, and when they are dry, glue them in place.

13. For the plug, cut a 3/32-inch length from a 1/8-inch dowel. Drill a small hole in the top of the "plug," and glue one end of the length of chain in the hole. Cut a 3/8-inch length of wire. Bend the wire into a U-shape. Thread the last link on the loose end of the chain onto the wire, as in diagram 3. Twist the ends of the wire together, as in diagram 4. Make a small hole (F) on the top of the wash basin, between the two faucets, and glue the wire in place as in diagram 5.

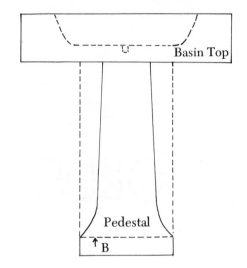

Basin Top

Pedestal

B

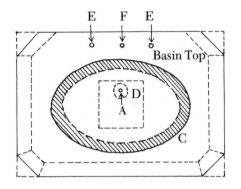

E F E

Basin Top

D
A

C

A

Pedestal Top View

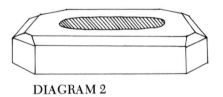

DIAGRAM 2

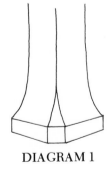

DIAGRAM 1

DIAGRAM 3

DIAGRAM 4

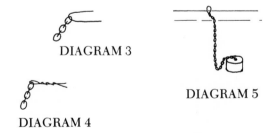

DIAGRAM 5

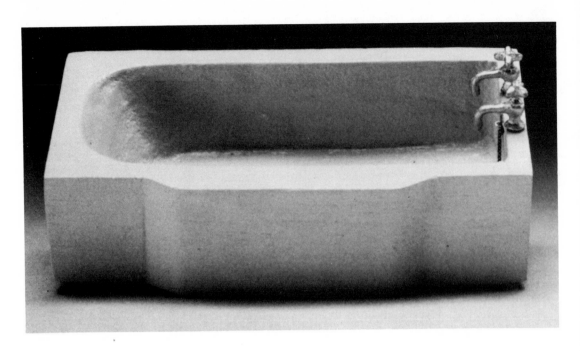

Bathtub

(Scale: 1 inch to 1 foot)

MATERIALS

A block of balsa wood 5 inches long x 1-3/8 inches high x
    2-7/16 inches wide, for the tub
3/16-inch dowel for the plug
Half of a small snap for the drain cover
1-1/4-inch length of thin, gold-colored chain
A flat, gold sequin
Two faucets
A small length of thin wire
White glue
Gesso
Acrylic paints
Gold paint
Gloss polymer medium
Tracing paper

In the Appendix (page 216) I give the names of dealers
who supply small faucets.
*See the general instructions for making wooden furni-
ture, page 59.*

1. Trace and transfer the patterns for the top and the
front side of the tub, to the block of wood.

2. Carve the rough shape of the front side of the tub.
Working on the top, retrace the inner rim of the tub (A)
with the blade of an X-acto knife, making a cut about 1/4
inch deep. Cutting from the rim toward the base, hollow
out the rough shape of the center of the tub using
gouges.

3. Dilute white glue with water (two-thirds glue and
one-third water). Paint the tub, inside and outside, with
the diluted glue. (This will improve and harden the surface of the balsa wood for sanding.)

4. When the tub is dry, sand it to shape.

5. Give the tub a coat of gesso.

6. Then paint the tub. Finish it with a coat of gloss
polymer medium.

7. Drill two holes (B) in the rim of the tub for the
faucets.

8. Drill a hole in the base of the tub for the drain cover
(C).

9. Paint the faucets and the drain cover (half of a small
snap) gold. Let them dry. Then glue the faucets and the
drain cover in place.

10. For the plug, cut a 3/32-inch length from a 3/16-inch
dowel. Drill a small hole in the top of the "plug" and
glue one end of the length of chain in the hole. Cut a
3/8-inch length of wire. Bend the wire into a U-shape.
Thread the last link on the loose end of the chain onto
the wire, as in diagram 1. Twist the ends of the wire
together as in diagram 2. Thread the twisted ends of the
wire through the hole in the sequin, as in diagram 3.
Make a small hole in the inside end of the tub (D) and
glue the sequin and wire in place, as in diagram 4.

Front Side

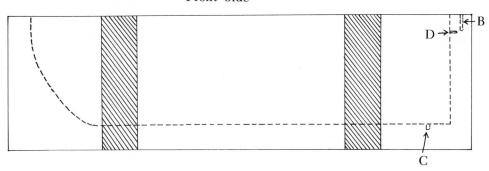

Top

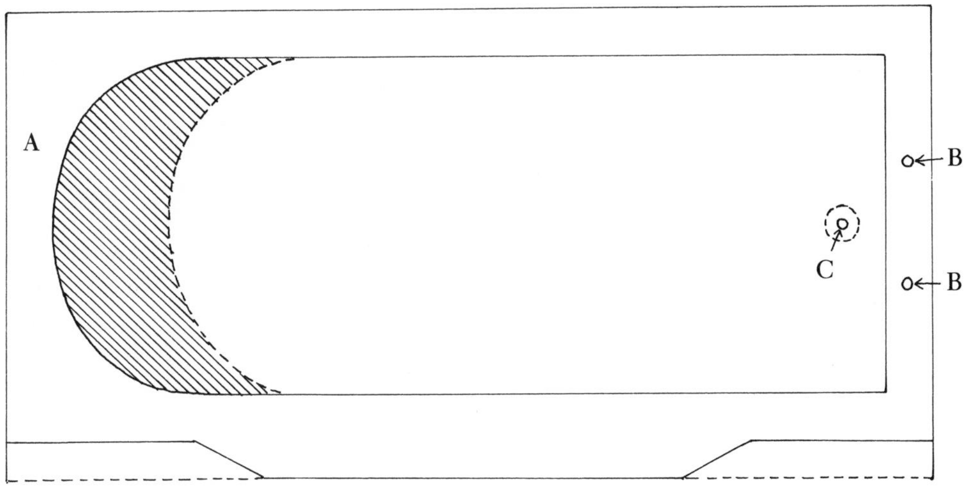

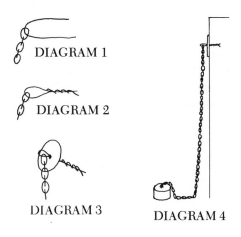

DIAGRAM 1

DIAGRAM 2

DIAGRAM 3

DIAGRAM 4

Toilet

(Scale: 1 inch to 1 foot)

MATERIALS

A block of balsa wood 1-1/2 inches long x 9/16 inch high x 1-1/4 inches wide, for the bowl

A block of balsa wood 2-3/16 inches long x 15/16 inch high x 3/4 inch wide, for the pedestal

A block of balsa wood 1-3/4 inches long x 1-3/8 inches high x 3/4 inch wide, for the tank

3/16-inch-thick balsa wood for the base

3/32-inch-thick balsa wood for the tank cover and toilet seat

1/8-inch-thick wood for the seat cover

For the seat and cover hinge: 1/8-inch-thick balsa wood, 1/8-inch dowel, and a length of thin wire

For the handle: 1/8-inch dowel and a round toothpick

White glue

Gesso

Acrylic paints

Gold paint

Gloss polymer medium

Tracing paper

I made the seat cover from mahogany wood. I did not stain the wood, but finished it with shellac and Butcher's wax. Looking at the photograph, you will notice that I have cut the corners off all the rectangular pieces of wood. This is not shown in the drawings, except for the tank top, because I wanted to show the true dimensions of each piece.

See the general instructions for making wooden furniture, page 59.

1. Trace and transfer the pattern pieces for the tank top, the seat, the base, and the seat cover, to the wood. Cut out the pieces.

2. Trace the patterns for the top, side, and front of the bowl. Transfer the patterns to the tops, sides, and front of the block of wood. Carve the rough shape of the outside of the bowl. Cut from the top to the bottom. (As you carve, refer to the photograph and patterns.) Now work on the top part of the bowl. Retrace the oval shape (A) with the blade of an X-acto knife, making a cut about 1/4 inch deep. Cut and gouge out the rough shape of the inside of the bowl. Work from the oval (A) toward the circle (B) which is the flat center part of the bowl.

3. Dilute white glue with water (two-thirds glue to one-third water). Paint the inside and outside of the bowl with the diluted glue. (This will improve and harden the surface of the balsa wood for sanding.) When the bowl is dry, sand it to shape.

4. Trace the patterns for the top, side, and front of the pedestal. Transfer the patterns to the top, sides, and front of the block of wood. Cut the shape for the pedestal. Note the curve at point C: this curve must fit the curve at the back of the bowl.

At the front of the pedestal, diagonally cut 3/16 inch off each vertical edge. At the back of the pedestal, diagonally cut 3/32 inch off each vertical edge. Paint the pedestal with diluted glue, and when it is dry, sand the pedestal smooth.

5. Take the block of balsa wood for the tank. Diagonally cut 1/8 inch off each vertical edge. Paint the tank with diluted glue, and when it is dry, sand it smooth.

6. Take the tank top and diagonally cut 1/8 inch off each corner. Sand smooth.

7. Take the toilet base, and diagonally cut 5/16 inch off the front corners, and 1/8 inch off the back corners. Sand smooth.

8. Glue the bowl and the tank to the pedestal. Glue the tank top to the tank. (*Note:* The back edge of the top is flush with back of the tank.) Glue the toilet to the base.

9. Take the toilet seat, and paint it with diluted glue. Let it dry. Bevel and gently sand the outer rim of the seat. Sand the top edge of the inner rim of the seat, rounding it off.

10. Take the toilet seat cover, and bevel and sand the outer rim.

11. To hinge the seat and cover to the toilet, proceed as follows: Cut a strip 1/4 inch long by 3/32 inch wide from 1/8-inch-thick balsa wood (D). Glue the strip of wood in position on the toilet. Cut a 1/4-inch length from 1/8-inch dowel. Glue the piece of dowel (E) on top of the balsa strip. Cut two 1/8-inch lengths from 1/8-inch dowel. Glue

each length in position on the toilet seat. Put the seat on the toilet, and the cover on the seat. Hold these two parts firmly in position, and drill a hole through the sides of the cover and the lengths of dowel, as shown in diagram 1. (Do not fix the length of wire through the holes yet.)

12. For the toilet handle, cut a 5/16-inch length from 1/8-inch thick dowel. Carve a 1/16-inch peg at one end of the dowel. Sand the top edges of the other end of the dowel, rounding them off. Cut a 1/4-inch length from a round toothpick. Drill a hole in the side of the dowel, 1/16 inch deep, as shown in the drawing. Glue the length

of toothpick into the dowel. Drill a hole 1/16 inch deep in the tank. Glue the handle into the tank.

13. Give the entire toilet, except the seat cover, a coat of gesso.

14. Paint the toilet (except the seat cover) a color, and the handle and hinges gold.

15. Finish the painted parts of the toilet with a coat of gloss polymer medium.

16. Now fix the seat and seat cover to the toilet, by threading a length of wire through the holes in the seat cover and lengths of dowel. Bend the ends of the wire to secure it in place.

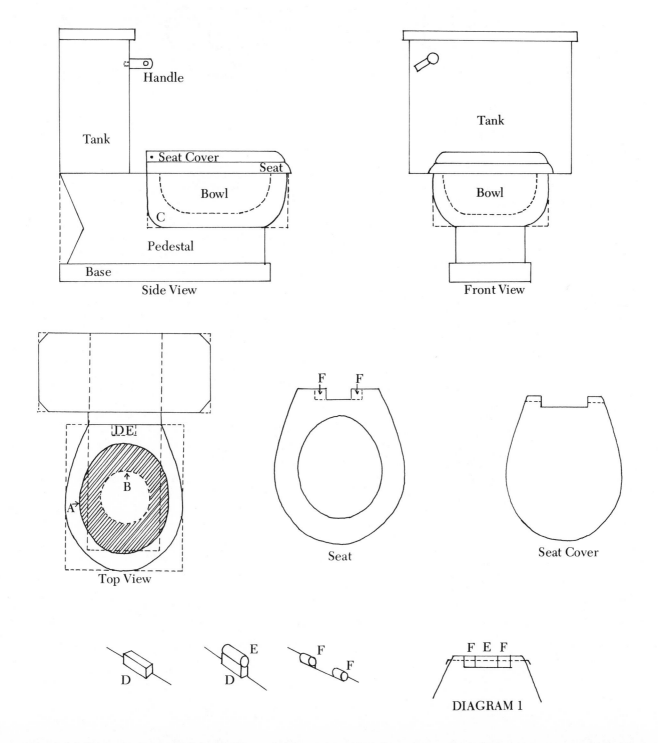

Side View

Front View

Top View

Seat

Seat Cover

DIAGRAM 1

Bathroom Chair

(Scale: 1 inch to 1 foot)

MATERIALS

3/16-inch-thick wood for the legs
1/8-inch-thick wood for the seat, slats, and stretchers
A straight pin
White glue
Gesso
Acrylic paints
Gloss polymer medium
Tracing paper

I made the chair from basswood. To identify the chair I have called it the bathroom chair, but with various appropriate finishes, it could be a dining or kitchen chair. *See the general instructions for making wooden furniture, page 59.*

1. Trace and transfer the patterns to the wood. Cut one seat, two back legs, two front legs, three slats, two side stretchers, a back stretcher, and a front stretcher. (When cutting the stretchers, remember to include 1/16

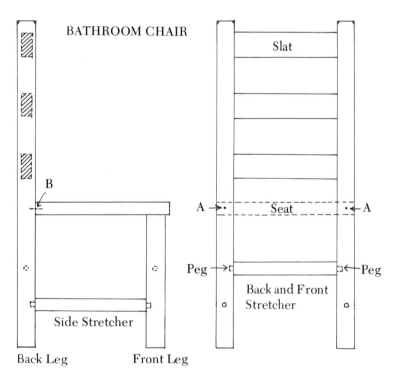

BATHROOM CHAIR

Slat

B

A ▸ Seat ◂ A

Peg ▸ ◂ Peg

Back and Front
Stretcher

Side Stretcher

Back Leg   Front Leg

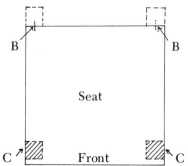

B   B

Seat

C ↗   Front   ↖ C

inch extra wood at both ends of each stretcher for the pegs, as indicated in the drawing.) At the tops of the back legs, cut a sliver of wood off each corner.

2. Whittle the pegs on the ends of each stretcher (each peg 1/16 inch long and 1/16 inch in diameter).

3. Drill holes in the legs for the stretcher pegs, as indicated in the drawing. Drill two pin-sized holes, 1/16 inch deep, one in each back leg (point A in the drawing).

4. Take a back leg and lay it on a flat surface (pin-sized hole and side-stretcher peg hole up, and the back-stretcher hole facing to your right). Glue one end of each slat, and the peg on one end of the back stretcher, in place.

Take the other back leg (pin-sized hole and side-stretcher hole up, and the back-stretcher hole facing to your left). Glue the leg to the free ends of each slat, and the peg on the free end of the back stretcher.

5. Take the seat. Drill two pin-sized holes (B), 1/16 inch deep, in the back edge of the seat. Cut two 1/8-inch lengths of steel from a pin. Glue a length of steel in each hole in the back edge of the seat.

6. Glue the pegs on each end of the front stretcher between the two front legs.

7. Glue a peg on the end of each side stretcher into the appropriate hole in each front leg.

8. Glue the tops of the front legs (C) to the underside of the seat.

9. Glue the pegs and pins (on the free ends of the side stretchers and the seat) in the appropriate holes in the back legs.

10. Give the chair a coat of gesso.

11. Paint the chair, and finish it with gloss polymer medium.

An A to Z
of
Dolls' House Furnishings

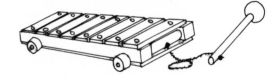

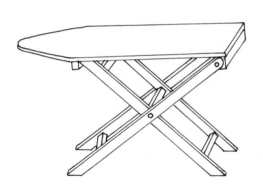

From an alarm clock, a dog dish, and a rolling pin
to umbrellas and wine glasses—illustrated instructions
for making 106 household objects
that will give your dolls' rooms a lived-in look.

In this chapter you will find drawings and instructions for the extras, the finishing touches, the small objects, that make a dolls' house look inhabited. An alarm clock to make sure that John Bead will get to work on time; mirror, comb, brush, and perfume bottles for Sarah Bead; toys and books for the children. And lots of food for everybody.

When I considered what I needed to make for this section, I realized that many of the things could be adapted from already existing objects. Every bottle cap, paper clip, and button I came across I scrutinized for its possibilities as something miniature for a dolls' house. I stopped seeing everyday objects for what they really were—a lamp finial was obviously an andiron, the heads of some kinds of push pins were candlesticks. I spent hours searching through the supplies in hardware stores. When asked whether I needed assistance, I answered, "I'm just looking;" the salesperson would seem puzzled, as though my response was suitable for a rack of dresses, but not for a display of screws and nails.

Therefore, in making these small items (described in alphabetical order in this chapter), besides using balsa wood, dowel, and tooth-picks, I utilized an assortment of miscellaneous objects from my magpie collection which includes buttons, beads, scraps of fabric, embossed gold paper, lace, thumbtacks, stiff clear plastic (the kind that comes in store packaging), and bits of string.

Alarm Clock

For the clock, cut a 1/4-inch length off a 1/2-inch dowel. Either draw a clock face on paper or cut one out of a magazine. (Having seen just the clock face I wanted to use on the clock page of an old Montgomery Ward catalog, I mutilated the page, only to find that I could have had the page photocopied.) Glue the clock face to the flat front of the dowel. Cut a piece of thin card 1/16 inch wider than the dowel and the length of the dowel's circumference. Glue the card strip around the outside of the dowel. Drill two holes in the top of the clock for the small brass nails which will hold the bells in place. Drill another hole in the center of the top of the clock for the hammer. And drill two holes in the bottom of the clock for the feet. Use trimmed-down straight pins for the hammer and the feet. Cut a small wooden bead in half for the bells. After the feet, bells, and hammer have been glued in place, paint the clock.

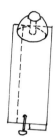

Alarm Clock

Antimacassar

Take a piece of lace, and look for an oval, round, or oblong shape, which is part of the woven design. Cut the shape out carefully, and use as an antimacassar.

Ashtray

Use a small bowl-shaped button as an ashtray. Fill the holes with plastic wood. When the plastic wood is dry, paint the filled holes the same color as the button. Cut and shape a piece of toothpick to look like a cigarette. Paint the "cigarette," and glue it to the rim of the button.

Ball

Use a bead for a ball. Fill the bead hole with plastic wood (or sawdust mixed with white glue). Paint the bead. I made a baby's ball from a large flocked bead. I divided the bead into eight sections, drawing pencil lines from top to bottom, and then painted the sections in four alternating bright colors.

Bathing cap

This is my eight-year-old daughter's idea. Cut off the top of a finger of an old rubber glove. Use the finger top as a bathing cap for a small doll.

Blackboard

(Drawing actual size)
Make a square, mitered frame from 3/32-inch-thick balsa wood. Smooth the edges of the balsa wood frame with sandpaper, and give it a coat of shellac or varnish. Paint a square of card black. When the paint is dry, mount the frame on top of the blackboard. Using a small paintbrush and white paint, "draw" on the blackboard. Sort out some letters from a box of alphabet pasta. So that they will lie flat, sand the backs of the letters gently (they break easily). Paint the letters in bright colors, keeping the paint as dry as possible. When the paint is dry, glue the letters around the frame.

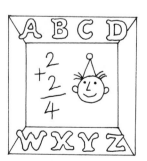

Blackboard

Blocks

Cut 1/4-inch-square blocks from balsa wood. Paint each block, using several different colors (on each block paint four sides, and when the paint has dried, paint the remaining two sides). On the blocks draw letters and simple shapes (e.g., circles, squares, hearts). Paint the letters and shapes in colors that contrast with the backgrounds on the blocks.

Book No. 1

(Drawings actual size)

Using typing paper, cut eight rectangles the size shown in pattern A for the pages. Fold each rectangle in half. Hold the pages firmly together and apply a small amount of glue along the backs of the folds (B). Gently rub the glue in with the tip of your finger. Take care that the glue does not seep through along the pages. Cut two boards from card, pattern C. Use paper with a small printed pattern for the book cover. Cut two book covers, pattern D. Fold the book covers over the boards and glue them in place, as shown in diagram E. Cut four triangles from thin glove leather, pattern F. Then fold and glue the leather triangles to each book-cover corner following the procedure in diagram G. Cut a strip of glove leather 1-5/8 inches long by 1/2 inch wide for the spine of the book. Glue the leather spine to the book covers as shown in diagram H. Note the space of 3/16 inch between the book covers in the center. Cut two end papers from colored paper, using the pages pattern (A). Glue an end paper to the inside front cover and the front of the first page, as shown in diagram I. When the glue has dried, glue the other end paper to the inside back cover and to the last page.

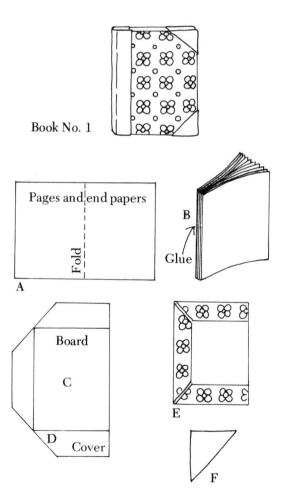

Book No. 1

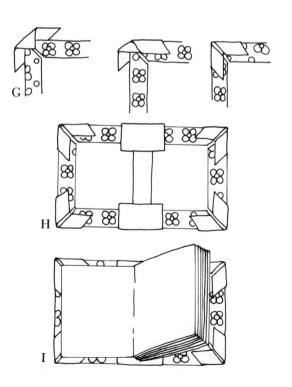

Book No. 2

From 1/8-inch-thick balsa wood cut a rectangle 1 inch long and 3/4 inch wide. Using sandpaper round off the edges of the "spine" end of the book. Sand a shallow groove along the top, the bottom, and the end of the book (opposite the spine)—giving the illusion of pages. Paint the bottom, the top, and the end of the book white or gold. Cover the book with colored paper, or thin glove leather, or a small photo of a book cut from a magazine advertisement. (Make other books using this method and varying the length, width, and thickness of the wood.)

Book No. 2

Breadboard

(Drawing actual size)

Trace the drawing onto tracing paper. Use either 3/32-inch hardwood or balsa wood for the breadboard. Transfer the traced pattern to the wood, and cut it out. (If you are using balsa wood, cut the rectangle shape of the breadboard. Then cut two small squares at the top, either side of the handle, and *sand* the curves to shape.) Sand all the surfaces of the breadboard, so that they are smooth. Drill a small hole about 1/16 inch in diameter in the handle. Thread a piece of embroidery floss through the hole and tie a knot in the floss.

Broom

For the handle, cut a 3-inch length from a 1/8-inch dowel. Round off the top of the dowel with sandpaper. For the brush cut a bunch of straw, about 1-1/2 inches long, from a straw broom. Split each piece of straw in half down the middle, to make narrower lengths. Glue the straw to the handle. Twist thread around the straw as shown in the drawing. Drill a small hole about 1/16 inch in diameter at the top of the handle. Thread a piece of embroidery floss through the hole, and knot the floss.

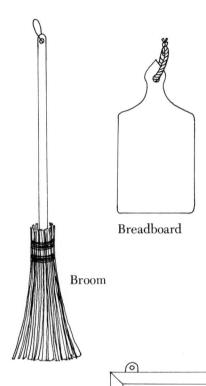

Breadboard

Broom

Bulletin Board

(Drawing actual size)

Make a mitered frame from 1/32-inch-thick wood. Stain the frame and finish it with a coat of varnish or shellac. Mount the frame on thin cork. (I found 6-inch-square pieces of 1/16-inch-thick cork at a hardware store.) Make two small, hanging tabs from card, and glue them to the back of the bulletin board. Make a tiny shopping list, a drawing, a newspaper clipping, et cetera, and pin them to the bulletin board with cut-down straight pins. Paint the heads of the pins in bright colors so that they will look like thumbtacks.

Butterfly in a Case

Draw a butterfly on paper, with a wingspan of about 3/4 inch; then paint the butterfly. Cut the butterfly out. Glue a V-shaped piece of thread to the back of the head of the butterfly for the antennae. Use the top of an inch-square clear plastic box for the top of the display case, and cut a square piece of card for the backing. Mount the butterfly on a square of white felt, and glue the felt to the backing. Glue the case backing onto the plastic box top. Frame the case with strips of shiny black tape. Make a tiny label with the name of the species of butterfly and its country of origin to glue on the back of the case.

Bulletin Board

Butterfly in a Case

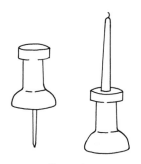

Candlestick No. 1

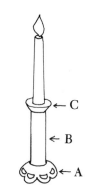

Candlestick No. 2

Canister Set and Shelf

Calendar

Many Christmas card catalogs (the most attractive come from museums and UNICEF) have a page or two of photographs of calendars. They are reproduced in the correct size to cut out and hang on dolls' house walls. See the calendar I cut from a catalog, in the photograph of the children's room, facing page 17.

Candlestick No. 1

The candlestick is a silver-colored push pin from which the pin has been removed with wire cutters. Make the candle from a round toothpick, sanded to shape. Paint the candle white or a color. Make a tiny hole in the top of the candle. Glue a small piece of thread in the hole for the wick. The tiny wax matches that are made in Italy are ideal to use as candles, too.

Candlestick No. 2

Starting at the base of the candlestick, use a gold-colored, filigree jewelry finding (A). Using quick-drying epoxy glue, stick the jewelry finding to a 1/2-inch length of brass tubing (B). Then glue a concave, faceted gold sequin (C) to the top of the brass tubing. (A length of 1/8-inch dowel, painted gold, can be substituted for the brass tubing.) Make the candle from a round toothpick cut to size. Sand the top of the "candle" flat. Paint the candle and make a small hole in the top of the candle. Cut the shape of a flame from an unfaceted, flat red sequin. Glue the "flame" to the top of the candle.

Canister Set, Shelf, and Brackets

The lids of the canisters are not removable. For the largest canister, cut a 7/8-inch length from a 5/8-inch dowel. For the middle-sized canister cut a 3/4-inch length from a 1/2-inch dowel. And for the smallest canister cut a 5/8-inch length from a 1/2-inch dowel. Make the sides of the canister lids from 1/8-inch-wide strips cut from 1/32-inch-thick card. Glue a strip of card around the top of each length of dowel. Cut typing paper (not card) circles for the tops of the canister lids. Make the paper circles the correct size to come to the *edge* of the card strips. (Do this by making each paper circle 1/16 inch wider in diameter than the diameter of the dowel it will cover.) Glue the tops of the lids in place. Paint the canisters with gesso, and then with one or two coats of acrylic paint. To seal the paint and give it a slight shine, brush on gloss polymer medium. Make a small hole in the top of each canister lid. Use bead-headed pins for the canister knobs. Cut the pins down, and glue them in the holes. Make small labels to identify the contents of each canister, and glue them on the front of the canisters. For the shelf, cut a rectangle 2-1/2 inches long by 1 inch wide from 1/8-inch-thick wood. Bevel the two sides and the front of the shelf as indicated in the drawing. Give the shelf whatever finish you choose. The brackets are made from strips of tin cut from an empty food can. Cut several 1/4-inch-wide strips of tin. For the support part of the bracket cut a strip of tin 1-1/2 inches long and bend it to form a right angle. For the C-shaped curlicues, cut two 1-inch-long strips of tin. Bend the strips to shape with pliers. Using quick-drying epoxy glue, fix the curlicues to the support part of the bracket as shown in the drawing. Make the second bracket in the same way. Glue the top of each finished bracket to the bottom of the shelf. The brackets should come flush with the back of the shelf, and they should be set in about 1/4 inch at either side of the shelf. Glue the brackets to the wall.

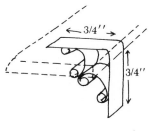

Bracket

Checkers Set

Make the checkerboard from a 1-1/2-inch-square piece of white card. Draw and then paint a narrow black border 1/16 inch in from the edge of the card. Divide the area beyond the border of the card into sixty-four small squares. Paint alternate squares black to make a checkerboard design. Paint a stiff piece of clear plastic (from store wrapping) white on both sides, and another piece of plastic black on both sides. Using a paper punch, cut small circles from the plastic to make the checkers.

Christmas Tree and Ornaments

For the trunk of the tree, cut a 7-inch length from 1/8-inch dowel, and paint it brown. Make the tree branches from green pipe cleaners. (I dyed white pipe cleaners green.) Starting about an inch from the bottom of the trunk, place the center of a pipe cleaner horizontally across the trunk, twist the right side of the pipe cleaner to the left, and the left side to the right—securing the pipe cleaner to the trunk and forming the two lower branches. Continue making branches in the same way, at 1/2-inch intervals up the trunk to the top of the tree. To get the graduated effect, cut the lengths of pipe cleaners a little shorter with each new set of branches. For the small boughs, cut 1-1/4-inch lengths of pipe cleaner, and twist them in place along the arms of the larger branches. For the tub, cut a solid cylinder shape from Styrofoam, 1 inch in diameter and 1 inch high. For the tub planks, cut lengths 1-1/4 inches long and 1/4 inch wide from 3/32-inch-thick wood. Stain the planks, and when they are dry, glue them around the Styrofoam cylinder to form the tub. Make a hole in the center of the Styrofoam, and glue the end of the tree trunk in place. Pack a small quantity of soil on top of the Styrofoam in the tub. (In the tree-trimmings department in some stores at Christmas time, you can buy seven- or eight-inch-high artificial Christmas trees. Use this kind of tree, if you don't want to make one from scratch.) Cover the tree with different kinds of ornaments: apples, pears, heart shapes, gingerbread men, and candy canes made from the special dough (see recipe on page 144); colored bows, made from narrow ribbon; tiny packages made from squares and rectangles of balsa wood, gift-wrapped in colored shiny paper; various shapes and sizes of sequins. And make a star or an angel or a fairy for the top of the tree. An angel or fairy can be made as follows: Glue a small wooden bead onto a length of round toothpick. Paint the hair and features on the bead. Glue a tiny rhinestone to the hair for decoration. For the dress make a paper cone, and glue it (at the neck) to the toothpick. Make the wings from stiff clear plastic, and glue them in place. Cut slivers of wood for the arms, and glue them to the dress.

Christmas Tree

Crayon

Find a real crayon to use as a model. Cut a 3/8-inch length from the end of a round toothpick. Lightly sand the pointed end of the piece of toothpick. Paint the "crayon." Cut a piece of paper 1/4 inch long and a little wider than the circumference of the crayon. Glue the paper wrapper around the crayon. Using the same color paint which was used for the crayon, paint a narrow border around the circumference of the paper wrapper, at the top, and at the bottom. Make a few small paint marks along the side of the wrapper to resemble letters.

Cushion No. 1

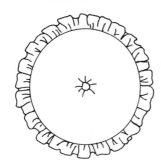

Cushion No. 1

(Drawing actual size)

Cut four circles, all the same size, two from card, and two from about 3/8-inch thick foam rubber. Cut two circles of fabric for the cushion cover. Cut them 1/2 inch wider in diameter than the card and foam-rubber circles. Using fabric glue, stick each foam-rubber circle to a card circle. Then place a foam-rubber and card circle on top of one of the fabric cushion covers. Fold the fabric over the edge of the card and glue the fabric down. Thread a needle and make a knot in the end of the thread. Push the needle through the card and foam rubber to the front of the cushion. String a small bead on the thread and then bring the needle back through the fabric to the card. Pull the thread so that the bead is fixed firmly in the center of the cushion. Finish the thread off. Make the other half of the cushion using the method I have just described. Take a piece of narrow ribbon about 6 inches long, and sew small running stitches along one edge. Pull the thread, and as the ribbon gathers, it will form a circle. Glue the gathered ribbon to one half of the cushion as shown in the diagram. Last, glue the two parts of the cushion together.

Ribbon —

Card —

Fabric —

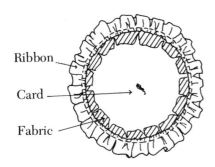

Cushion No. 2

(Drawing actual size)

Use the following directions to crochet a small square cushion cover, from two colors of lightweight yarn (crochet abbreviations: ch = chain; sl/st = slip stitch; dc = double crochet; sp = space): Starting at the center with the first color, ch 6. Join with sl st to form a ring. Round 1: ch 3, in the ring make 2 dc, ch2 and (3dc, ch2) 3 times. Join with a sl st to top of ch 2. Break off and fasten. Round 2: Attach second color to any ch-2 sp, ch3, in same sp make 2 dc; ch2 for corner sp and make 3 dc; (ch 1, in next sp make 3 dc, ch 2 for corner sp and 3dc) 3 times; ch 1. Join as before. Break off and fasten. These directions will make the first two rounds of the traditional granny-square motif. Make a felt-covered cushion, the same size as the crocheted square. Stuff the cushion with cotton. Sew the crocheted square to one side of the cushion.

Cushion No. 2

Dog Dish

Use a button with a deep bowl and high rims.

Doily

Cut a tiny section from a large paper doily.

Doll under a Glass Dome

The base of the dome is a cut-down screw cap from a soda bottle. The "glass" dome is the larger part of an egg-shaped plastic container, the kind that comes from vending machines. Paint the screw-cap base gold or black. Cut a small circle of felt for the doll's skirt. Assemble the doll in the following way: Take a bead-headed pin. On the pin, thread and then glue together a round wooden bead for the head, a small jewelry finding (or sequin) for the collar, a square wooden bead for the chest, the circle of felt for the skirt, and finally an oval bead for the base. The skirt will stick out; so glue it in folds to the oval-bead base of the doll. Use small beads for the dress sleeves; use slivers of wood for the arms, as shown in the drawing. Glue the sleeves and arms to the doll's body. Paint the doll's hair and features (the bead-headed pin is her bun). Then glue the doll to the screw-cap base. Fit the dome over the doll, and glue the rim of the dome to the screw-cap base.

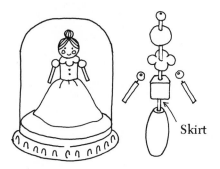

Doll Under a Glass Dome

Draining Board
(Drawing actual size)

Trace and transfer the pattern for the draining board onto 1/16-inch balsa wood. Cut it out. By sanding, bevel the end indicated by the arrow. Give the draining board a coat of shellac or varnish. Let the shellac or varnish dry. Using the point of a blunt darning needle, make indentations around the border and three horizontal lines on the draining board, as shown in the drawing. Cut a small rectangle-shaped wedge from 1/16-inch balsa wood. Glue the wedge under the draining board to raise one end slightly.

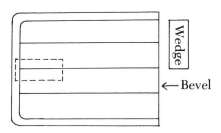

Draining Board

Eyeglasses
(Drawing actual size)

Use a length of thin brass wire for the eyeglasses frames. Make two loops in the wire (A). Then make a slipknot with the wire at the side of each loop (B). Pull the knots tightly, being careful not to lose the round shapes of the loops. Bend the ends of the wire back to form the side pieces of the glasses, and trim the wire to the correct length (C). Make the "lenses" by putting a drop of clear paper glue into each frame of the glasses. When the glue has dried, the effect will be of lenses in the frames.

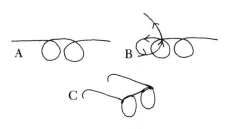

Eyeglasses

Eyeglass case
(Drawing actual size)

Make the eyeglass case from felt. Use pattern A to cut the back and front of the case. Embroider the flower on the front piece of the case with a single thread of embroidery floss. Stitch the back and front of the case together (on the outside) leaving a space at the top. Make narrow cording from twisted threads of embroidery floss. (For cording instructions see page 42.) Glue the cording around the edge of the eyeglass case.

Eyeglass Case

Fences

Cut the slatted sides from plastic tomato or berry boxes. Paint the box sides first with gesso and, when they are dry, with acrylic paint.

Flowerpot

Flowerpot

Use a toothpaste cap for the flowerpot and a button for the saucer. Give both the button and the toothpaste cap a coat of gesso. Then paint them a terra cotta color, so that they look like a real flowerpot and saucer. Cut a 1/2-inch-thick circle of foam rubber, soak it with glue, and put the foam rubber in the bottom of the "flowerpot." Take a bunch of tiny dried flowers and arrange their stems in the foam rubber so that they stand firmly. Fill the flowerpot with earth, pressing the earth gently down around the flowers' stems.

Food

(All drawings actual size)
I have found that the following dough recipe produces the best modeling material for making miniature food. (The dough can be stored in a plastic bag in the refrigerator for several weeks.)

DOUGH RECIPE
   3 slices of white bread with the crusts removed
   3 tablespoons of white glue
   1 teaspoon of white acrylic paint

Crumble the bread into small pieces in a bowl. Add the glue and paint, and mix them thoroughly with the bread.
Knead the mixture until it has a smooth texture and no longer sticks to your fingers.
Take small pieces of dough and shape them into food, using as sculpting tools an X-acto knife, a pin, a toothpick, and your fingers. Keep the dough that you are not using in a plastic bag. Unless otherwise instructed, paint the dough after the food is made and when it is hard and dry. I paint the food with concentrated (liquid) watercolors. And when the paint is dry, I give the food a coat of shellac. Use real food, photographs in magazines, and pictures in recipe books as models when sculpting food.

Chicken, French Fries, and Tomatoes

CHICKEN, FRENCH FRIES, AND TOMATOES
Form a ball of dough into the shape of a chicken leg. Roll a piece of dough flat, and cut the "French fries" with a knife. For the tomato slices, make a small dough ball and cut it into slices. Then with a pin, draw lines and dots, to indicate the texture of the food. Glue the food to a plate (see page 155). Paint the food, and then give it a coat of shellac.

Fish, Baked Potato, Carrots, and Peas

FISH, BAKED POTATO, CARROTS, AND PEAS
Model the fish, potato, and carrots from dough. Use green-colored sprinkles (cake decorations) for the peas. Decorate the fish with slices of lemon cut from a small ball of dough. Draw lines with a pin to indicate the fish's scales and tail. Glue the food to a plate. Paint the food. Make the fish silver, and highlight the scales and tail with touches of black paint. Give all the food, except the baked potato, a coat of shellac.

CHEESE

Flatten a ball of dough into the shape of a cheese. Cut a wedge shape from the "cheese." Paint the outside of the cheese black or red, and the inside part that shows, yellow. Shellac the cheese.

SALAMI

Mix some red and brown acrylic paint into a piece of dough, to get the color of salami. Mold the dough into a sausage shape, and wrap it in clear plastic food wrapping. Twist the ends of the plastic. Then tie a piece of thread around each end of the salami.

EGGS

From little balls of dough make egg shapes, and paint them brown or white. Shellac the eggs. Make the fried egg on a slice of bread in layers. First, mold the bread, then mold a small, flat, irregular shape for the egg white, and a flattened ball for the egg yolk. Paint and shellac the fried egg on bread.

Cheese, Salami, and Eggs

CANAPÉS

Roll some dough flat, and cut squares, circles, triangles, and oblongs for the pieces of bread. Cut the small circles, by removing the eraser from a pencil, and using the metal eraser holder at the end of the pencil as a cutter. Lightly press tasty morsels on each slice of "bread": black caviar made of poppy seeds; hard-boiled eggs sliced from a thin, sausage-like shape of dough (paint the centers of the egg slices yellow and the outsides white); sardines made from dough and painted silver and black; small triangles of cheese made from dough, and painted yellow. Glue the canapés to a plate. Decorate the plate with green olives made from tiny green beads. Paint slivers of wood red—and stuff them in the bead holes to look like pieces of pimento.

Canapés

JAM JAR AND GLASS CANISTER

Make both the jam jar and the canister using clear plastic tubing (I used the plastic container from a ball-point pen refill) for the cylinders, and circles of stiff clear plastic cut from wrappings for the bases. Fill the jam jar with a mixture of red paint and clear glue, to resemble jam. Cut a small circle of white tissue paper and tie it to the top of the jam jar with a piece of thread. Make a label for the front of the jar. Use a button with a shank for the lid of the canister, and a tiny bead for the lid knob. Fill the canister with flour, or salt, or sprinkles, or instant coffee, or millet.

Jam Jar and Glass Canister

PIES

For the latticed-top fruit pie, roll a piece of dough flat. Cut a circle of dough and press it into the bottom of a metal soda-bottle cap. Fill the pie case with little red beads for a cherry pie, or wedges of dough for an apple pie, or a solid piece of dough for a pumpkin pie. Cover the pie with interwoven narrow strips of dough to form a lattice design. Paint and shellac the pie. Make the meat pie from a solid lump of dough rolled into an oval shape. Flatten the oval at the top and bottom. Encase the bottom and sides of the oval in another piece of dough which has been rolled flat. Pinch the two pieces of dough together along the edge of the circumference of the pie. Cut small leaves from dough to decorate the top of the pie. Paint and shellac the pie.

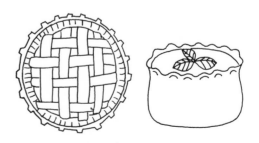

Pies

Cookies

Chocolate Cake

Bread

Fruit

Vegetables

COOKIES

Cut the crescent-shaped cookie from dough, using as a cutter the metal end of a pencil with the eraser removed. Finely crumble little pieces of cork, and press them into the top of the cookie for chopped nuts. Cut the heart-shaped cookie from dough. Paint a heart on the cookie using thick pink acrylic paint which will look like icing. For the round sugar cookie, glue two pieces of sandpaper together, rough sides showing. Cut a circle either with scissors or with a paper punch. Cut the leaf-shaped cookie from dough. Make the center indentation with the end of a metal tube used with cake-decorating cones. Cut the round cookie from dough using the metal end of a pencil as a cutter. Decorate the cookie with acrylic "icing" and stick a small red bead in the center for a cherry. For the gingerbread man, knead some brown paint into the dough. Roll out the dough and cut the gingerbread man shape. Make a hole in the top with a pin, and thread a strand of embroidery floss through the hole and tie it with a knot. Decorate the gingerbread man with light-colored acrylic "icing." Make the candy cane from dough by rolling a thin sausage shape and bending the top over. Paint red stripes on the candy cane. You can use the gingerbread man cookie, and the candy cane as decorations for your dolls' house Christmas tree.

CHOCOLATE CAKE

Cut a 5/8-inch length from a 1-inch-diameter piece of dowel (or use a small spool). Paint the sides of the dowel with a thick layer of dark brown acrylic paint. While the paint is still wet, roll the dowel in sawdust, which will adhere to the paint, and look like finely grated nuts. Paint the top of the dowel with thick acrylic "icing." Mold a small rose and leaves from dough, and glue them to the top of the chocolate cake. Paint the rose and leaves. The cake stand is made from gold-colored jewelry findings and a long, gold-colored bead, fixed together with epoxy glue.

BREAD

Make the bread from dough. Cut small slashes in the top of the bread with an X-acto knife before painting and applying shellac.

FRUIT

Shape the fruit from dough. Cut slivers from the stalks of real apples and pears to use as the stalks for the miniature fruit. Texture the lemons, oranges, and grapefruit with tiny pinpricks. Use a large fancy button for a fruit bowl.

VEGETABLES

Make a cabbage or lettuce in the following way: Glue a piece of red or green crepe paper to a bead, so that the bead is entirely covered. Tear the leaf shapes from another piece of crepe paper; glue and overlap the leaves around the bead to form the shape of a cabbage or lettuce. Shape the carrot from dough, and use small sprigs of dried fern or dillweed for the stalk. Use dough to make the other vegetables.

The possibilities for making miniature food are endless. The yellow or red wax which encases some kinds of cheese becomes quite malleable with the heat from your hand if you knead it for several minutes; it can be formed into bananas, lemons, and tomatoes. For a dish of spaghetti, force dough through a garlic press.

Garbage Can

Use the round container that rolls of film come in. Make two holes in the top of the lid and attach a large metal staple for the handle.

Grater

Cut a length, 1-1/4 inches long and 3/4 inch wide, from a piece of heavy aluminum foil (the type used for oven pans). Turn the edges about 1/16 inch at the top and bottom of the width of foil, as indicated by arrows in the drawing. Prick holes in the foil with a pin. With the rough surface of the foil outside, form the cylindrical shape of the grater around a length of dowel or a pencil. Secure the ends together with quick-drying epoxy glue. Cut a strip of foil 3/4 inch long by 3/16 inch wide for the handle of the grater. Turn the sharp edges of the strip of foil toward the center. When the edges are turned, the strip will be about 1/16 inch wide. Glue the handle to the grater.

Grater

Groceries

Before you trade in the special-purchase coupons received in the mail, cut out the small colored photographs of the products. Glossy magazines also have small photographs in advertisements for cereal, cake mixes, paper towels, pet foods, coffee, et cetera, which can be cut out. I made a can of coffee from a length of dowel, which I covered in red shiny paper. I cut the label from a small photograph of a can of coffee and glued it to the front of the dowel can. For the lid I used a white button, which I sanded to make thinner. Cut various-sized oblongs of balsa wood, and cover them with colored paper. Glue small photographs of cereal packages or cake mix boxes onto the colored paper.

Grocery Bag

(Pattern actual size)

Trace and transfer the pattern to a piece of brown paper cut from a real grocery bag. Cut the pattern out. Make folds in the brown paper where indicated by the dotted lines. Glue the backs of the bag together, with A overlapping B. Fold and glue the bottom of the bag as shown in the diagram. Paint a store name on the front of the bag.

Hammer and Pegs Set

(Patterns actual size)

Cut the peg shelf and the end supports from 1/8-inch-thick wood. Drill 6 holes in the shelf, each 3/32 inch in diameter. Cut a dado 1/16 inch deep, where it is indicated by the dotted lines, in each end support. Glue the shelf to the end supports. Cut 6 pegs from round toothpicks. Test the pegs to make sure that they fit into the peg

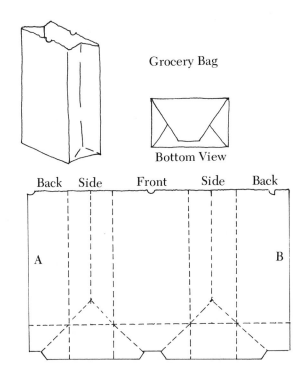

Grocery Bag

Bottom View

Back　Side　　Front　　Side　Back

A　　　　　　　　　　　　　　　　B

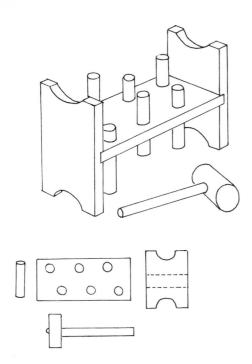

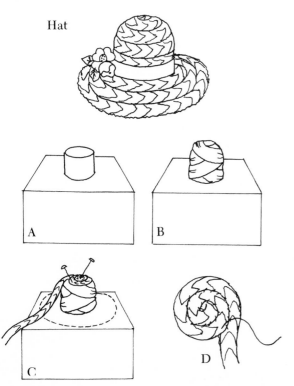

Hat

Hammer and Pegs Set

holes. Make the head of the hammer from a length of 1/8-inch dowel, and the handle from part of a round toothpick. Drill small holes through the center of the hammer head and the top of the handle. Join the head to the handle with a straight pin. Paint the pegs, the end supports, and the hammer head in bright colors.

Hanger No. 1
(Drawing actual size)
Cut the hanger from 1/8-inch-thick wood, and the stretcher from a round toothpick. Note that the ends of the stretcher are cut at an angle. Round off the top edge of the hanger by sanding. If you wish, stain the wood. Glue the hanger to the stretcher. Use the end of a hairpin for the hanger hook. Make a hole in the top of the hanger, and glue the hook in place. Shellac or varnish the hanger.

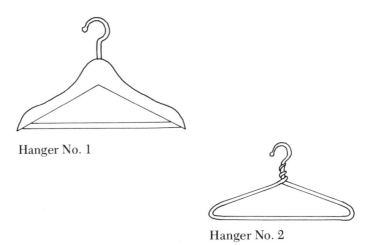

Hanger No. 1

Hanger No. 2

Hanger No. 2
(Drawing actual size)
Make the wire hanger from a hairpin. Use small pliers to bend and twist the hairpin into shape.

Hat
First make a hat block: Cut a 1-1/2-inch length from a 5/8-inch dowel. Push the dowel into a block of Styrofoam, leaving about 1/2 inch of the dowel protruding (A). Wrap a strip of nylon stocking around the dowel to pad and shape it (B). For the hat use 3/16-inch-wide braided millinery straw. Start making the hat by pinning the end of the length of straw to the top of the hat block. Begin to coil the straw, going around in slightly overlapping circles. Pin the straw to the block as you go; coil the straw around two or three times (C). Then, using matching thread, starting at the center of the crown, join the circles with tiny slip stitches (D). (Tuck the end of the length of straw inside the center of the crown.) Continue coiling and joining the straw until the crown and the brim of the hat are completed. Remove the hat from the block. Trim with fabric flowers and narrow ribbon.

Hatbox

(Patterns are *not* drawn to scale)

Glue shiny colored paper, or paper with a small print, to a piece of card. First, make the bottom of the hatbox. Using a pencil in a compass, draw a circle on the card 1-11/16 inches in diameter. Keeping the point of the compass in the center of the circle, increase the reach of the pencil by 1/8 inch and draw another circle. Cut the bottom of the box out around the outer circle. Cut tabs around the rim of the circle as shown in diagram A. Bend the tabs down as shown in diagram B. Cut a length of card for the sides of the box, 5-3/4 inches long by 7/8 inch wide. Make two small holes in the card as shown in diagram C. Bend the length of card to form a circle, and glue the ends together allowing 1/4-inch overlap. Glue the bottom of the hatbox to the sides (the tags go inside). Cut two lengths of narrow ribbon. Make knots at one end of each length of ribbon. Thread a length of ribbon through each hole in the sides of the box. Make the diameter of the lid 1-3/4 inches, and then follow the same instructions that I gave for the bottom of the hatbox. (For the rim of the lid, diagram D, cut a length of card 6 inches long by 3/8 inch wide.) Make a narrow cord from one strand of embroidery floss (for cording instructions see page 42). Glue a length of cord around the bottom of the box and around the top of the lid. Place the lid on the box, and tie the ribbons in a bow.

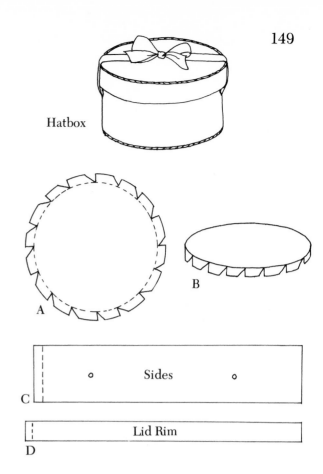

Hatbox

Ironing Board

(Patterns are *not* drawn to scale)

Make the ironing board to a scale of 1 inch to 1 foot, by using the measurements given with the directions: Cut the board (4-1/4 inches by 1-1/4 inches) and the four legs (each leg 4 inches by 3/16 inch) from 1/16-inch-thick balsa wood. Shape the board and the legs as shown in the drawings. Make a pin hole through the center of each leg. Cut a length 1/8 inch wide by 5-1/4 inches long from 1/8-inch-thick balsa wood. From this strip of wood, cut one stretcher (A) 1-1/8 inches long, the other three stretchers (B) each 1 inch long, and the brake bar (C) 1-1/8 inches long. Glue the stretchers between the ironing-board legs as shown in the drawing. Glue the brake bar (C) to the underside of the board. Cut a length 1-1/8 inches long by 1/8 inch wide from 1/4-inch-thick balsa wood (D), and glue this strip in place on the underside of the board. Place the inner set of legs (with the three stretchers) inside the outer legs, forming a cross. Align the pin holes. Join the sets of legs together with two straight pins for hinges. Using two more straight pins, hinge the legs to the board as shown in the drawing. The ironing board folds down flat. If you wish, make a cover for the ironing board from a piece of cotton fabric painted silver.

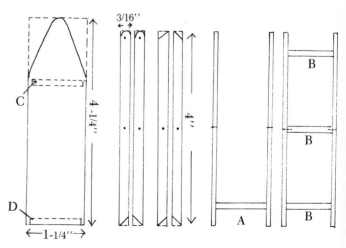

Ironing Board

Jack-in-the-Box

(Patterns drawn to scale)

Use a small wooden bead for Jack's head. Paint the features on the bead. Make Jack's hat and his star-shaped collar from felt. Using darning yarn, trim the hat with a band and a tassel. Glue the hat and the collar to the bead head. Cover a narrow 1-inch-long piece of

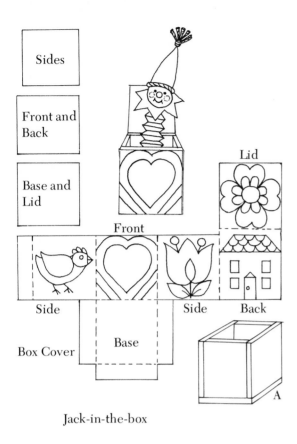

Jack-in-the-box

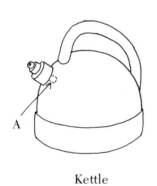

Kettle

Knife

metal spring (from the inside of a dried-out retractable ball-point pen–or coil thin wire around a piece of narrow dowel) with a strip of cotton fabric. Glue the spring to the head. Trace and transfer the patterns for the box onto 1/16-inch-thick balsa wood. Cut out a front, back, base, lid, and two sides. Following the method of construction illustrated in diagram A, glue the box together (the lid is attached later). Trace and transfer the pattern for the box cover onto typing paper. Draw the designs on the paper, and color them with felt markers. Fold the paper box-cover where indicated by the dotted lines. Starting with the base, glue the cover to the box. Glue the wooden lid to the paper lid-cover. Glue the end of the spring to the inside base of the box.

Kettle

Take the smaller half of an egg-shaped plastic container (the kind you get from vending machines that contain small favors). Using a pin-vise drill, make three holes in the top (two for where the ends of the handle will be inserted, and one for the spout). For the handle: Cut a length of plastic-covered electrical wiring, and glue it in place. For the spout: Cut a 5/32-inch length from a 3/16-inch dowel, and a 1/8-inch length from a 1/8-inch dowel. Carve a peg 1/16 inch long on the larger piece of dowel (A). Glue the peg into the hole. Complete the spout by gluing on the smaller piece of dowel and a tiny bead. Paint the completed kettle, first with gesso, and then with silver paint.

Knife

Make the blade either from the top part of a keyhole saw blade (the kind used in X-acto knives) or from heavy aluminum foil. For the handle cut two small oblong lengths, 5/8 inch by 1/8 inch, from 1/32-inch-thick balsa wood. Glue a piece of wood on either side of the blade (leaving 5/8 inch of blade protruding). When the glue is dry, sand the handle to shape, and paint it. Make a small pin hole at the top of one side of the handle. Cut a straight pin, leaving just enough of the shank to glue in the pin hole.

Knitting on Needles

Some of my friends can knit on straight pins with darning yarn, but I can't. For those of you who also can't knit on pins, make "fake" knitting in the following way. Cut a length of ribbing, about 1 inch long and 5/8 inch wide, from the top of an old sock. Use small bead-headed pins for knitting needles. Using one of the "knitting needles," pick up the loose stitches at the top of the piece of ribbing. Pull out a length of yarn from the sock. Make a small ball out of paper tissue. Wind one end of the yarn around the paper ball, covering it completely, and thread the other end of the yarn onto the needle with the knitting.

Lamp No. 1

I bought the Mickey Mouse I used for this lamp by mail order from The Enchanted Doll House in Vermont. But you can use the special dough (recipe, page 144) to model a Mickey Mouse, teddy bear, or other type of doll. When the dough is dry and hard, paint the modeled figure. For the base of the lamp cut a circle 3/4 inch in diameter from a piece of 1/16-inch-thick balsa wood. For the support cut a length 1-3/8 inches long from a piece of 1/8-inch dowel. Drill two holes in the top of the dowel support, and glue two straight pins in the holes, as shown in diagram A. The lampshade will rest on the pins. Paint the base and the support. Glue the Mickey Mouse (or teddy bear) to the base of the lamp. Glue the dowel support to the base. Drill a pin-sized hole through the support and the dough figure. Push a pin through the hole, securing the dough figure to the support, as indicated in the drawing. The pattern for the shade is the actual size. Stick a strip of plastic-coated cloth tape (at least 1-3/4 inches wide) onto a piece of index card. Trace and transfer the pattern for the lamp shade (B) to the tape-covered card, and cut it out. Glue the shade together (overlap one end to cover the other end to the dotted line). Put small dabs of glue on the pinpoints and pin heads at the top of the support. Place the shade over the pins. Glue a small bead to the front of the base for a "switch."

Lamp No. 2

Pull apart the two ends of a bobby pin, to form a right angle. Cut a small oblong from 1/8-inch-thick balsa wood, for the base of the lamp. Paint the base and the bobby pin. Make a small hole in the base, and glue one end of the bobby pin in the hole. Make a cone-shaped shade from colored paper. Make two holes at the top of the shade, as shown in the drawing. Put the end of the bobby pin through the holes in the shade, and glue the shade in place. Glue a small bead to the base for a "switch."

Lamp No. 3

Make a shade for this hanging lamp: Use half of an empty concentrated lemon juice container. Make a pencil line around the circumference of the plastic lemon, and cut it in half using an X-acto knife. Make a hole at the top of the "shade." Wind a piece of thin wire around the end of a flashlight bulb. Thread the wire, from the inside, through the hole in the shade leaving about 1/2 inch of wire protruding. Wind the end of the wire around a length of keychain. See the Appendix for names of dealers who supply electrical fittings and tiny light bulbs specially suitable to use in dolls' houses (page 216).

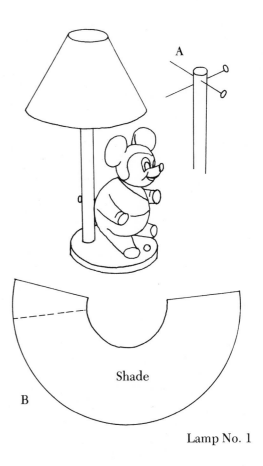

Lamp No. 1

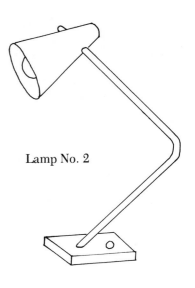

Lamp No. 2

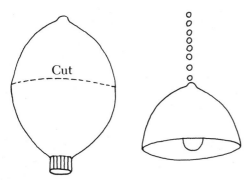

Lamp No. 3

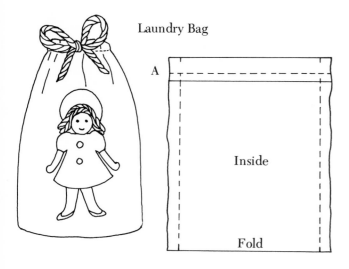

Laundry Bag

Laundry Basket

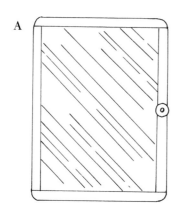

A

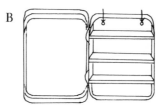

B

Medicine Cabinet

Laundry bag
(Drawings actual size)

Cut a strip of lightweight cotton fabric 4-1/2 inches long and 1-3/4 inches wide. (These measurements allow 1/8-inch seam allowances at the sides, and 1/4 inch at both ends.) Fold the strip of fabric in half, and sew the side seams together. Turn the top edge of the fabric over 1/4 inch, and stitch it down. The bag will then look like diagram A. Turn the bag right side out. Cut the design for the "girl" motif from pieces of colored felt, the hair from darning yarn. Glue the pieces of felt and the yarn to the front of the bag with fabric glue. Using a darning needle, thread a length of lightweight yarn through the top hem of the bag, leaving about 2 inches of the ends of the yarn hanging loose at the front of the bag. Pull the ends of the yarn to close the bag, and tie a bow.

Laundry Basket
(Drawing actual size)

I used an empty plastic Tic-Tac candy box for the basket. Remove the lid from the box. Starting at the top of the outside of the box, coat 1/2 inch around the circumference with glue. Wind thin string around the glue-covered part of the box. Keep applying glue and winding string until the box is completely covered. Cover the lid starting with a small circle of string in the center and working out toward the rim. Decorate the front of the laundry basket by gluing on a second layer of string wound into simple shapes. Paint the laundry basket with acrylic paints, using contrasting colors for the basket and the decoration. For the knob push a pin with a bead on it through the top of the lid.

Magazines

Cut out small photographs of magazine covers, and mount them on sheets of folded paper.

Medicine Cabinet
(Drawing A actual size)

Use a small empty aspirin tin for the cabinet. Glue a piece of mirror to the front of the tin. (I found the correct-size mirror in a hobby store. But you can use silver paper mounted on card, instead of a mirror.) Glue a frame to the mirror with strips of 1/16-inch-thick balsa wood, as shown in the drawing. Paint the frame, the sides, and the inside of the cabinet to match your bathroom fixtures. Make three shelves from 1/16-inch-thick balsa wood, paint them and then glue them inside the cabinet as shown in drawing B. If you wish to "nail" the medicine cabinet to your bathroom wall, drill two pin holes where indicated by the arrows and insert cut-down straight pins. Otherwise use epoxy glue to fix the cabinet to the wall. Use a bead for the knob on the front of the cabinet door.

Mirror, Comb, and Brush Set

Cut the rough shapes of the mirror, comb, and brush from 1/16-inch-thick balsa wood. Gently sand the pieces of wood into shape. Cut small lines along one side of the comb to indicate teeth; but don't cut right through the wood. Glue a small circle of silver paper to the front of the mirror. For decoration, glue tiny beads and filigree jewelry findings to the backs of the mirror and the brush. Paint the mirror and brush (including the beads and jewelry findings) silver. Paint the teeth of the comb brown, and the edge silver. Make small holes in the front of the brush, with a pin-vise drill, taking care not to go right through the wood. For bristles take hairs from a mascara brush or an old artist's paintbrush. Glue small clumps of bristles into the holes in the front of the brush. When the glue is dry, cut the bristles down, so that they measure about 1/8 inch. (Trying to glue the bristles into the holes is an exasperating job, but a pair of tweezers helps.)

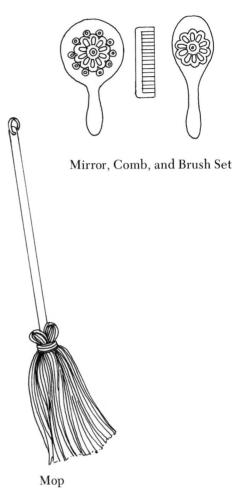

Mirror, Comb, and Brush Set

Mop

Cut a length 3-1/2 inches long from 1/8-inch dowel for the handle. Wind thin string around a book of matches. Take the loops of string off the book of matches and arrange and glue them to the end of the handle. Wind a length of string around the loops to secure them in place. Cut the bottom ends of the loops. Round off the top of the handle by sanding. Drill a hole about 1/16 inch in diameter at the top of the handle, and insert a small metal jump-ring (for jump-ring description see page 24). The length of the finished mop is 4-1/2 inches.

Napkin Rings

Use the plastic tubing that covers electrical wiring. Cut 1/8-inch-wide lengths from 3/16-inch tubing.

Notebook

(Drawing actual size)

For the covers cut two pieces of colored construction paper 1 inch long and 7/8 inch wide. Using typing paper, cut six rectangles 1-11/16 inches wide by 15/16 inch long. Fold each rectangle of paper in half. (The pages are a fraction smaller than the covers.) Put the folded pages between the covers, and clamp them together with a spring-type clothespin to keep them in place while you work on the spiral binder. Make small holes through all the thicknesses of paper, along one side of the notebook. Thread thin wire through the holes to bind the book together. Remove the clamp. Make a small label for the front of the notebook. It can serve as a recipe book, too.

Mop

Oven Mit

(Drawing actual size)

Trace the shape of the mit onto tracing paper, and cut it out to use as a pattern. Cut the scalloped border from a double thickness of felt, and the main part of the mit from a double thickness of felt in a contrasting color. Slipstitch a scalloped border to the bottom edges of the back and front of the mit. Whipstitch the back and front of the

Notebook

Oven Mit

Paddle and Ball

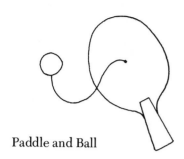

Paper Toweling

Perfume Bottles

mit together. Make a thin cord from embroidery floss (see page 42). Glue a length of cord around the seam which joins the border to the mit. Make a hanging loop from cord, and glue the ends inside the mit. Cut the flower and two small circles (for the center of the flower) from different-colored pieces of felt. Glue the circles to the flower. Place a damp cloth over the felt flower, and press it with a warm iron. Glue the flower to the front of the oven mit.

Paddle and Ball

Cut the rough shape of the paddle from 1/32-inch-thick wood. Refine the shape by gently sanding. Cut two pieces of 1/32-inch-thick wood for the handle. Glue the paddle between the two sides of the handle. Make a small hole in the center of the paddle. Thread a length of narrow rubber band through the hole. Knot one end of the rubber band, to secure it to the paddle. Push and glue the loose end of the rubber band into the hole in a small wooden bead. Paint the paddle and the ball.

Paper Toweling

Cut the label for the paper toweling from a small, colored photograph in a magazine, or a special-purchase coupon. Wind an inch-wide strip of toilet paper around a length of round toothpick, and glue the end down. Glue the label onto the roll of paper. Then cover the "paper toweling" with a piece of clear plastic food wrap, securing it envelope-style at the top and bottom of the roll.

Paperweight

Try to find a round, clear-glass button which has a colored glass design embedded in it. (It is actually called a "paperweight button." This type includes Victorian hand-blown buttons and others that were mass-produced in Czechoslovakia in the period 1910–1920. A small quantity of paperweight buttons are still being manufactured.) Remove the wire eye-shank from the glass button, and mount the button either on half of a small snap or on a tiny flat button.

Perfume Bottles

For the bottles use faceted crystal, round or rondelle-shaped beads. Make the stoppers from tiny metallic beads, fixed to the "bottles" with cut-down pins and glue.

Pictures

There are many sources for small dolls' house pictures: photographs cut from magazines, Christmas card catalogs, embroidery kit catalogs, and old books. I used a postage stamp for the picture in the living room, and my daughter drew the pictures which are on the wall in the children's bedroom. Make a simple picture frame from strips of wood, or use a metal brooch setting for a frame. (Metal brooch settings come in a great variety of shapes, styles, and sizes, and can be bought from suppliers of costume jewelry parts.)

Piggy Bank

Make the pig from the special bread dough (see recipe on page 144). Roll a small piece of dough into a ball, and then mold the ears and snout. Cut the legs from a round toothpick and press them into the dough. Using snipe-nose pliers, curl a short length of wire for the pig's tail. Make a small indentation in the pig's back for the money slot. When the dough is hard and dry, paint the pig with acrylic paints. For the "coin" in the slot in the pig's back, cut a tiny circle from card and paint it silver. Glue the coin in place.

Piggy Bank

Plates

Using the point of a knife, gently pry out the white plastic discs to be found inside certain soda bottle caps. As these discs are slightly concave they look like small plates. Paint designs on the plates using acrylic paints.

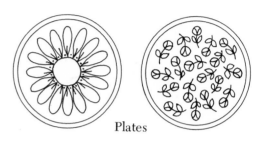

Plates

Pot No. 1

The pot and lid are made from white plastic coasters. (I bought a packet of these coasters at the hardware store. They are meant to be used on the bottom of metal chair legs as a protection against scratched floors.) For the lid, cut the bottom from a coaster. Make two holes in the lid for the wire handle. Use a length of plastic-covered electrical wiring for the handle. Use a complete coaster for the pot. Cut a small slit in each side of the coaster for the plastic handles. Cut the handles from the surplus parts of the coaster used for the lid. Insert and glue a handle into the slits on each side of the pot. Paint the design on the front of the pot using acrylic paint.

Pot No. 1

Pot No. 2

This pot is made from a brass drawer pull or cupboard pull (the kind that is concave, and set *into* the piece of furniture). For the wooden part of the handle, cut a length 3/8 inch long from a round toothpick. Paint the length of wood black. Drill a hole in each side of the pot where the handle will be inserted. Using a pin vise, drill a hole about 1/16 inch deep in each end of the wooden handle. Cut two lengths of brass wire and attach each length to the pot and the wooden handle, as shown in the drawing.

Pot No. 2

Quill Pen

(Drawing actual size)
Cut the shape of a small feather from the top end of a large feather. Glue the "quill pen" into the hole of a crystal-faceted rondelle bead, which will look like a fancy inkwell.

Records and Record Jackets

For records, either mount shiny black paper onto both sides of a piece of card, or use the thin, flexible sample records that come as advertisements in the mail. Draw circles, with a compass, on the black paper or sample records, and cut them out. Cut circles of

Quill Pen

colored paper with small printing on it (from magazines) to use for the record labels. Glue the labels onto both sides of a "record." Make a hole with a pin through the center of the record and label. Cut small photographs of actual record jackets from magazine advertisements. Cut two pieces of card the same size as the photograph of a record jacket. Glue the two pieces of card together along their edges, but leaving the top open. Glue the photograph to the cover.

Rolling Pin

(Drawings actual size)

Cut a 1-inch length from a 3/16-inch piece of dowel. Drill a pin-sized hole, about 1/8-inch deep, in the center of each end of the dowel. For the handles, cut two 5/16-inch lengths from a 1/8-inch piece of dowel. Whittle the handles into shape. Drill small pin-sized holes in the blunt end of each handle. Cut two small lengths of steel from a straight pin, and glue a length in each handle hole (A). Glue the pins on the handles into the pin holes at the ends of the 1-inch length of dowel. Paint the handles red.

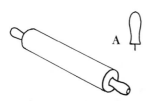

Rolling Pin

Salad Bowls

There are high-rimmed wooden buttons which look as if they had been specially made to use as tiny salad bowls. Use 1/2-inch buttons for the individual small bowls, and a 1-inch button for the larger serving bowl. Fill the holes in the buttons with plastic wood and give them a coat of varnish or shellac. Acorn caps are also suitable for small salad bowls; and a half shell of a walnut or pecan can be used for the serving bowl. Sand the bottoms of the acorn caps and nut shells to make them "sit" properly.

Salad Tossers

Cut lengths from flat toothpicks, the right size for your salad bowl. Moisten (to make pliable) the wider, rounded ends of the toothpicks, and bend them into a slight curve; this will make the "spoon" ends. Stain the tossers to match the color of the salad bowl.

Scales

The scales are made from two oval-shaped pieces of wood, one glued on top of the other. Cut the rough shape of the top oval (A) from 1/16-inch-thick balsa wood. Refine the shape by sanding. Drill a small hole in the wood (B), and enlarge it into an oval shape using a needle file. Cut the rough shape of the bottom oval (C) from 1/8-inch-thick balsa wood. Refine the shape by sanding. Draw the dial for the scale (make small lines and numbers) on a piece of typing paper. Place the dial on the bottom piece of wood (C). Lay the pieces of wood one on top of the other and align the hole with the dial. Note the correct position for the dial so that it shows through the hole. Glue the dial in place on the bottom piece of wood. Glue the top and bottom pieces of wood together. Cut an oval from stiff, clear plastic wrapping, a fraction larger than the hole in the top of the scales. Glue the plastic oval over the hole. Glue a length of embroidery floss around the circumference of the plastic oval to make it look neater. Paint the scales with acrylic paint.

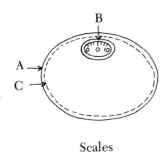

Scales

Shoe Bag

Shoe Bag

Shoe Bag

(Drawings actual size)

Cut a rectangle (A) from orange felt. Cut three strips of felt using pattern B (cut two from turquoise felt, and one from pink felt.) Sew the strips of felt to the rectangle (the pink strip in the center) as shown in the drawing. As you sew a strip in place, try to distribute the slackness in the fabric evenly between the four pockets. Cut the clown's arms and face from pink felt. Cut his hands, collar, and pompom from turquoise felt; his hat from orange felt; his cheeks and nose from dark red felt; the whites of his eyes from white felt; and his pupils and hair from brown felt. Glue the pieces of felt together to make the clown. Draw the mouth with a thin-tipped felt marker. Glue the clown to the rectangular shoe bag. (Note that the clown's collar is glued to the front of the bag.) The shoe bag will hang better if it is backed with a piece of card. Cut the shapes of just the soles and heels of shoes, from balsa wood, to put in the pockets of the shoe bag.

Slippers

(Patterns actual size)

For a slipper, first make the inner sole. Cut pattern A from card, and pattern B from thin glove leather. Glue the leather to the card, as shown in diagram C, clipping the leather so it will lie flat. Cut patterns D and E from leather. Place the strip of leather (E) across the top of the slipper, and glue each end under the inner sole. Glue the sole (D) to the bottom of the slipper. Cut and then shape the heel (F) from 3/16-inch-thick balsa wood. Cut a strip of leather (G), and glue it around the heel. Glue the heel to the sole. Trim the slipper. I used cording made from embroidery floss for the edging (for cording instructions see page 42), and tiny ribbon rosettes, with beads sewn in the centers, for the trimming on the tops of the slippers.

Soap

Cut a small rectangle of soap from a large bar of soap. With your fingers smooth the rectangle of soap to shape in a basin of water. Use a small scallop-shaped shell as a soap dish.

Stool

Use a large thread spool as the base for the stool. Cut a length of fabric 7 inches long and about 1-3/4 inches wide (the width will depend on the height of your spool). Sew a line of running stitches, 1/4 inch in, along the top of the length of the fabric. Leave the end of the thread loose. Sew the side seams together. Place the "skirt" over the spool, and pull the loose thread to form gathers. Glue the raw edge of the fabric (just above the gathers) to the top of the spool. Make the padded top of the stool (following the directions for half a cushion under the heading Cushion No. 1, page 142). Glue the top of the stool to the top of the spool. Tie a narrow length of ribbon around the stool as shown in the drawing. Flatten, by sanding, the tops of three map pins, and push them into the base of the spool for the feet. Adjust the length of the "skirt" so that it just skims the floor. Hem the skirt.

Slippers

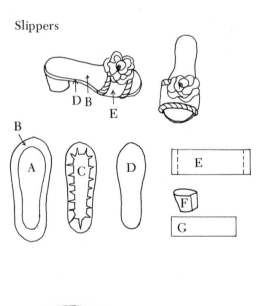

Stool

Teapot, Cup, and Saucer

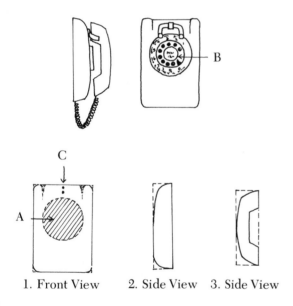

1. Front View   2. Side View   3. Side View

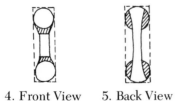

4. Front View   5. Back View

Telephone

Table Mats
Using a sharp knife, cut thin discs from a wine-bottle cork.

Teapot, Cup, and Saucer
For the body of the teapot (A) sand a large wooden bead flat at the top and at the base. Glue buttons to the top (B) and the base (C). Cut the rough shapes of the handle and spout from 1/8-inch-thick balsa wood. Refine the shapes by sanding. Glue the spout and handle to the teapot. For the lid (D), put a wooden bead in a table vise and saw it in half. For the lid knob, I used a tiny shank button from a Barbie doll's dress (E). Use a button for the saucer. For the cup use a wooden bead. Sand the base of the bead flat, so that it will sit in the saucer. Saw off about 1/3 of the top of the bead. Gouge out the center of the bead (a dangerous and laborious task!). Make two holes in the side of the bead for the handle. Cut a small length of wire for the handle, and glue it in the holes. Give the completed teapot, cup, and saucer a coat of gesso, and then paint them with acrylic paint. Finish the tea set with a coat of gloss polymer medium.

Telephone
(Drawings actual size)

Cut two rectangles from 1/4-inch-thick balsa wood, one for the main body of the telephone 7/8 inch long by 5/8 inch wide, and the other, for the receiver 3/4 inch long by 1/4 inch wide. Whittle and sand the main part of the telephone, following the shape indicated in diagrams 1 and 2. Note the indentations at the top of the phone. Draw a circle on the front of the body of the telephone (A). Draw the same size circle on a piece of card and cut it out. Retrace the circle on the front of the telephone with the tip of an X-acto knife blade, making a cut about 1/32 inch deep. Gently gouge out the wood in the circle, making it sufficiently deep (about 1/32 inch) for the card circle to fit flush with the front surface of the telephone. Glue the card circle to the front of the telephone. For the dial, cut a card circle 1/4 inch in diameter (B), and glue it to the first circle. Drill two small holes in the front of the telephone (C). Cut two short lengths of wire. Using small pliers, bend one piece of wire into a C-shape and the other into a narrow U-shape. Secure the C-shaped piece of wire (the holder for the receiver) to the front of the phone, by using the U-shaped piece of wire as a staple. Whittle and sand the receiver to the shape shown in diagrams 3, 4, and 5. Give the main part of the telephone and the receiver a coat of gesso, and then paint them with acrylic paint. Using a fine paintbrush, paint a circle in the center of the dial, and small dots in a circle to represent the dialing holes. To make the telephone cord, thread a needle with three strands of embroidery floss. Stick the point of the needle in a block of wood, so that the needle stands firmly. Wind the strands of floss many times around the needle to form a dense spiral. Pull the ends of the strands of floss taut, and secure them to the block of wood with a thumbtack. Paint the floss-spiral the same color as the telephone. When the paint is dry, cut the floss and remove it from the needle (the floss will retain its spiral shape). Drill a small hole in the bottom of the main part of the telephone, and another small hole at the bottom of the receiver. Glue the ends of the spiral telephone cord into the holes. Give the entire telephone (except the cord) a finishing coat of gloss polymer medium.

Toilet Paper and Holder
(Patterns actual size)

Cut the back and the two sides of the toilet-paper holder from 3/32-inch-thick balsa wood. Sand the pieces of wood smooth. Give the pieces of wood a coat of gesso, and then paint them with acrylic paint. Drill a hole (the circumference of a round toothpick) in each side piece of the holder. Glue *one* side to the back section of the holder. Cut a length 3/4 inch long from a round toothpick. Cut a length of toilet paper 9/16 inch wide. Wind the toilet paper around the toothpick. Place one end of the toothpick into the hole in the side that is glued to the back of the holder. Then glue the other side of the holder in place. Paint the ends of the toothpick that show.

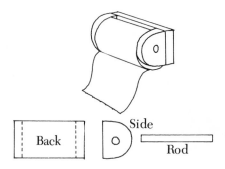

Toilet Paper and Holder

Toothbrush, Toothpaste, and Mug

For the toothbrush handle, cut a 5/8-inch length from a round tooth-pick. Slightly taper one end, and sand down the length of the tooth-pick, so that there are two flat sides. Cut a narrow groove 1/8 inch long on a flat side of the wider end of the toothbrush handle. For the bristles, cut a thin rectangle from wood 1/8 inch long, and glue it into the groove in the handle. Paint the handle a color and the bristles white. For the toothpaste tube, from a strip of thin lead (the kind that is wrapped around corks on wine bottles), cut a length about 1/2 inch wide and 5/8 inch long. Form a small sausage shape from clay or Plasticine. Wrap the lead strip around the clay and using epoxy glue stick the strip together to form a tube. Pinch the end of the tube closed. For the cap, cut a small length from a round toothpick, and push the "cap" into the top of the tube. Paint the tube white and the cap red. With a fine paintbrush, paint a brand name on the front of the toothpaste tube. Finish the tube and cap with a coat of gloss polymer medium. Make the mug by forming a small length of card into a cylinder, and gluing the ends together. Cut a circle from card for the base. Glue a length of embroidery floss around the top of the mug for the rim. Paint the mug and finish it with a coat of gloss polymer medium.

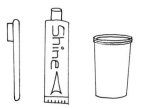

Toothbrush, Toothpaste, and Mug

Towel Rack
(Pattern actual size)

Cut two side pieces from 3/32-inch-thick balsa wood. Sand the pieces of wood smooth. Drill the holes in the sides the circumference of a round toothpick. Try not to go right through the wood. Cut five 1-1/2-inch lengths from round toothpicks. Take one side of the towel rack and lay it down on a flat surface, holes up. Glue an end of each of the five toothpick rungs into each of the holes. Place the holes in the other side of the towel rack over the free ends of the toothpick rungs and glue in place. Make sure that the towel rack stands square. When the glue is dry, paint the towel rack, with acrylic paints, in a color to match your bathroom fixtures. Finish the rack with a coat of gloss polymer medium.

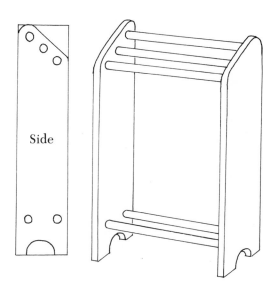

Towel Rack

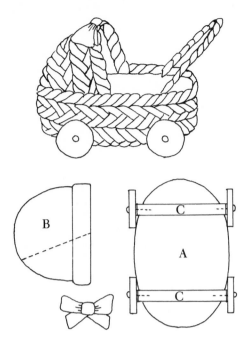

Toy Baby Carriage

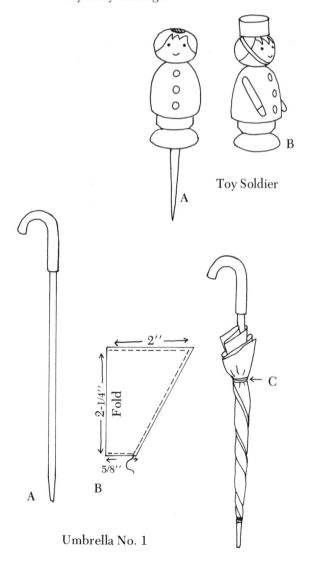

Toy Soldier

Umbrella No. 1

Toy Baby Carriage

(Drawings actual size)

Cut the oval base (A) from 1/8-inch-thick balsa wood. For the sides of the carriage cut a strip of card about 4-1/2 inches long and 1/2 inch wide. Glue lengths of narrow millinery straw to the card. Bring the straw over the edge to bind the top of the card. When the glue has dried, bend the straw-covered card into shape and glue the long ends together to form an oval which will fit snugly over the base. Glue the sides to the base. The hood is made from half of a small, egg-shaped, plastic container (but it could also be made from a piece of bent card). With an X-acto knife cut the shape for the hood along the dotted lines as shown in diagram B. Then glue strips of straw to the hood. Glue the hood to the sides (note the angle). For the handle, cover a length of wire with straw, and glue it in place to the sides. Cut the two wheel supports (C), 1 inch long by 1/8 inch wide, from 1/8-inch-thick balsa wood. Glue the supports to the bottom of the base. Cut the four wheels, each 3/32 inch thick, from 3/8-inch dowel. Paint the wheels. Drill a pin-sized hole through the center of each wheel. Drill a pin-sized hole into the end of each support. Attach the wheels to the supports with pins. As a finishing touch, make a bow from narrow ribbon, and glue it to the top of the hood.

Toy Soldier

Drawing A is a birthday-candle holder. Drawing B shows the conversion into a toy soldier. Cut off the pointed stick at the bottom of the holder. Cut the arms from flat toothpicks and glue them in place. For the hat, cut a length 3/16 inch long from 3/8-inch dowel, paint it, and glue it on the head. Finally paint the chin strap.

Tray

Cut the metal end from a Parmesan cheese tube (or use the round lid from a cocoa or drinking chocolate box). Give the "tray" a coat of gesso. Paint the main part of the tray one color and the rim a contrasting color, using acrylic paints. Cut two heart shapes from shiny colored paper, and glue them to the center of the tray. Finish the tray with a coat of gloss polymer medium.

Tire Swing

Remove the tire from an old "Match Box"-size toy car. Tie a piece of string through the hole in the tire.

Umbrella No. 1

(Drawing actual size, but diagram *not* drawn to scale)

For the handle, cut a 1-inch length of plastic-covered electrical wire. Paint a round toothpick. Fix one end of the plastic-covered wire to the end of the toothpick. Bend the wire into a handle shape (A). For the umbrella cover, cut a length of lightweight fabric 4 inches long and 2-1/4 inches wide. Fold the fabric in half and cut the diagonal line as shown in diagram B. Make a line of running stitches at the bottom and leave the thread loose. Sew the side seam, and turn and sew the top 1/4-inch hem in place. Turn the cover right side out. Place the cover on the toothpick. Pull the thread so that the cover is secured to the end of the toothpick. Fold and twist the cover around the toothpick. Wind several turns of thread around the top of the umbrella cover (C). Wind the *loose* thread several times around the bottom of the umbrella cover, and finish it off.

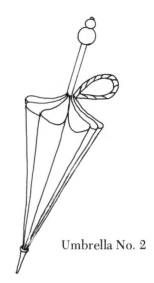

Umbrella No. 2

Umbrella No. 2

(Drawing actual size, but diagrams *not* drawn to scale)
Draw a circle on paper (with a compass) 3 inches in diameter (A). Draw a circle on cotton fabric 3-3/4 inches in diameter (B). Draw a third circle the same size as A on aluminum foil. Cut out the three circles. Fold each circle into eights along the dotted lines (so you have three triangle shapes). Cut a curved line, from point to point, at the top of each triangle. Unfold the three triangles, and the circles are now octagons. Glue the foil octagon to the fabric octagon as shown in diagram C. The paper octagon is used as a template. Place the paper octagon over the foil octagon. Turn the hem of the fabric over the paper and baste it down as shown in diagram D. Whip stitch the edge of the fabric, making tiny stitches, as shown in diagram E. Remove the basting and the paper template. Cut one of the pointed ends off a round toothpick. Paint the toothpick. Push the pointed end of the toothpick through the center of the foil and fabric umbrella cover. Arrange the folds, and then glue the eight points of the octagon to the toothpick, as shown in the drawing of the umbrella. Drill a pin hole in the top of the toothpick, and pin two beads in place for the umbrella handle. Make a length of cording from two strands of embroidery floss (for cording instructions see page 42). Make a loop from the cording, and glue it to the umbrella for an arm strap.

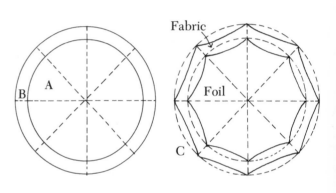

Valentine Cards

(Drawings actual size)
Make small cards from paper. Either draw and color designs on the cards, or cut motifs from magazines and glue them to the cards. Decorate the cards with pieces of narrow lace and fancy gold embossed paper.

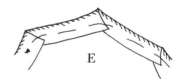

Valentine Cards

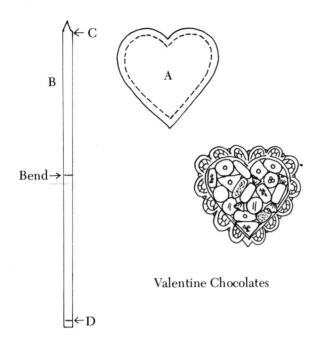

Valentine Chocolates

Vase

Waste Paper Basket

Wine Glass

Valentine's Day Box of Chocolates

(Drawing and patterns actual size.)

For the base of the box, cut the heart-shaped pattern (A) from card. For the rim of the box, cut a strip of card as shown in diagram B. Cut a point at one end of the strip (C), and cut a slit at the other end (D). Bend the card strip in half, and put the pointed end through the slit. Glue the rim to the box along the dotted lines (the bend in the rim at the point of the heart). Line the chocolate box with a piece of paper doily or some embossed gold paper. To make the chocolates, use the special dough (see recipe on page 144). Roll small pieces of dough into the shapes shown in the drawing. Wrap some of the "chocolates" in aluminum foil and colored metallic-type paper. Paint the rest of the "chocolates" with dark brown acrylic paint. Roll some of them in sawdust (while the paint is still wet), so that the "chocolates" look as if they are covered with chopped nuts. Press sprinkles into the top of some of the chocolates. Paint tiny chips of wood green to look like bits of angelica and press them into the top of some of the "chocolates." Fit the decorated chocolates in the box.

Vase

Make the vase from a tiny Christmas tree ball (remove the hanging wire), and two small colored buttons. First paint the ball with gesso to cover the shininess. Then give the ball one or two coats of paint. Glue one button to the base of the ball, and the other to the top. Use small cloth flowers for the floral arrangement. Put small dabs of glue on the stems of the flowers, and push them in place through the holes in the button. You can also use large wooden beads and clear plastic tubing for vases.

Waste Paper Basket

Make the basket from a small picnic (or airline) salt or pepper container. Turn the container upside down and remove the card base. For the rim, glue a length of elastic band around the top of the "basket." Give the "basket" a coat of gesso, and then paint it inside and outside with acrylic paint. Paint a design on the front of the basket. The small plastic cream containers you sometimes get in restaurants can also be used for waste paper baskets.

Wine Glass

Some vitamin pills and cold medicines come in gelatin capsules that can be taken apart to use for wine glasses. For the bowl of the glass, use the smaller half of the capsule; for the stem a clear bugle bead; and for the base a circle of clear stiff plastic. Glue the parts of the glass together, using quick-drying epoxy glue. When the glue is dry, pour a few drops of gold paint on a piece of paper, and dip the rim of the glass in the paint. (This method is easier than trying to paint a thin gold line around the rim.) The first time I made these glasses, I thought, why not wine too? — and filled them with some red-tinted water, forgetting they were made from gelatin. I ended up with small pools of red water and distorted little wine glasses.

Xylophone

(Patterns actual size)

For the base, cut from 1/16-inch-thick balsa wood a trapezoid 1-7/8 inches long by 1/2 inch wide (at the top) and 3/8 inch wide (at the bottom). Cut two side supports 1-7/8 inches long by 1/8 inch wide from 1/8-inch-thick balsa wood. Glue the side supports to the top of the base. Paint the supports and the base white. Cut two cross bars—A, 1/4 inch long and B, 1/8 inch long—from a length of round toothpick. Paint the cross bars red, and glue them between the side supports. For the bars, cut eight 1/8-inch-wide strips (graduating them in length as shown in the drawing) from 1/32-inch-thick wood. Paint the bars different colors. For the nails, cut down sixteen straight pins, so that each meaures 1/8 inch long. Fix the bars to the side supports with "nails" as shown in the drawing. For the wheels cut four 3/32-inch lengths from 1/8-inch dowel. Paint the wheels red. Drill a hole through the center of each wheel and attach them to the xylophone with cut-down straight pins. Make the hammer from a length of round toothpick and a bead. Drill a small hole through the base of the xylophone, and drill a small hole toward the bottom of the hammer handle. Join the hammer to the xylophone with a piece of thread as shown in the drawing.

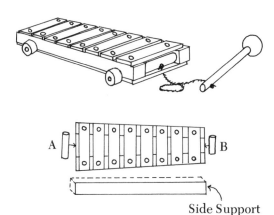

Xylophone

Yardstick

Cut a length 3 inches long by 1/8 inch wide from 1/16-inch-thick wood. With a fine-nibbed pen, mark off the inches and feet along the length of the yardstick in black ink.

Yardstick

Yarn

Make small balls from pieces of paper handkerchiefs. Take lengths of crewel embroidery yarn, or darning yarn, and wind a different color around each paper ball. Keep the ends of yarn from unraveling with a dab of glue.

Zebra Rug

Enlarge the pattern to make the rug about 6 inches long. Cut the shape of the zebra rug from white felt. Paint the stripes on the felt with black acrylic paint.

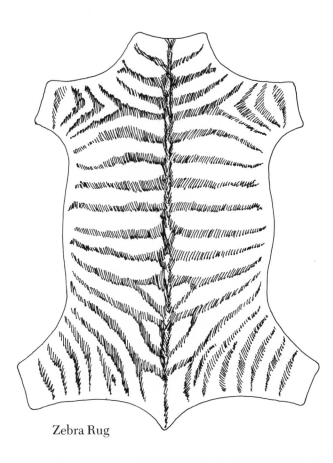

Zebra Rug

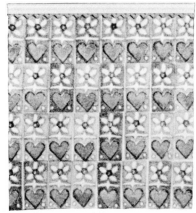

Floors, Walls, and Soft Furnishings

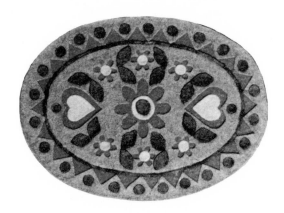

How to print wallpapers . . . lay floors . . . make doors . . .
windows . . . rugs (woven, braided, appliqué) . . .
sew and hang curtains. How to make a patchwork quilt.
With patterns and complete instructions.

I was pleasantly surprised to find that simple crafts learned in childhood, such as spool knitting and potato-block printing, could be applied in dolls' house decoration. My third grade teacher, Mrs. Williams, might be disappointed that I remember no simple algebra, but her instruction on how to cut a potato block has stayed with me. I remember we used to print with our potato blocks on yesterday's newspapers, as paper was in short supply. And during a summer in the country when I was about nine, Mrs. Brown, the farmer's wife, taught me to bake apple pies and spool-knit. Mrs. Brown gave me a small wooden painted doll, with a hole through the center and four nails in the top. That summer I made more pot holders than we had pots.

In this chapter I have used some of the crafts I learned as a child. I describe floor coverings, wallpapers, and soft furnishings I have made for my rooms, but first I have included a list of some ideas friends of mine have used in their dolls' houses.

Walls

- The small prints on the insides of some envelopes for wallpaper
- Gift-wrap paper for wallpaper
- Printed fabric instead of wallpaper
- Plastic contact paper (which I don't like) for wallpaper
- Paint mixed with sand for a textured wall
- Ice-cream sticks for the wainscoting around the walls
- Felt fabric instead of wallpaper

Floors

- Kitchen matchsticks cut to size and arranged in patterns to make parquet floors
- Linoleum
- Oilcloth (which is hard to find these days)
- Ice-cream sticks for random floorboards

Rugs and Carpets

- Velvet for a carpet
- Needlepoint embroidery for rugs
- Ready-bought woven straw coasters and place mats for mats

- Knitted and crocheted rugs
- Straw-cloth for rugs and carpets

In all the rooms that I decorated, I applied the floor coverings first, then the wallpapers, and last, the moldings and baseboards.

A Simple Room

If you do not own a dolls' house, you may wish to make simple four-sided boxes similar to those I used for my rooms.

MATERIALS

From 3/8-inch-thick plywood, cut the following lengths:
11-3/8 inches by 22 inches for the back
14 inches by 22 inches for the base
11-3/8 inches by 14-3/8 inches for the sides
White glue
A dozen brads

1. Glue the back edge of the base to the back.
2. Glue the sides to the side edges of the back and base. Check that the box is square.
3. Use a few brads to reinforce the box.

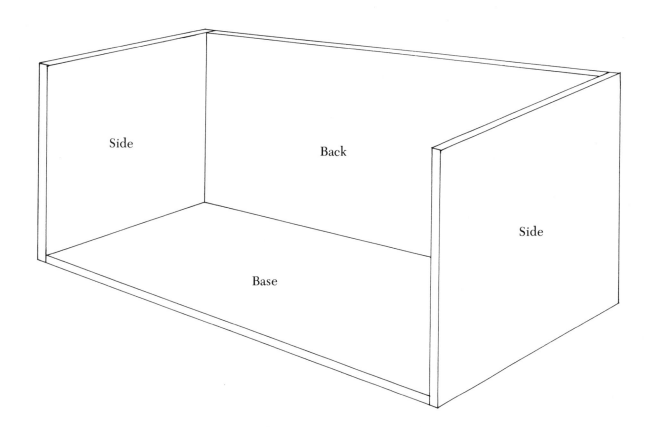

FLOORS

The easiest method for covering a dolls' house floor is to use felt, paint, or paper. With the growing interest in dolls' houses and miniatures, many attractive floor papers are now available, and the designs are scaled to dolls' house size. Some of the prettiest designs I've seen are colored reproductions of actual Victorian tiles. Papers with prints of floorboards, parquet, and flagstones are also available.

For the bathroom floor I used printed paper place mats, which were cut up and pieced together to cover the floor. I also used strips of the paper for the molding at the top of the bathroom walls.

The bedroom floor was laid with random flooring—precut lengths of wood 1/16 inch by 3-1/2 inches by 22 inches that have been scored lengthwise, giving the impression of floorboards. (See the Appendix, page 216, for mail-order dealers who supply random flooring.) I glued the lengths of wood to the floor surface with white glue and weighted the floor down with books until the glue was dry. I then finished the floor with stain, shellac, and Butcher's wax.

For the children's room floor I cut Pantone colored paper to the size of the floor, and then stenciled the border design. (The design for the border is an adaptation of the wallpaper design.)

In the living room I used one of the simplest methods for covering a dolls' house floor—wall-to-wall carpet made from a piece of felt cut to the size of the room and glued in place.

I used Venetian glass tiles, bought at a hobby store, for the kitchen floor. The tiles are usually used for mosaic table tops. I glued the tiles to the floor with a heavy coat of white glue. I then filled in the cracks between the tiles with grout. The grout, which I bought at the hardware store, comes in a powder that is mixed with water to form a paste. The directions for mixing and applying are printed on the packets.

RUGS

Spool-knitted Rug

I made the kitchen rug on a homemade knitting device consisting of four nails hammered into the top of an empty wooden thread spool.

MATERIALS

> An empty spool and four small round-headed nails
> Thick cotton embroidery floss, or two-ply knitting yarn,
> in three or four colors
> A darning needle

1. Hammer the nails into the top of the spool as shown in the drawing.

2. Thread the end of the first color of yarn through the spool, leaving a 2-inch tail protruding.

3. Cast on as shown in drawing A. The yarn is looped around each nail. As each loop is formed, pull the "tail" to make the loop firm. When there is a loop on each of the four nails, pull the yarn taut across the first nail, and above the loop. Using a darning needle, lift the loop over the taut yarn and the nail head. Tug the tail. (This makes the first stitch.) Pull the yarn taut across the second nail and make the second stitch. Continue knitting, going around the nails to make stitches as shown in drawing B. Remember to tug the tail after each stitch.

4. Join new colors of yarn, with a knot, to the yarn already on the spool. (The knot is pushed inside the tube of knitting, and therefore does not show.)

5. Continue knitting until the tube, when coiled into a circle, measures about 4 inches in diameter.

6. Cast off as follows: Cut the yarn about 4 inches from the last stitch. Carefully remove the knitting from the spool. Then thread the end of the yarn through each of the four loops on the top of the stitches. Pull the yarn firmly.

7. Starting at the center of the rug, begin coiling the tube of knitting to make a flat circle. Pin the edges of the knitting together as the circle is being formed. Edge-stitch the coils of the rug together. If the completed rug doesn't lie flat, press the rug lightly with a steam iron.

SPOOL KNITTING

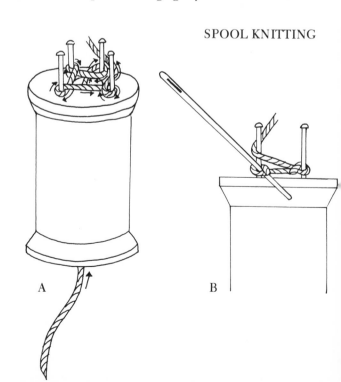

A   B

Woven Felt Rug

(See the photograph of rugs in color section following page 80.)

MATERIALS

    Four different-colored pieces of felt

    Dressmaker's chalk

1. Cut a rectangle of felt 6 inches wide by 7 inches long.

2. Using a ruler and dressmaker's chalk draw a border around the felt rectangle, 1/2 inch in from the ends and 1/4 inch in from the sides.

3. Divide the rectangle within the border, with horizontal lines drawn every 1/4 inch as shown in diagram A. (The diagram is drawn half size.)

4. Fold the felt in half as shown in diagram B. Cut slits along the lines, taking care not to cut the border. When the slits have been cut, unfold the piece of felt.

5. Cut the three remaining pieces of felt into 1/4-inch- and 1/2-inch-wide by 6-inch-long strips. (The arrangement of the colors and widths of the felt strips forms the pattern of the rug.)

6. Weave the strips of felt over and under the bars on the background piece of felt, as shown in diagram C. Keep the strips straight and even.

7. When the rug is completed, cut slashes in the 1/2-inch-wide border to make a fringe. Also, glue down the ends of each strip.

A

WOVEN FELT RUG

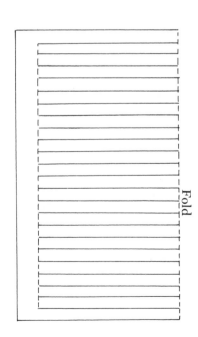

B

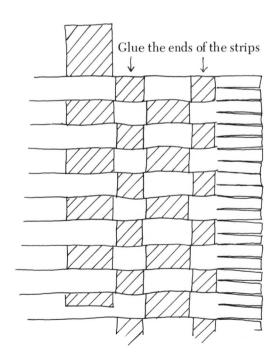

C

Braided Oval Bedroom Rug

MATERIALS
Old pairs of tights and pantyhose

1. Try to find old stockings, pantyhose, and tights in an assortment of light, medium, and dark colors. Cut the hose into long strips about 1/2 inch wide.

2. Divide the strips into light, medium, and dark colored sets of three strips.

3. Tape the ends of three strips to the edge of a table. Braid the strips. Turn in the raw edges as you braid. Continue to braid sets of hose strips until there are sufficient lengths to make an oval rug approximately 3-3/4 inches by 5 inches.

4. Draw an oval shape (the size of the rug) on a piece of paper.

5. Starting at the center of the oval, begin to pin and coil the first length of braid. Make two or three rounds, and then sew the rounds in place. Before starting a new color combination, finish off the previous length of braid by completing a full round. Cut off any extra braid. Continue to shape the rug by adding more rounds of braid until the rug is the size of the drawn oval. (Pin and then sew the braid as you make the rounds.)

6. Steam press the finished rug. As you press, block the rug into a perfect oval by pulling the edges slightly.

Woven Living Room Rug

This rug is woven on a simple, homemade matte-board loom.

MATERIALS
1/8-inch-thick matte-board
Thin string for the warp
Knitting yarn in five or six different colors

1. Cut a piece of matte-board 3-3/4 inches wide by 10 inches long.

2. Cut 12 slits in each end of the board as shown in diagram A. (Note that the diagram is drawn half size.) Start cutting the slits 1/2 inch in from the sides. Space the slits at 1/4-inch intervals.

3. Cut two strips of board 3/4 inch wide by 3-3/4 inches long. Glue a strip 1/2 inch in from each end of the "loom" as shown in the diagram.

4. For the warp support, cut a strip of board 1/2 inch by 3-3/4 inches long. Cut 12 slits in the warp support to correspond with the slits cut in the ends of the loom.

5. Cut a length of string about 10 feet long.

6. Set up the warp on the loom as follows: Make a knot in one end of the string. Pull the knotted end of the string through the first slit in the left end on the loom. (The knot will secure the end of the string to the underside of the loom.) Take the string across the length of the loom to the right end. Push the string through the first slit. Bring the string up through the second slit. Take the string across the loom back to the left end. Push the string through the second slit. Bring the string up through the third slit. (See diagram B.) Continue in this way until the warp is completed. Finish off the string with a knot on the underside of the loom.

7. Plan the order in which the various colors of the yarn will be woven to make the design for the rug.

8. Take the warp support and place it across the loom, fitting the warp strings into the slits in the support. (This raises the strings and makes weaving easier.) Move the support to about 2 inches from where you will start weaving.

9. Weave the yarn threaded on a darning needle to form the woof. Take the yarn over and under the warp strings. Finish off the loose ends of the yarn by weaving them neatly into the sides of the rug, with a needle. (As you weave, move the support along the loom.)

10. When the rug is completed, remove the rug from the loom by cutting the strings at the ends of the warp. Tie the first string to the second string, and the third string to the fourth string, et cetera, at each end of the rug. (The tied strings will form part of the fringes.)

11. To finish off the sides of the rug, blanket-stitch the edges with yarn.

12. Make a fringe for each end of the rug in the following way: Cut 2-1/2-inch lengths of the different colored yarns. Double each length of yarn to form a loop. At the end edge of the rug, in the first space in the weaving, insert a crochet hook, and draw a yarn loop through the space. Draw the ends of the yarn through the loop and pull up tightly to form a knot. Continue to knot a length of yarn in each space along the edge of the rug.

13. Steam-press the rug to shape.

LOOM FOR WOVEN RUG

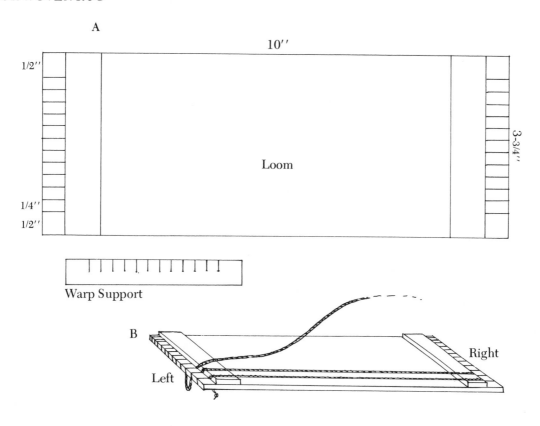

Appliqué Children's Room Rug

MATERIALS

    4 pieces of felt in different colors (red, rust, blue, and
       pink)
    Fabric glue
    Tracing paper
    A 5B pencil

See the photograph of rugs (in the color section following page 80) for the arrangement of the different colors in this rug.

1. Trace the pattern for the rug with the 5B pencil.

2. Place the tracing paper, drawn-side down, on the red background piece of felt. Tape the tracing in place. Retrace the outer oval shape on the back of the tracing paper, taking care not to puncture the paper with the pencil.

3. Remove the tracing paper and cut out the oval.

4. Place the tracing paper on the rust-colored felt. Retrace the outer oval shape again. Retrace the tri-angles, the inner oval shape, the outer lines on the hearts, and the flowers.

5. Remove the tracing paper. Cut the outer oval shape. Fold the felt in half and cut the inner oval shape. (You now have two pieces of rust-colored felt—the border, and the inner oval.) Cut the triangles from the border. Cut the flowers and the hearts from the oval.

6. Glue the rust-felt border and oval to the red background felt. (Note that there is a 1/8-inch space between the border and the inner oval.)

7. Place the tracing paper on the pink felt, and retrace the inner heart shapes and the round flower centers.

8. Remove the tracing paper and cut out the hearts and flower centers.

9. Glue the hearts and flower centers in place on the red felt.

10. Place the tracing paper on the blue felt. Retrace the leaves, the dots, and the large flower center.

11. Remove the tracing paper, and cut out the leaves, dots, and flower center. Also cut several 1/8-inch-wide

strips of felt to glue between the border and the inner oval.

12. Glue the 1/8-inch strips onto the red felt, between the border and the inner oval. Glue the blue flower center onto the pink flower center. Glue the blue dots and leaves to the rust felt.

13. Cover the completed rug with a damp cloth, and press the rug with an iron. Put pressure on the iron. (The heat and moisture will flatten and bond the various thicknesses of felt together.)

APPLIQUÉ FELT RUG

Fur Bedroom Rug

I pinked the edges of a rectangle of felt, and then mounted a piece of rabbit fur on the felt.

WALLPAPERS

For the wallpaper in all the rooms except the bedroom, I used Pantone colored paper, which can be bought at art-supply stores, and comes in hundreds of different colors, shades, and tones. The paper has a suitable surface for acrylic paints, which I used with a stencil-cut for the children's room and for concentrated water colors, which I used to print the design on the kitchen walls. When you print with translucent colors such as watercolors, the paper must be lighter in tone than the paints. I used a commercial wallpaper for the bedroom. A large variety of pretty wallpapers is now being produced specially scaled for dolls' houses. (See the Appendix, page 216, for the names of mail-order suppliers of dolls' house wallpapers.)

Applying Wallpaper

Measure the height and width of each wall in the room. Cut the paper for the back wall, 1 inch wider at each end than the width, but the same height as the wall. Cut the paper for the side walls the same width and height as the walls. Take the paper for the back wall. Fold back an inch of paper at each end, and make a crease line. For the glue, use book-binder's glue or wallpaper glue. (White glue is not suitable to use for wallpapering, as it makes the paper wrinkle.) I find applying the glue to the walls easier than applying the glue to the paper. Apply an even coat of glue to the back wall of the room. Glue the paper in place, pressing the crease lines at the ends of the paper into the corners. Smooth the paper down with your hands, getting rid of any air bubbles or wrinkles. Glue the extra inch of paper at each end of the back wall to the side walls. (This will ensure that there are no gaps, where the side and back wallpapers meet.) Glue each side piece of wallpaper in place.

Kitchen Wallpaper

MATERIALS

A large, firm baking potato (Do not use new potatoes, as they are too watery.)

Colored paper in a light shade

Concentrated (liquid) watercolors

Two 3-inch-square pads of foam rubber

1. Cut the potato in half with a kitchen knife. Leave the potato halves, cut sides down, on paper towel to drain off some of the moisture.

2. Using a soft-leaded pencil, draw the oblong block and the design onto one half of the potato.

3. With an X-acto knife, cut the block, raising it about 1/2 inch from the surrounding surface of the potato.

4. Cut the design, using various gouge blades in an X-acto knife. Make the cuts about 1/8 inch deep. (Note that the background of the block will print positive, and the area that is cut away will be negative.) Cut registering notches (to help align the motif when you print) on the edge of the potato as shown in the drawing A.

5. Cut two blocks (B) and (C) for the second color, from the other half of the potato. (Note that these blocks will print positive.)

6. Mark the height and width of each wall on the colored paper. Allow a 2-inch margin at the sides, top, and bottom, and then cut the paper for each wall.

7. Divide each piece of paper into rectangles 5/8 inch wide by 1-1/4 inches long (the size of the block). Draw the dividing lines *lightly*.

8. Put newspaper on a flat surface, and then lay a piece of the colored paper on top of the newspaper ready for printing.

9. Mix the paint for the first color. (Most of the concentrated watercolors have to be diluted with water, as the undiluted colors are too intense and brilliant.)

10. Put a pad of foam rubber on a plate. Soak the pad with some of the paint. (Keep the extra paint covered so that it won't evaporate.)

11. Press block A onto the paint-soaked pad. Test the block on a spare piece of paper, to check that it prints well. (You will learn to judge exactly how much paint to get on the surface of the block, so that the paint prints clearly yet does not flood.)

12. Start printing, aligning the notches on the potato with the lines drawn on the paper. (Note that you will

never get perfectly even printing with a potato block.) Continue printing until the paper is covered with the design.

13. For the dot and heart blocks, soak the other foam rubber pad with the second color of paint.

14. Use block B to print a dot in the center of each flower and block C to print the second color in each heart. (See the photograph of wallpapers, in color section following page 80.)

Potato-cut Blocks

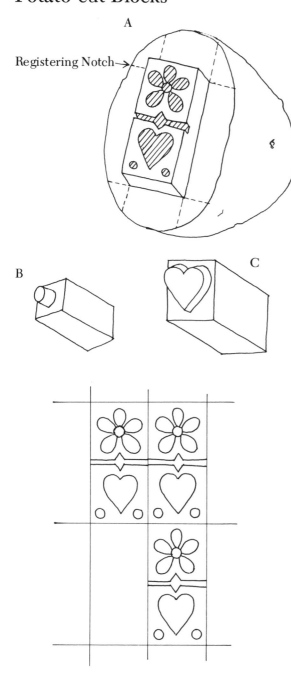

A

Registering Notch→

B

C

Stenciling Children's Room Wallpaper

MATERIALS
    Stencil paper
    Colored paper
    Acrylic paints
    A sponge
    Tracing paper

Two kinds of stencil paper are available at art-and hobby-supply stores—an off-white paper that looks like heavy wax paper and a thicker, brown stencil paper. If possible, use the off-white paper; it is easier to cut.

1. Trace and transfer the motifs for design A onto the stencil paper. Enclose the motifs in a square 3 inches by 3 inches as shown in the drawing. Cut out the square.

2. Using a sharp blade (no. 11) in an X-acto knife, cut around the lines of the motifs in the following way: Use a ruler for the straight lines. For the curved lines, place the point of the blade on the line and, keeping the blade stationary, move and turn the paper, pulling it under the blade to make the cuts. Take care not to cut the joining bars. (If you cut the stencil, as shown in the drawing, the set of motifs when they are printed will be repeated every two inches, both across and up and down the paper.)

3. Mark the height and width of each wall on the colored paper. Allow a 2-inch margin at the sides, top, and bottom, and then cut the paper for each wall.

4. Divide each piece of paper into 2-inch squares. (Make *light* pencil lines.)

5. Draw eight registering marks on the stencil, as shown in the drawing.

6. Mix the paint for printing. Put a small amount of paint on a plate. (Keep the rest of the paint in a covered container so that it will stay moist, and add more paint to the plate as needed. The consistency of the paint should be quite thick. If the paint is too watery, it will spread under the stencil.)

STENCILED WALLPAPERS

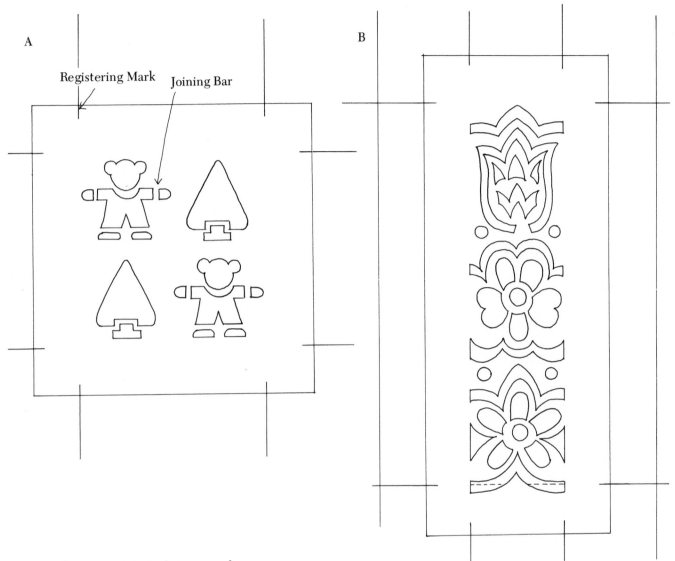

A

Registering Mark   Joining Bar

B

7. Cut the sponge into inch-square cubes.

8. Cover a flat surface with newspaper, and place a sheet of the colored paper on the newspaper, ready for printing.

9. Place the stencil on the paper, aligning the registering marks with the lines drawn on the paper. Hold the stencil firmly in place. Dip a cube of sponge in the paint on the plate, dab off any excess paint. With the sponge, stipple the paint through the design in the stencil, onto the paper. Use a light patting motion with the sponge. Miss a square, so as not to smudge the wet paint, and print another set of motifs. Continue printing until the design covers the entire area of the paper. Note that it is

useful to cut two stencils if you are printing a large area. When a stencil begins to get clogged with paint, wash the paint off gently. Allow the stencil to dry between two sheets of paper towel and under the pressure of a book. While the first stencil is drying, use the second stencil for printing.

Drawing B shows the stencil I used for the design in the lower right-hand corner, in the photograph of wallpapers in color section following page 80.

Moldings

1. Woven Braid

2. Embossed Paper

3. Wooden Trim

4. Rickrack

MOLDINGS

Here are some of the trimmings that I used for wall moldings. I took two of the motifs from the braid design, the teddy bear, and the tree, and adapted the motifs for the stenciled wallpaper. I combined all the trimmings with either strips of balsa wood or precut moldings.

CURTAINS

I have noticed that even in some beautiful old dolls' houses exhibited in museums, a room has been spoiled by badly hung curtains. Dolls' house curtains lack weight and therefore do not fall into folds naturally, but have to be forced into shape. Whatever fabric is used, the curtains should be arranged and draped before they are put onto a window. I would not recommend using synthetic crease-resistant fabrics for dolls' house curtains; these fabrics *resist* falling into folds. For heavy silk, taffeta, or velvet curtains, you may find the following method for draping useful: Make the curtains to the correct size. Press the curtains. Cut lengths of aluminum foil, 1/2 inch smaller than the curtains. Lightly spray the foil with an adhesive such as Scotch Spra-ment, and then stick the wrong side of the fabric to the foil. Let the adhesive dry. As the foil backing can be molded easily, the curtains can be draped, and the folds will stay in place. Needless to say, this method is only suitable for curtains that do not show through the outside of a window. To make sure the glue doesn't leave a stain on the front of the fabric, test a scrap of material with the adhesive, before using the glue on the actual curtains.

Living Room Curtains

MATERIALS

 1/4 yard cotton fabric

 Approximatey 1/2 yard of narrow cord

 A piece of cardboard to use for a mount

 Thin card for backing the valance

 Fabric glue

 Tracing paper

 Two straight pins and two small decorative buttons for the tiebacks

 1. Cut the curtains double the width of the window and about 7 inches long.

 2. Turn the raw edges along the sides of the curtains, and glue them down with fabric glue.

 3. Turn the bottom hem once, and glue it down.

 4. Sew a row of running stitches 1/4 inch from the edge, along the top of the curtains. Also sew a row of running stitches, two-thirds down the curtain, from points A to B. Gather the curtains at the tops and points A and B, but leave the threads loose.

 5. Cut a piece of cardboard the width of the window and a little longer than the curtains.

 6. Draw lines on the cardboard to indicate the bottom and center of the window.

 7. Pin and drape the curtains on the cardboard. Finish off the loose gathering threads.

 8. Set the curtain folds with steam from an iron. Leave the curtains pinned to the cardboard until they are thoroughly dry.

 9. Carefully remove the curtains from the cardboard.

 10. Glue the top edges of the curtains to the top of the window frame.

 11. Make two cord loops. Slip the end of each curtain through a cord loop. Push the loops up to point A.

 12. Secure a loop in place with a pin slipped through the shank of a small decorative button.

VALANCE

 1. Trace and transfer the patterns for the valance to the card and the fabric, and cut them out.

 2. Bend the card part of the valance along the dotted lines, and then smooth the card flat again.

 3. Place the card on top of the fabric as shown in the drawing. Turn the edges of the fabric, and glue them to the card.

 4. Bend the top of the valance down and the ends back. Glue flaps C inside the tops of the ends.

 5. Place the valance in position over the top of the curtains. Glue the back flaps of the valance to the back of the window.

 6. Glue cord trimming to the top and bottom edges of the valance.

 7. Glue the curtained window to the wall.

LIVING ROOM CURTAINS

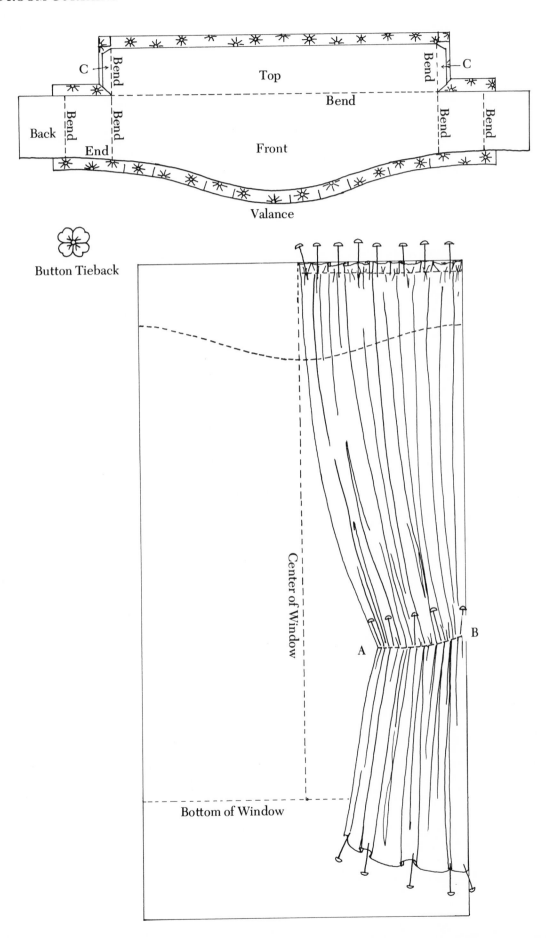

Kitchen Curtains

MATERIALS

1/4 yard of cotton fabric

1/2 yard rickrack trimming

18 S-shaped jump-rings (for description see page 24) for the curtain rings

A piece of wire for the top curtain rail

1/8-inch-thick brass tubing or dowel for the lower curtain rod

A piece of cardboard to use as a mount

2 brass or wooden beads for the rod knobs

Thin wire for the rod-holders

Fabric glue

Gold paint if dowel and wooden beads are used for the rod

1. For the top curtain frill, cut a length of fabric 3/4 inch long (plus hem allowances) and twice the width of the window. For the lower curtain cut a length of fabric 1-1/2 inches long (plus hem allowances) and twice the width of the window.

2. Turn the top and side edges of the curtains. Glue all the turns except the one on the top of the frill; sew this one. Turn the hems and glue them down.

3. Trim the bottom edges of the curtains with rickrack.

4. Cut a piece of cardboard the width of the window, and a little longer than the curtains.

5. Draw lines on the cardboard to indicate the bottom and center of the window.

6. Thread the frill onto the curtain rail, which has been bent into the shape shown in the drawing.

7. Make two holes at the top of the cardboard for the ends of the rail. Fix the rail into the cardboard. Arrange the gathers of the frill evenly, and pin the frill in place to the cardboard.

8. Take the lower section of the curtain. Using a darning needle, make eighteen evenly spaced holes along the top edge of the curtain for the rings. Attach the rings to the curtain.

9. Pin the lower section of the curtain to the cardboard in folds.

10. Set the gathers and folds with steam from an iron. Leave the curtains pinned to the cardboard until they are thoroughly dry.

11. Carefully remove the curtains from the cardboard.

12. Drill two holes at the top of the window frame for the rail. Glue the rail with the frill in place.

13. Drill two small holes in the center of each side section of the window frame, for the wire rod-holders.

14. Thread the rings on the curtain onto the length of brass tubing or dowel rod. Fix the bead knobs to the ends of the rod.

15. For the rod-holders, cut two lengths of thin wire. Loop a length of wire around each end of the curtain rod.

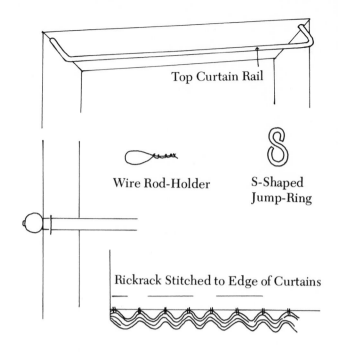

Top Curtain Rail

Wire Rod-Holder

S-Shaped Jump-Ring

Rickrack Stitched to Edge of Curtains

DETAILS FOR KITCHEN CURTAINS

Twist the ends of the wire together to secure them to the rod. Glue the twisted ends of the wire into the holes in the window frame.

16. Glue the curtained window to the wall.

Shower Curtain

I laminated plastic wrap to a piece of cotton fabric for the shower curtain. On the fourth attempt I got the laminating right. I think using material from an old shower curtain liner or a piece of plastic from a shopping bag would have been just as effective, and far less frustrating. Nevertheless, here is my method for laminating fabric.

1. Cut a piece of fabric the width and length of the curtain, plus hem allowances. Cut a piece of plastic wrap the same size as the curtain.

2. Lightly spray one side of the plastic wrap with an adhesive such as Scotch Spra-Ment.

3. Glue the plastic wrap to the fabric.

4. This is the tricky part—place the fabric, plastic side down, on a flat surface. Cover the fabric with a cloth, and press it with a warm iron. If the iron is too hot, the plastic will shrivel up. And if the iron is too cool, the plastic will not laminate with the fabric.

5. Turn the edges and hem of the curtain, and using fabric glue, stick them in place.

6. With a darning needle, make holes along the top edges of the curtain for the rings.

7. Attach S-shaped jump-rings to the top of the curtain.

8. Thread the rings through a wire curtain rail. Attach the rail to the walls.

DOOR

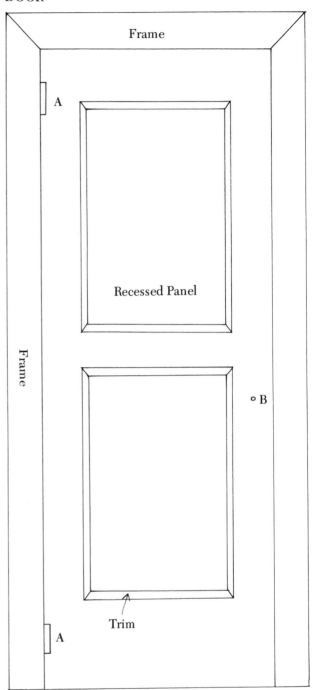

DOOR AND WINDOWS

The doors and windows I made for the rooms are "fake" and they were glued onto the walls after wallpapering.

Door

MATERIALS

    1/16-inch-thick balsa wood for all the parts of the door
    The screw from an earring for the doorknob
    Narrow brass tubing or a round toothpick for the hinges
    Two straight pins
    White glue
    Acrylic paints
    Gesso
    Gloss polymer medium
    Tracing paper

For the door frames, rather than strips of balsa wood you can use precut baseboard, rail, or mullion moldings, which are obtainable in 1/16-inch thicknesses. (See the Appendix, page 216, for mail-order dealers who supply dolls' house moldings.) The door is built up on top of a length of balsa wood backing that is the width and length of the entire door frame.

1. Trace and transfer the patterns to wood.

2. Cut the length of balsa wood the width and length of the door frame for the backing. Cut the sides and top of the frame, mitering the top corners. Cut the door. Cut the panels from the door; and the two recesses (A) for the hinges. Cut the strips for the panel trim, mitering each corner.

3. Glue the frame to the backing.

4. Glue the door in place. (The backing, showing through the rectangular holes cut from the door, forms the recessed panels.)

5. Glue the trim on the door.

6. Cut two 1/4-inch lengths from narrow brass tubing or a round toothpick, for the hinges. (If you use a toothpick, drill a hole through the lengths of toothpick, using a thin bit in a pin vise to make the holes, and paint the hinges gold.)

7. Cut two straight pins, a fraction longer than the hinges. Glue a pin in each hinge.

8. Give the door a coat of gesso. Paint the door, and finish it with gloss polymer medium.

9. Drill a hole (B) for the doorknob.

10. Glue the doorknob and hinges in place.

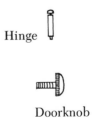

Hinge

Doorknob

Windows

MATERIALS

    1/16-inch-thick wood for all the parts of the windows except the sills

    3/32-inch-thick by1/8-inch-wide balsa wood for the sills

    Card for backing the windows

    Gesso

    Acrylic paints

    Gloss polymer medium

    White glue

    Tracing paper

Both the windows are made in the same way; here is just one set of directions:

1. Trace and transfer the patterns to the wood. Cut the four sides of each frame, mitering the top corners. Cut upper and lower rails, two sashes for each window, a window jamb, and for the long window, two mullions. Cut a sill for each window.

2. From card, cut the backing the same length and width as the entire window, including the frame.

3. Paint the backing light blue. Let the backing dry.

4. Glue the frame onto the backing.

5. Glue the other parts of the window in place, as shown in the drawing. (The sills protrude 1/8 inch, and they are glued onto the frames, not onto the backing.)

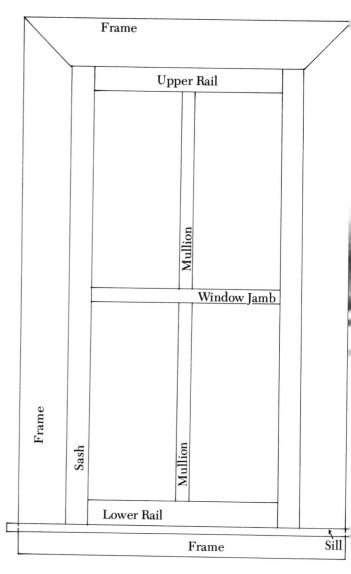

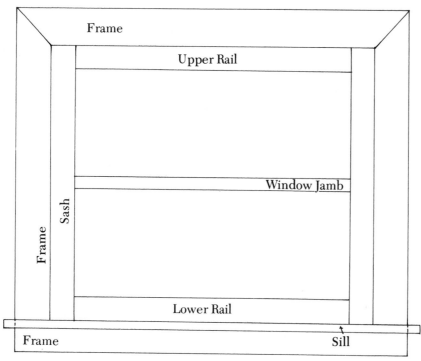

BEDDING AND LINEN

Mattresses

I prefer foam rubber to cotton as filling for mattresses and pillows, and lightweight cotton fabric for the covers.

1. Cut a rectangle the same width and length as the bed, from 3/4-inch-thick foam rubber.

2. The cover is made from two lengths of fabric (one to cover the bottom and the other to cover the top of the mattress) joined together by a strip of fabric that goes around the four sides. Cut two lengths of fabric, 1/2 inch wider and 1/2 inch longer than the foam rubber.

3. Cut a 1-1/4-inch-wide strip on the bias of the fabric, the correct length to go around all the sides of the mattress, plus 1/4 inch at each end of the strip for the seam allowance.

4. Take the top cover for the mattress. Working on the wrong side of the fabric, pin one edge of the strip around the entire edge of the top cover. Sew the strip to the top, keeping the edges aligned and leaving a 1/4-inch seam allowance.

5. Sew the ends of the strip together to make the side seam.

6. Take the bottom cover for the mattress. Pin the free edge of the strip around the entire edge of the bottom cover. Sew the strip to the bottom, but leave one side unstitched.

7. Turn the mattress cover right side out.

8. Stuff the foam rubber filling into the opening in the side.

9. Tucking the seam allowances in, slip stitch the opening in the side of the mattress.

10. Glue a thin length of cord, for piping, around the top edge of the mattress. And glue another length of cord around the bottom edge of the mattress.

11. If you wish to give a "tufted" effect to the mattress, cut down straight pins, so that each pin measures about 1/2 inch; paint the heads of the pins either white or a color to match the mattress cover; press and glue the pins into the top of the mattress in a diamond pattern. (I have found that regular tufting, using thread, distorts the shape of the mattress.)

Pillows

1. Cut a rectangle, 1-1/4 inches wide by 2-1/4 inches long, from 3/8-inch-thick foam rubber.

2. Cut two lengths of fabric 1/2 inch wider and 1/2 inch longer than the foam rubber, for the pillow cover.

3. Working on the wrong side of the fabric, pin and then sew three sides of the pillow cover together. Leave a 1/4-inch seam allowance.

4. Turn the cover right side out. Stuff the foam rubber filling into the opening in the pillow cover.

5. Tucking the seam allowance in, slip stitch the opening in the side of the pillow cover.

6. Glue a thin length of cord, for piping, around the edge of the pillow. See the drawing.

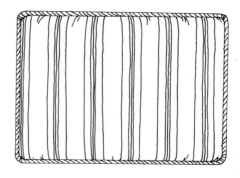

PILLOW

Sheets, Pillow Cases, and Blankets

Use fine cotton or linen handkerchiefs for sheets and pillow cases. A handkerchief can be left intact and put on the bed for a sheet. The pillow case can be made in the same way as for a normal-sized one.

For the sheets and pillow case on the brass bed I used unbleached muslin trimmed with ecru-colored lace. For the sheets and pillow cases in the children's room I used pale blue and floral seersucker, cut from a baby's old coverlet. If there is a spread over the bed, you don't need blankets, as they would make the bed look too bulky. But if the bed is uncovered, make a blanket from flannel cut from an old nightgown. (Blanket fabric, such as wool, is too thick to use on dolls' house beds.) Turn the selvage edges of the flannel blanket, and sew the hems using blanket stitch.

Bedspreads

Crocheted and knitted bedspreads, made from fine yarn, look attractive on dolls' house beds. (A friend of mine crocheted an afghan spread of granny square motifs, using different-colored darning wools.) The pattern I have drawn for a spread (note that the drawing is half size) is for a 4-inch by 6-inch bed. For the spread on the brass bed, I used 2-inch-wide strips of heavy lace, sewn together edge to edge to form the shape of the spread. I did not turn the raw edges of the lace (at the top and bottom corners of the spread), but ran a small amount of fabric glue along the edges using a toothpick to apply the glue. (Use just enough glue to stop the lace from fraying.) If you use a length of fabric for the spread rather than lace, cut along the *dotted* lines of the pattern, which will give you the hem allowances.

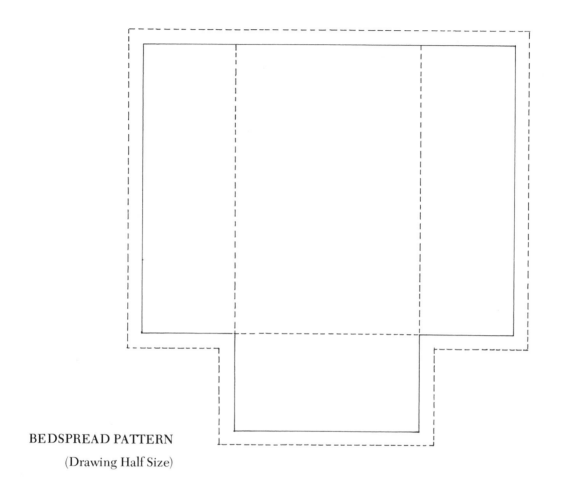

BEDSPREAD PATTERN

(Drawing Half Size)

Patchwork Quilts

Any simple traditional patchwork design can be adapted and reduced to make a miniature patchwork quilt. I make dolls' house quilts the same length and width as the bed. If a quilt is larger than the bed, it sticks out and does not hang properly over the sides. Use lightweight fabric with small prints for patchwork. Make a simple patchwork quilt by blocking out the design with tailor's chalk on a plain piece of fabric, and then drawing in the patterns using fine-tipped felt markers. For an easy-to-sew patchwork quilt use a checkerboard design. Choose a light and dark patterned fabric. Cut inch-square blocks from the fabric (this allows 1/8 inch for the selvage, so the finished blocks will measure 3/4 inch square). Pin and then sew together a strip of alternating dark and light blocks. Make the strip the same length as the bed. Sew enough strips of blocks to cover the width of the bed. Then pin and sew the strips together. Line the quilt following the directions in the next section.

RAIL-FENCE PATCHWORK QUILT

1. Choose four pieces of lightweight patterned fabric, graded in shades from dark to light.

2. Cut a rectangle from each piece of fabric 3 inches wide by 5 inches long.

3. With the wrong side of the fabric up, using a pencil and a ruler mark the cutting lines and the sewing lines as shown in diagram 1 (the drawing is half-size) on each piece of fabric. Note that there is an 1/8-inch seam allowance around each small rectangle.

4. Cutting carefully along the solid lines, cut 24 small

rectangles from each of the 4 pieces of fabric.

5. Arrange the rectangles in four-line units, as shown in diagram 2. (Always keep the patterns in the same order with the darkest pattern at the top and the lightest pattern at the bottom.)

6. Place strip A over strip B, right sides together. Align the strips and hold them in place with a pin. Backstitch the strips together, allowing 1/8-inch selvage. Take strip C and place it over strip B, right sides together. Pin and then back stitch the strips together. Complete a block by stitching strip D to strip C. Make 24 blocks.

7. Spread the blocks flat, wrong side up, and press the seam allowances toward the first strip on each block.

8. Sew the blocks into six block-strips, arranging the blocks as shown in the drawing. (You will have four strips.)

9. Sew the four strips together to complete the patchwork.

10. Place the patchwork, wrong side up, and press the side seam allowances flat.

11. To line the quilt, cut a length of fabric 5-1/8 inches wide by 7-1/8 inches long. Place the lining wrong side up on a flat surface. Center the patchwork right side up on top of the lining. Pin the patchwork to the lining. Turn the top and bottom edges of the lining first. Turn under the raw edges of the lining 1/8 inch, and then make a second turn of 3/16 inch for the border. Attach the edges of the border of the lining to the front of the patchwork (1/16 inch in from the outer edge of the patchwork) with small slip stitches. Attach the sides of the lining to the patchwork in the same way, but tuck each corner in at an angle to form a miter.

QUILT

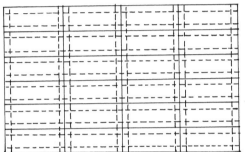

DIAGRAM 1 (Drawing Half Size)

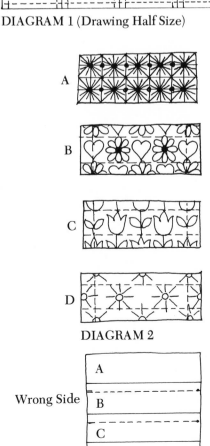

A

B

C

D

DIAGRAM 2

Wrong Side

A

B

C

D

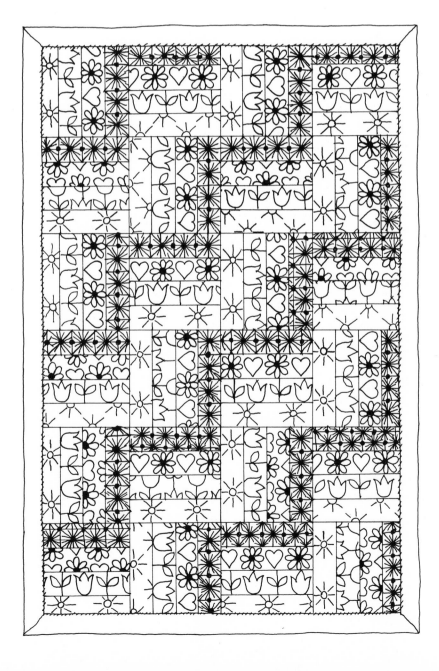

Tablecloths and Napkins

Use lightweight fabrics or lace-trimmed handkerchiefs for tablecloths and napkins. For the kitchen cloth and napkins I used gingham in the smallest available checks. Rather than sewing hems, I pulled threads from the edges of the cloth and the napkins, making fringed borders. To make the tablecloth hang over the edges of the table (rather than sticking out at right angles), I backed the fabric with a rectangle of card, glued down with fabric glue and cut 1/2-inch smaller all around than the cloth. See diagram.

Towels

Use lightweight terrycloth for towels. As terrycloth does not "fray" well, use embroidery floss for the fringes on the ends of the towels. Also glue two or three strands of embroidery floss to the towels, about 1/4 inch in from each end, making borders as shown in the drawing. Using a single thread of embroidery floss, stem stitch a monogram, or GUEST, or HIS, or HERS on some of the towels.

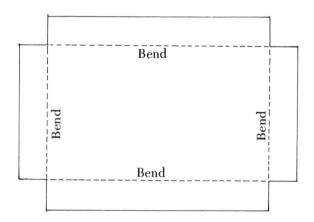

TABLECLOTH BACKING

Paper and Matchbox Furniture

Patterns and complete instructions for making a
paper dining table, a paper and matchbox chest of drawers,
a drinking-straw bed, a paper and matchbox
bedside table, a matchbox sofa and armchair,
a paper "glass"-top coffee table, a paper crib,
a drinking-straw-and-paper chair and table, a paper
stove, a paper-and-matchbox kitchen sink and
cupboard, a paper bathtub, a paper wash basin and toilet.

There is a long tradition of simple, homemade, not necessarily wooden dolls' house furniture. Victorian ladies and their children made small furniture using feathers, "conkers" (horse chestnuts), straw, and paper. Braids, ribbons, embossed paper, beads, and buttons were used as trimmings. I have a reprint of a Victorian book on making paper furniture called *How to Make Dolls' Furniture and Furnish a Dolls' House*, written especially for children. In it there are charming and carefully drawn patterns for furniture; the instructions are cautionary and slightly condescending:

> But one thing, my dear children, I wish you to remember, or else your kind and indulgent parents might regret having placed this book in your hands; that is, in cutting out your furniture, have near you a small basket or box, or if either of these are not at hand, take a large plate, in which to put your pieces of waste-paper. I do not think it is necessary for little children, while amusing themselves, to have things in confusion about them, or to litter the floor with bits of paper. It is just as easy, and much more agreeable to those around you, to be neat and orderly in your amusements.

The book is full of good ideas. The paper dining table I designed is an adaptation of one of the tables in this book.

What I particularly like about paper and matchbox furniture is that it is quick, easy, and inexpensive to make. You can furnish a room in an afternoon. Probably you have all the tools and most of the materials already. Basically, you will need a ruler, scissors, an X-acto knife, white glue, tracing paper, paints, paintbrushes, pencils, thick paper or card—and lots of matchboxes.

The tabs or flaps I have drawn on the paper patterns are to reinforce the furniture and make it sturdier. Use an X-acto knife, to lightly score the dotted lines which show where the card or paper will be bent. (Use the knife along the edge of a ruler for straight lines.) If you intend to paint the paper furniture, paint the separate pieces before gluing them together, and allow them to dry flat. If the furniture is first glued and then painted, it may warp and go out of shape. Before painting apply a coat of gesso; this will give the paint a better finish. I use acrylic paints for the furniture, and gloss polymer medium to seal the paint and give it a slight shine.

Paper Dining Table

Scale: (1 inch to 1 foot)

MATERIALS
  Thick paper or card
  2 drinking straws
  Paper tissues
  White glue
  Tracing paper
  Felt markers or paints

1. Trace and transfer the table-top–cloth combination to the paper, and cut it out.

2. Cut a slit (A) in the top of the table, for the vase of flowers. Color the border, if you wish.

3. Bend the sides of the table down, fold the tabs in, and glue.

4. Cut the straws for the legs into 2-1/2-inch lengths. Stuff them with paper tissues (this makes them sturdier). Paint the legs. Glue one leg to each corner of the table top.

5. Trace and transfer the flowers to paper, and cut them out. Color the flowers.

6. Slip the tab on the vase through the slit in the table top, bend, and glue underneath.

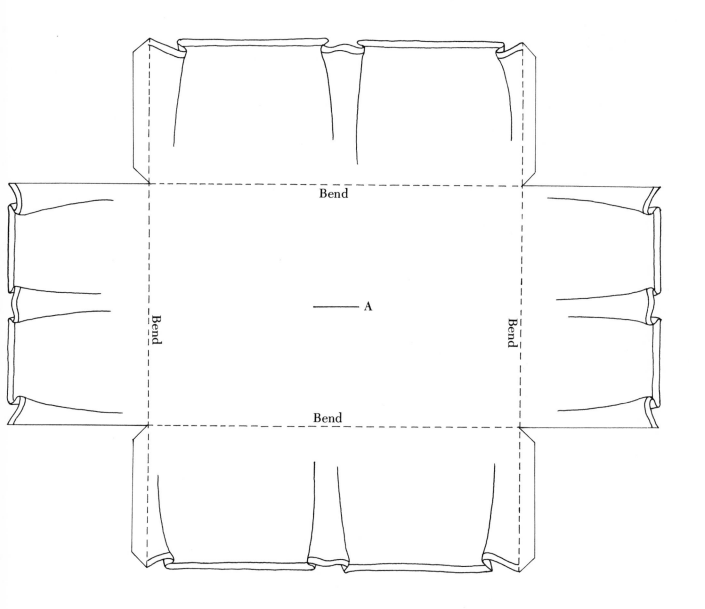

Bend

Bend

Bend

Bend

A

Paper and Matchbox Chest of Drawers

(Scale: 1 inch to 1 foot)

MATERIALS
  6 matchboxes
  Thick paper or card
  Tracing paper
  White glue
  Paint
  6 small beads and 6 straight pins, or 6 map pins

Matchboxes vary in size, so you may have to adjust the paper patterns to fit your matchbox size.

1. Glue two stacks of three matchboxes together. Then glue the two stacks together along their striking sides, to form the drawers as shown in the illustration.

2. Trace the patterns onto tracing paper, and adjust if necessary to fit your matchboxes.

3. Transfer the patterns to paper and cut them out.

4. Paint the pattern pieces. Remove the insides of the matchboxes, and paint the fronts of the "drawers." Also paint the rims of the outside parts of the matchboxes which will show. Make sure that the paint is dry before putting the matchboxes together again.

5. Take the base and the sides. Bend the base down as shown in diagram 1. Glue the set of matchbox drawers to the base. Bend the sides back, and glue them to the sides of the drawers.

6. Glue on the back of the chest.

7. Glue on the top, which should be flush with the back but protrude a little over the sides and front of the chest.

8. For the drawer knobs use either map pins or beads on straight pins. Put a dab of glue on the end of each pin before pushing it through the front of each drawer.

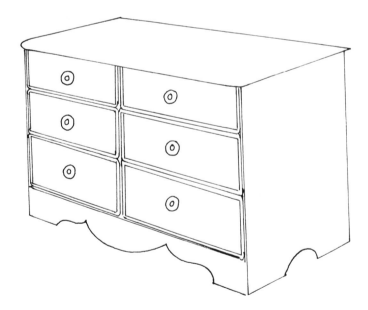

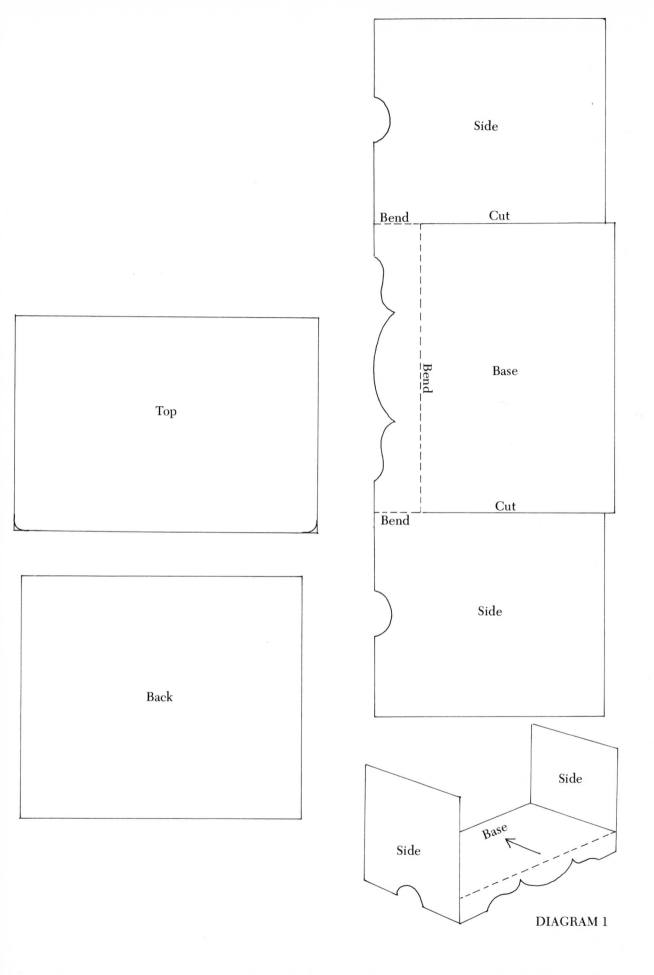

DIAGRAM 1

Drinking-Straw Bed

(Scale: 1 inch to 1 foot)

MATERIALS

 18 bendable drinking straws
 Thin string for the webbing
 Straight pins
 Paper tissues
 Gold paint (preferably spray paint)
 White glue

1. Fit and glue one end of a straw into the end of another straw for the top rail and legs. Bend the straws as shown in drawing 1. Cut the straws, so that the legs measure 5-1/4 inches. Fit and glue one end of a straw into the end of another straw for the bottom rail and legs. Bend the straws as shown in drawing 1. Cut the straws so that these legs measure 4-1/4 inches.

2. Stuff the top legs with paper tissues to points A. Stuff the bottom legs to points B. (The paper stuffing is to make the legs solid, so that the joining pins will hold.)

3. Make seven evenly spaced holes in the underside of the top rail. And make seven evenly spaced holes in the underside of the bottom rail.

4. Cut seven top bars from straws, each bar 4-1/2 inches long. Cut seven bottom bars from straws, each bar 3-1/2 inches long.

5. Push and glue the appropriate bars into the holes in the top and bottom rails.

6. For the cross bars, cut two lengths of straw.

7. For the sides of the bed, cut two 6-1/2-inch lengths of straw.

8. Stuff the bottom cross bar with paper tissues to points C. Stuff the top cross bar with paper tissues to points D.

9. Make seven evenly spaced holes, for the bars, in the top sides of both of the cross bars.

10. Push and glue the appropriate free ends of the bars into the holes in the two cross bars.

11. Pin and glue the cross bars to the legs as shown in drawing 1.

12. Pin and glue the side straws to the legs as shown in drawing 1.

13. Cut eighteen straight pins, so that each pin measures about 1/4 inch in length.

14. Pin and glue the pins to the sides as shown in drawing 2.

15. Cut a length of string about 7-1/2 feet long. Tie one end of the string to pin E. Take the string from side to side and around the pins as shown in drawing 2. Finish off the string by tying it to pin F. (Do not pull the string too tautly, as this will distort the shape of the bed.)

16. Spray or brush-paint the bed with two or three coats of gold paint.

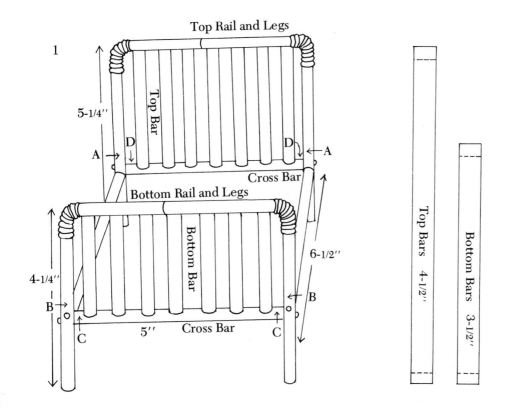

1

Top Rail and Legs

Top Bar

5-1/4''

D   D
A →   ← A
Cross Bar

Bottom Rail and Legs

Bottom Bar

6-1/2''

4-1/4''

B →   B

C   C
5''   Cross Bar

Top Bars   4-1/2''

Bottom Bars   3-1/2''

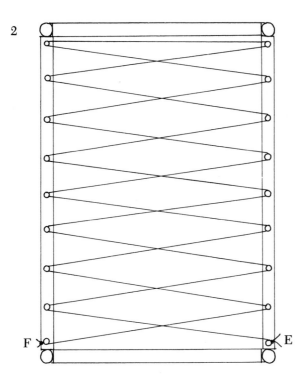

2

F   E

Paper and Matchbox Bedside Table

(Scale: 1 inch to 1 foot)

MATERIALS

    1 matchbox for the drawer
    Thick paper or card
    Tracing paper
    White glue
    Paint
    The "eye" from a hook and eye, and two straight pins for
        the handle

Matchboxes vary in size, so you may have to adjust the paper patterns to fit your matchbox size.

1. Trace and transfer the patterns to the paper, and cut them out. (If necessary, adjust the patterns to fit your matchbox.)

2. Paint the pattern pieces. Remove the inside of the matchbox, and paint the front of the "drawer." Also paint the rims of the outside parts of the matchbox which will show.

3. Take the pattern piece for the back, front, and sides of the table. Bend the vertical dotted lines. Glue flap A to the back, and flap B to the back leg.

4. Take the base, and bend the flaps down. Glue the flaps to the back, front, and sides of the table. (The base is glued inside the table, level with the bottom of the matchbox drawer.)

5. Glue the bottom of the matchbox to the base.

6. Bend the flaps C down, on the tops of the front, back, and sides of the table.

7. Glue the table top onto flaps C. (*Note:* The top is flush with the back of the table, but extends 1/8 inch over the front and sides.)

8. Pull the "eye" apart slightly, as shown in the drawing. Cut two straight pins, so that each pin measures about 1/4 inch in length. Make two pin-sized holes in the front of the table drawer. Pin and glue the "eye" handle to the drawer.

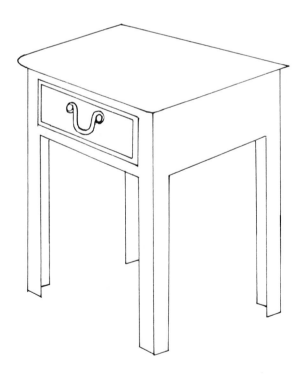

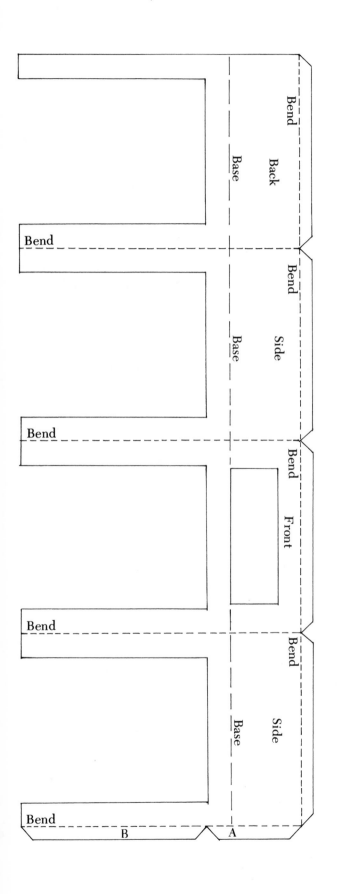

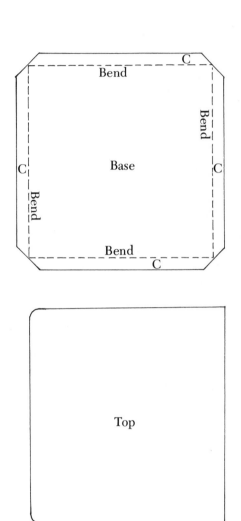

"Eye"

Matchbox Sofa

(Approx. 3 inches high by 6 inches long)

MATERIALS
  12 matchboxes
  4 wooden beads for the feet
  White glue
  A non-fraying fabric such as felt—or thin leather—for
    covering the sofa

I used chamois leather, which I bought at the hardware store. It was easy to work with, and made a very lush-looking sofa. I have not drawn the fabric patterns to scale, since matchboxes vary in size. Measure your matchboxes, and make your own patterns using the diagrams as a guide.

1. Glue four matchboxes together (along their striking sides) to form the bas Cut, and then glue a long strip of material to cover the top, sides, and bottom of the base, making the join underneath. (See drawing 1.)

2. Cut a strip of material and glue it to the front of the base.

3. Use one matchbox for each arm. Glue a strip of material to cover the sides and top of each arm (A). Glue a strip of material to the front of each arm (B). Glue the arms to the base.

4. Note that the back of the sofa is set at a slight angle. (See side view X.) Take three matchboxes to form the back. Cut three matchsticks the width of each box. Glue a matchstick to a matchbox as shown in the drawing 4. Glue the three matchboxes together (along their striking sides). The matchsticks will prop the matchboxes, and angle the back when it is glued to the base.

5. Cut the material for covering the front part of the back of the sofa, using the pattern shown in drawing 5 as a guide.

6. Glue the material to the front part of the back, fitting section C over the top, and sections D to the sides. Glue the back of the sofa to the base.

7. Cut a piece of material following the pattern in drawing 7, and glue it to the entire back of the sofa, including the base and the arms. Stretch and pull the material gently so that all the joins are covered.

8. The sofa cushions are made from only the *insides* of three matchboxes. Cut each box as shown in drawing 8, angled at the back, and long enough just to come over the edge of the base of the sofa.

9. Cut cushion covers, following the pattern shown in drawing 9. Glue the covers to the boxes. The E section will cover the front of each box and the F sections the sides.

10. Sand four wooden beads flat on the top, and glue them in place, for the feet of the sofa.

You can make an armchair to match the sofa. The main construction is the same, but for the armchair use two matchboxes for the base, and one matchbox for the cushion.

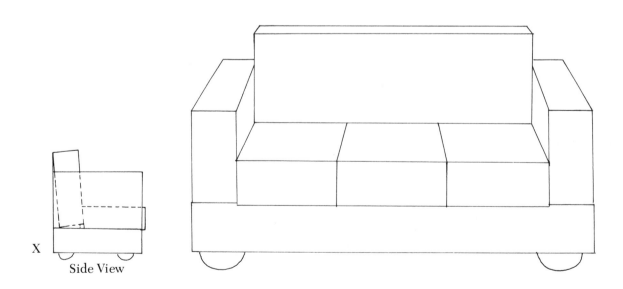

X
Side View

1

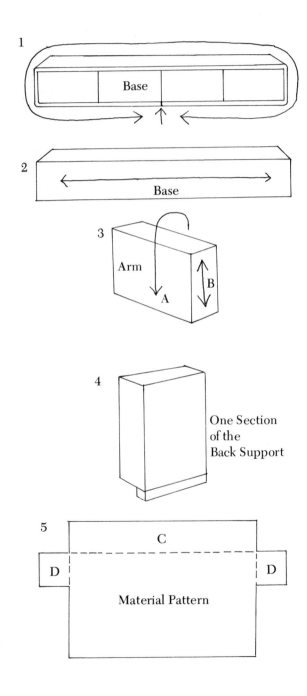

Base

2

Base

3

Arm

A

B

4

One Section
of the
Back Support

5

C

D

D

Material Pattern

6

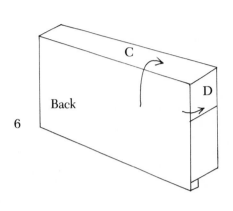

Back

C

D

7

Material Pattern

8

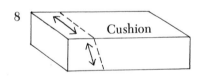

Cushion

9

F

Cushion
Cover

F

E

Matchbox Armchair

(Approx. 2-1/2 inches high by 3 inches long)

MATERIALS

    6 matchboxes
    4 wooden beads for the feet
    White glue
    A non-fraying fabric such as felt—or thin leather

I have not drawn the diagrams to scale here either. Measure your matchboxes, and make your own fabric patterns using the diagrams as a guide.

1. Glue two matchboxes together (along their striking sides) to form the base. Cut, and then glue, a long strip of material to cover the top, sides, and bottom of the base, making the join underneath. (See drawing 1.)

2. Cut a strip of material and glue it to the front of the base (drawing 2).

3. Use one matchbox for each arm (drawing 3). Glue a strip of material to cover the sides and top of each arm (A); glue a strip of material to the front of each arm (B). Glue the arms to the base.

4. For the back, cut a matchbox to the size of the space between the two arms (drawing 4). Cover the top and front of the back with material. Glue the back in place.

5. Cut a piece of material the height and length of the entire back of the armchair. Glue the material to the back, arms, and base (drawing 5).

6. Take the inside part of a matchbox for the cushion. Cut the inside part of the matchbox to the size of the space between the two arms (see drawing 6). Cover the top, front, and sides of the cushion with material.

7. Sand four wooden beads flat on the top, and glue them in place for the feet of the armchair.

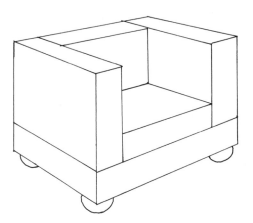

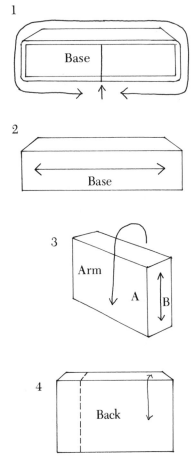

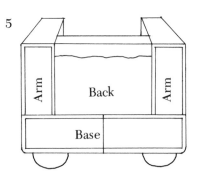

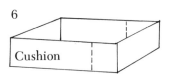

"Glass-Top" Coffee Table

(Scale: 1 inch to 1 foot)

MATERIALS

    Tracing paper
    Stiff, clear plastic (from wrappings)
    Thick paper or card
    White glue
    Paint

1. Place the clear plastic over the table top on the page. Draw the square on the plastic and cut it out.

2. Trace and transfer onto paper the patterns for the legs and sides of the table. Cut them out.

3. Paint the sides and legs. To get the look of stainless steel use silver paint.

4. Bend each leg section to form an L-shape.

5. Join and glue each A to each B to form a square, tucking the flaps inside so that they don't show.

6. When the glue has dried, turn the table upside down, and put it on a flat surface. Then glue the plastic table top in place.

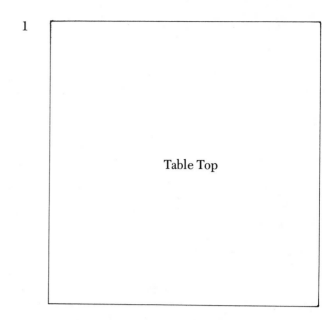

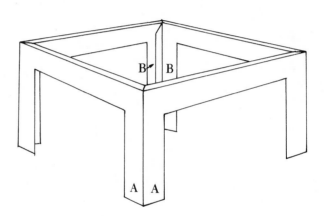

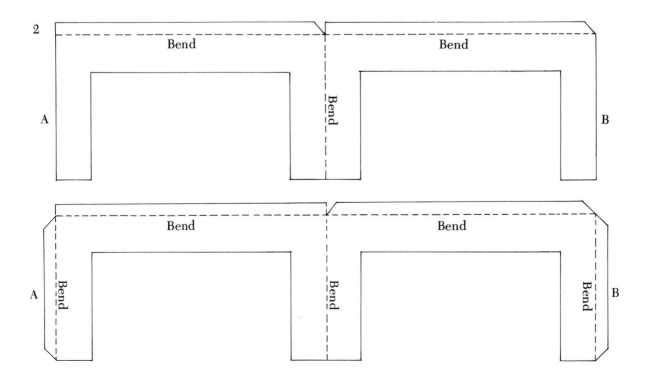

Paper Crib

(Scale: 1 inch to 1 foot)

MATERIALS

Tracing paper
Thick paper or card
White glue
Paint

1. Trace and transfer onto paper the patterns for the sides-and-base and the ends of the crib. Cut them out.

2. Paint the pattern pieces of the crib both on the back and on the front.

3. Paint a design (for example, a teddy bear, a panda, a heart, a flower) on both outside ends of the crib, or cut motifs from a magazine and glue them on.

4. Now put the pieces of the crib together. Bend the leg sections along the dotted lines and glue A to B to form the legs. Bend sections C down along the dotted lines, and tuck and glue the flaps inside the top of the legs.

5. Bend the sides of the crib up along the dotted lines. Bend flaps D up and flaps E in.

6. Glue the underside corners of the base of the crib to the tops of the legs (C). And glue the E and D flaps to the (inside) ends of the crib.

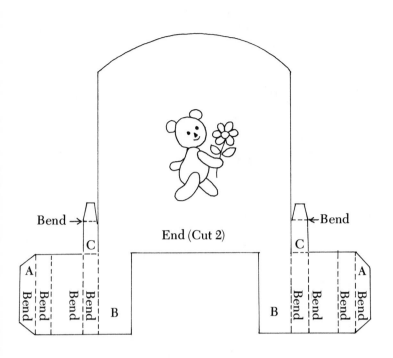

Bend →   ← Bend

C   End (Cut 2)   C

A   Bend   Bend   Bend   Bend   Bend   Bend   Bend   Bend   A

Bend   B   B

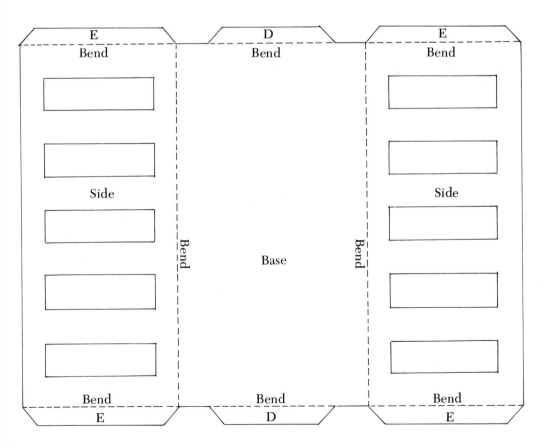

E   D   E

Bend   Bend   Bend

Side   Bend   Base   Bend   Side

Bend   Bend   Bend

E   D   E

Drinking-Straw and Paper Chair

(Scale: 1 inch to 1 foot)

MATERIALS
　　2 bendable drinking straws
　　Thick paper or card
　　Tracing paper
　　3 round toothpicks for the spindles
　　White glue
　　Paint

1. Trace and transfer the pattern for the chair seat to paper. Cut out the seat. Make the holes for the back legs and three spindles.

2. Paint the chair seat.

3. Bend the back, front, and sides of the seat down. Glue the flaps to the sides.

4. Fit and glue one end of a straw into the end of another straw. Bend the straws as shown in drawing 1. Cut the straws, so that the measurement from the bottom of the legs to the top of the back is 4 inches (see drawing 1).

5. For the front legs, cut two 1-1/2-inch lengths of straw.

6. With the pointed tip of a toothpick, make three holes for the spindles in the back of the chair, as indicated by the arrows.

7. Glue the toothpick spindles into the back of the chair.

8. Paint the back, back legs, and front legs.

9. Push the legs and the spindles through the holes in the back of the seat. Cut the spindles, so that only 1/8 inch of the spindles protrudes underneath the seat.

10. Glue a front leg to each corner of the front of the seat.

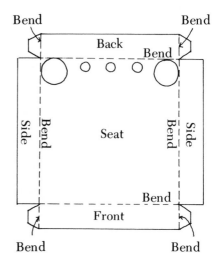

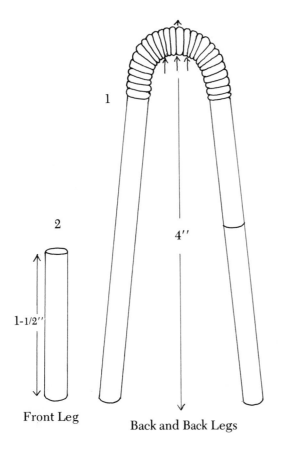

1

2

1-1/2''

4''

Front Leg

Back and Back Legs

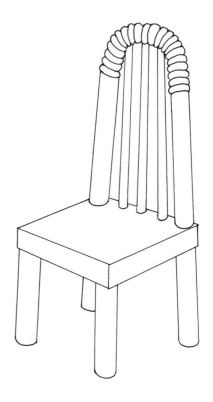

Bend　　　　　　　　　　　Bend

Back

Bend

Side　Bend　　Seat　　Bend　Side

Bend

Front

Bend　　　　　　　　　　　Bend

Drinking-Straw and Paper Table

(Scale: 1 inch to 1 foot)

MATERIALS
    3 bendable drinking straws
    Thick paper or card
    White glue
    Paint
    Tracing paper

1. Trace and transfer the pattern for the table top to the paper. Use a compass for drawing the circles. Cut out the pattern, cutting the flaps as shown in the drawing. Cut a strip of paper 1/4 inch wide by 12-3/4 inches long for the table rim.

2. For the legs cut three straws (including the bendable sections). Cut each straw 2-1/2 inches long. As the legs will cant out, cut the bottoms of the straws at a slight angle.

3. Glue the top 3/4 inch of each of the straws together as shown in diagram 1. Put a rubber band around the straws until the glue is dry.

4. Paint the pattern pieces and the straw legs.

5. Bend the flaps on the table top down. Glue the rim to the flaps on the table top.

6. Glue the top ends of the legs to the center of the underneath side of the table. Spread the legs of the table as shown in the drawing.

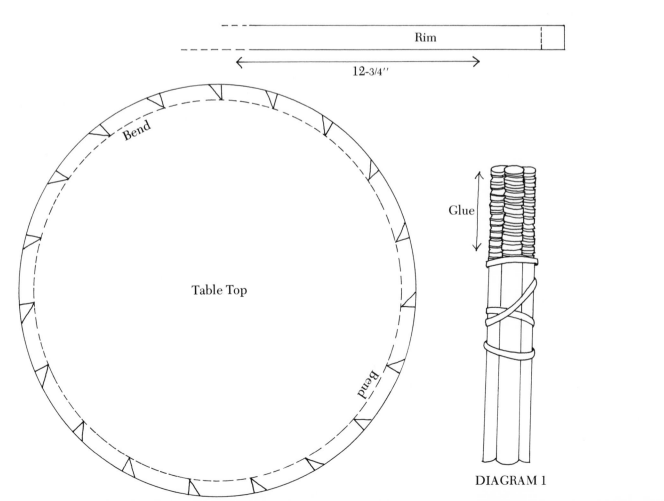

Rim

12-3/4''

Bend

Bend

Table Top

Glue

DIAGRAM 1

Paper Stove

(Scale: 1 inch to 1 foot)

MATERIALS

> Thick paper or card
> Tracing paper
> A piece of stiff, clear plastic for the oven-door front
> 5 map pins for the stove controls
> Wooden matchsticks for the oven-door and broiler-door handles
> White glue
> Paint

1. Trace and transfer the patterns to paper. (Transfer the "glass" oven-door front by placing the clear plastic over the pattern on the page. Draw the rectangle on the plastic.) Cut out the patterns.

2. Paint the pattern pieces.

3. Glue the "glass" to the rim of the inside of the oven door.

4. Take the main pattern piece of the stove. Bend the sides back, the top down, and the base up. Glue flaps A to the top, and flaps B to the base. Glue flaps C, D, and E to the back of the stove.

5. Draw or paint the four burners onto the top of the stove.

6. Pin and glue the map pins into the front of the stove for the controls.

7. Cut two 3/8-inch lengths of matchsticks for handles. Glue a handle to the oven door and to the broiler door. Paint the handles.

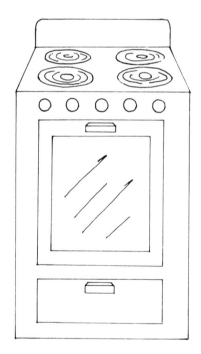

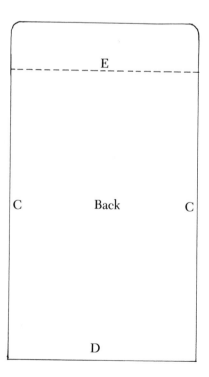

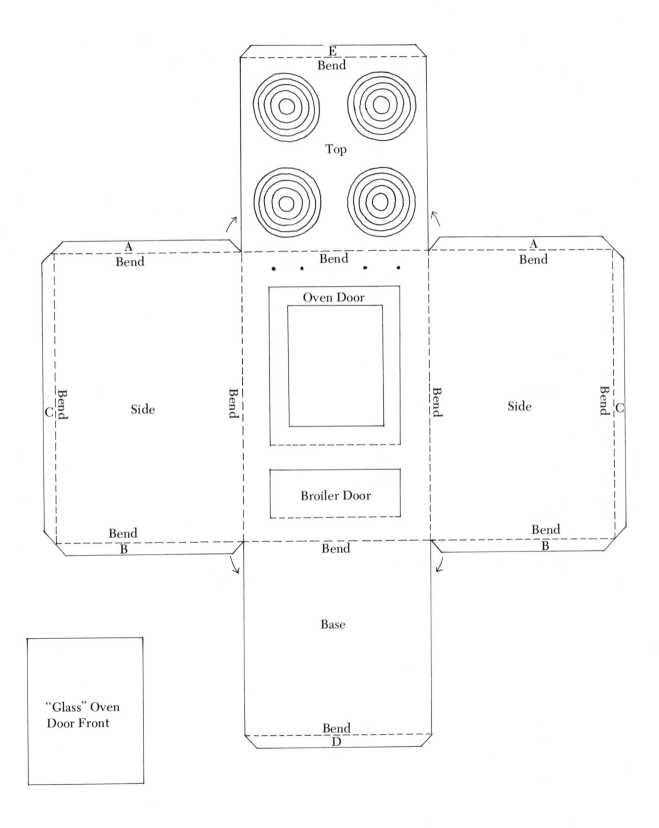

Paper and Matchbox Kitchen Sink and Cupboard

(Scale: 1 inch to 1 foot)

MATERIALS

4 matchboxes
Thick paper or card
Tracing paper
A plastic jelly container or the smaller part of a "cheese 'n crackers" container for the sink
Half of a small snap for the drain cover
Matchsticks for the drawer and cupboard handles
A piece of plastic-covered electrical wiring for the faucet
2 map pins for the taps
White glue
Paint

Matchboxes vary in size, so you may have to adjust the paper patterns to fit your matchbox size.

1. Glue a stack of four matchboxes together, for the drawers.

2. Trace the patterns onto tracing paper, and adjust if necessary to fit your matchboxes.

3. Transfer the patterns to paper and cut them out.

4. Paint the pattern pieces. Paint the plastic "sink" silver. Remove the insides of the matchboxes, and paint the fronts of the drawers. Also paint the rims of the outside parts of the matchboxes that will show. Make sure that the paint is dry before putting the matchboxes together again.

5. Take the front and sides of the sink and cupboard. Bend the base for the drawers down (the flap will be glued to the back of the cupboard). Bend the sides back.

Glue the bottom of the set of drawers to the base. Glue flaps A and B to the back part of the cupboard.

6. Glue the "sink" to the underneath side of the opening in the counter top.

7. Glue the counter top in place onto flaps C.

8. Take the top cupboard pattern piece. Bend the top down, bend the sides back, and bend the base under. Glue flaps D and E to the sides of the cupboard. Glue flaps F to the back of the cupboard.

9. Cut a length of plastic-covered wiring about 1 inch long. Bend one end into a curve, and glue the other end into hole G in the back of the cupboard.

10. Pin and glue two map pins into the counter top (H).

11. Make a hole in the center of the sink, and glue half of a snap in place.

12. Cut seven 3/8-inch-long lengths of matchstick. Glue the lengths of matchsticks in place for the drawer and cupboard handles. Paint the handles.

Glue top cupboard base here

Glue counter top here   ○ G

Back

Glue drawer base here

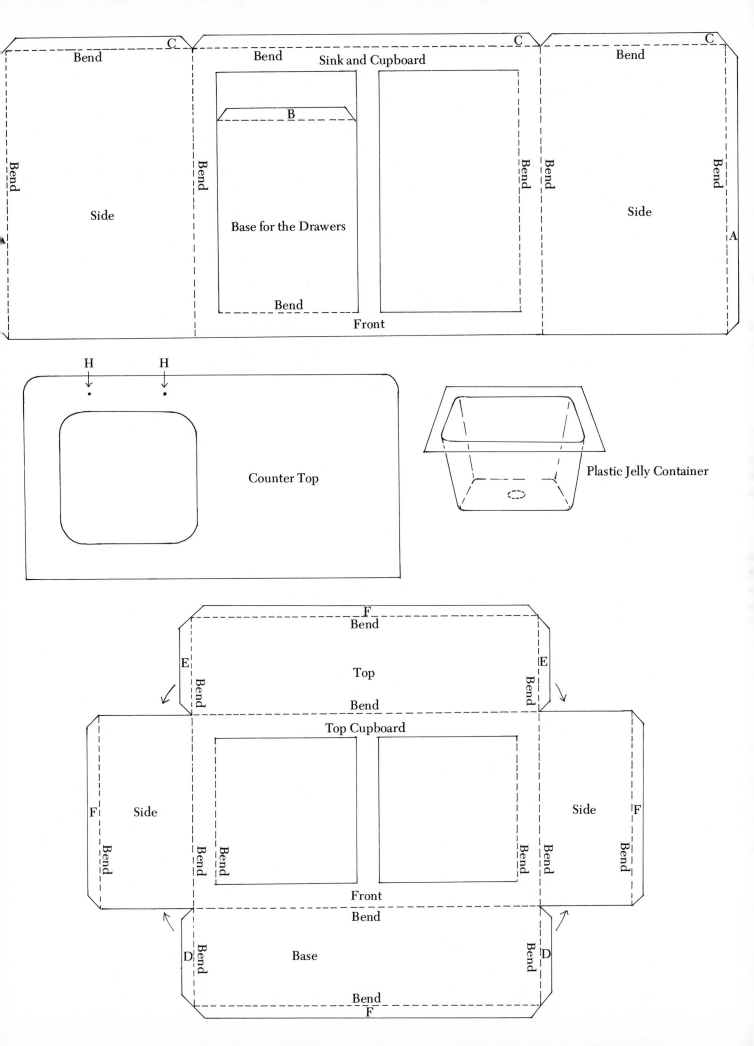

Paper Bathtub

(Scale: 1 inch to 1 foot)

MATERIALS
    Thick colored or white paper, or card
    Tracing paper
    White glue
    Paints
    2 gold or silver map pins for the taps
    One-half of a small snap for the drain cover

Smooth colored paper (shiny or matte) is good to use for bathroom fixtures. (It can be bought at art-supply stores.)

1. Trace and transfer patterns A and B to the paper, and cut them out. Make small slashes along the curved flap of A.

2. If you are not using colored paper, paint the pattern pieces.

3. Take the inside section of the bathtub (A) and bend the sides up. Then glue the corners together to form an oblong box which has one curved end as shown in diagram 1.

4. Bend down the sides of the outside section of the bathtub (B). Glue the corners together to form another oblong box. (Box A will fit inside box B.)

5. Turn the outside of the bathtub (B) upside down. Following the arrows in diagram 2, put glue around the rim. Now insert the inside of the bathtub (A) into the outside (B) and stick the flaps to the glued area. Check that the rims fit properly and that there are no gaps.

6. Press two map pins into the top of the rim for the taps.

7. Make a small hole in the bottom of the bathtub, and insert and glue half of a small snap for a drain cover.

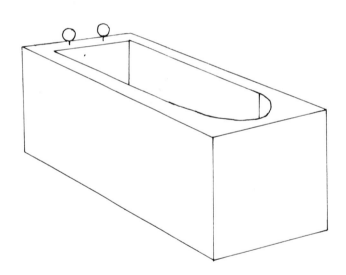

PAPER BATHTUB—PART I

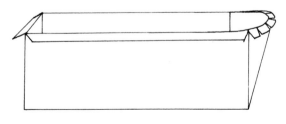

DIAGRAM 1

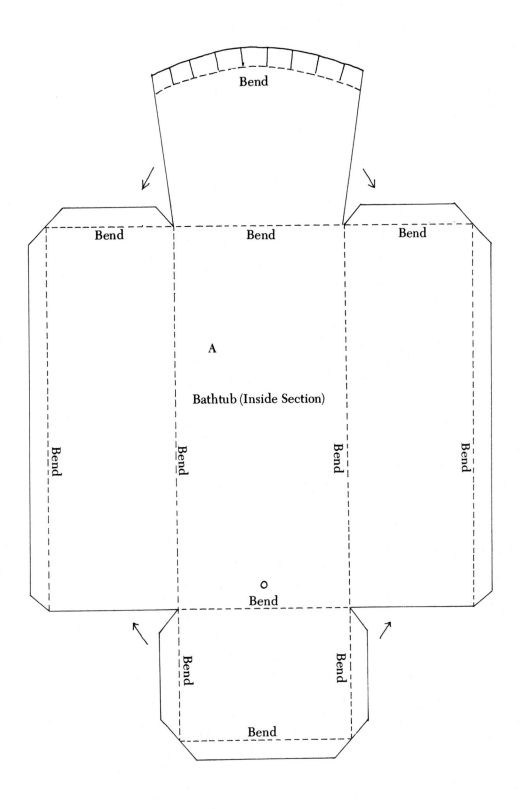

Bend

Bend   Bend   Bend

Bend   Bend   Bend   Bend

A

Bathtub (Inside Section)

Bend

Bend   Bend

Bend

PAPER BATHTUB—PART II

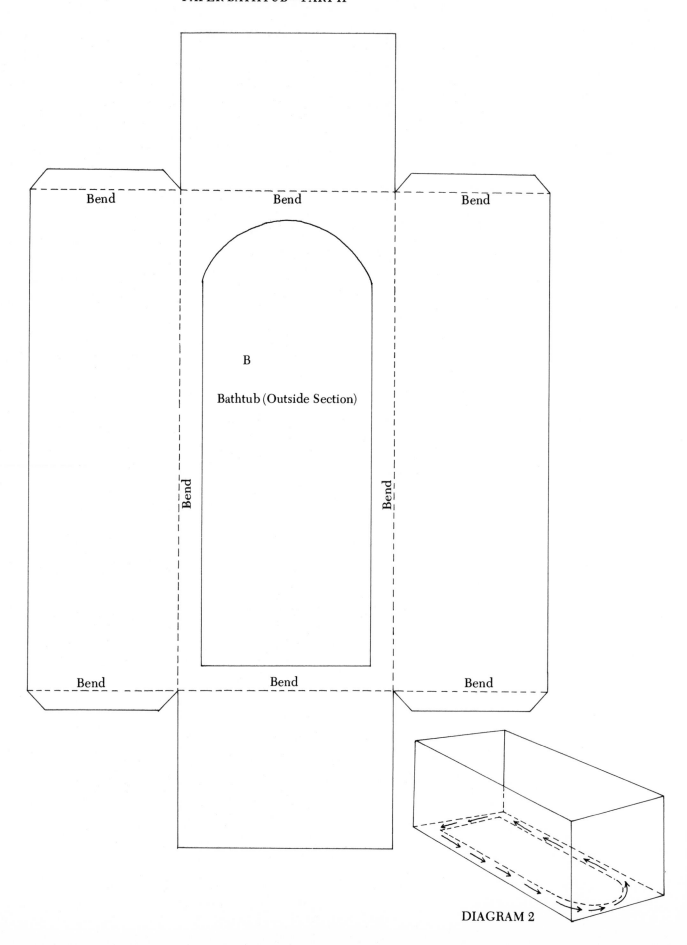

Bend

Bend

Bend

Bend

Bend

B

Bathtub (Outside Section)

Bend

Bend

Bend

DIAGRAM 2

Paper Wash Basin

(Scale: 1 inch to 1 foot)

MATERIALS

Tracing paper

Thick colored paper or white paper or card

White glue

Paint

2 gold or silver map pins for the taps

One-half of a small snap for the drain cover

For the bowl, use either the smaller half of an egg-shaped plastic container (the kind you get from vending machines that contain small favors) or a suitable plastic bottle cap. (The bowl should measure no more than 11/16 inch in height.)

Smooth colored paper (shiny or matte) is good to use for bathroom fixtures. (It can be bought at art-supply stores.)

1. Trace and transfer the pattern pieces to paper, and cut them out. *Note:* The outer rim of the plastic container or bottle cap must fit flush against the underneath rim of the circular hole in the top of the basin. Therefore, adjust the size of the circumference of the circle to fit the size of the "bowl" that is being used.

2. If you are not using colored paper, paint the pattern pieces. Also paint the "bowl" the same color as the rest of the wash basin.

3. Glue the rim of the "bowl" to the rim of the circular hole in the wash basin top, as shown in diagram 1.

4. Take the bottom of the wash basin and bend the

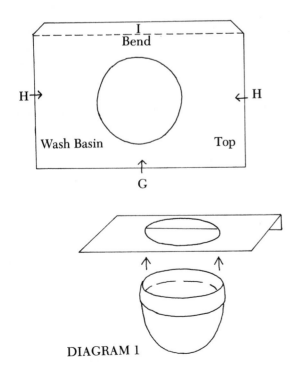

DIAGRAM 1

PAPER WASH BASIN—PART I

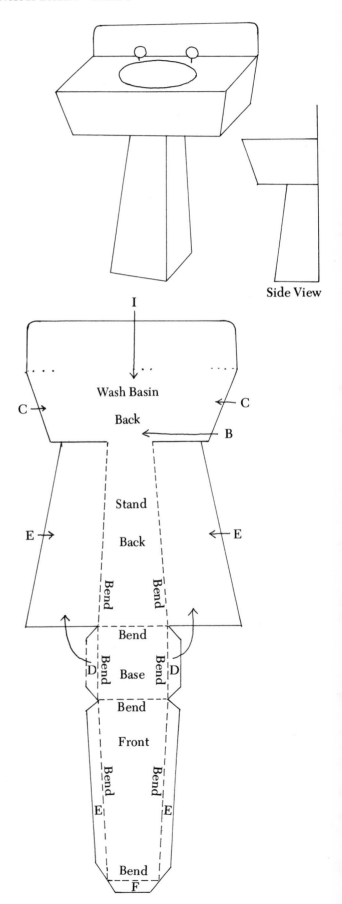

Side View

PAPER WASH BASIN—PART II

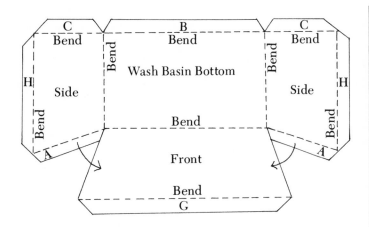

front and sides up. Bend all the flaps in. Glue flaps A to the front of the wash basin, as indicated by the arrows.

5. Now secure the bottom, sides, and front of the wash basin to the back section by gluing flaps B and C as indicated by the arrows.

6. Next form the stand part of the wash basin. Bend the sides in. Bend the base and the front of the stand up, gluing flaps D and E as indicated by the arrows. Glue flap F under the basin bottom.

7. Fit the wash basin top in place by first gluing flap I to the back of the wash basin, and then bringing the top down and gluing it onto flaps H and G.

8. Press two map pins into the top of the basin for the taps.

9. Glue half of a small snap to the center of the "bowl" for a drain cover.

Paper Toilet

(Scale: 1 inch to 1 foot)

MATERIALS
   Tracing paper
   Thick colored or white paper, or card
   White glue
   Paint
   A gold or silver map pin for the handle
   For the bowl, use either the smaller half of an egg-shaped plastic container (the kind you get from vending machines that contain small favors) or a suitable plastic bottle cap

Smooth colored paper (shiny or matte) is good to use for bathroom fixtures. (It can be bought at art-supply stores.)

1. Trace and transfer the pattern pieces to paper, and cut them out. *Note:* The outer rim of the plastic container or bottle cap must fit flush against the underneath rim of the circular hole in the top of the seat. Therefore, adjust the size of the circumference of the circle to fit the size of the "bowl" that is being used.

2. If you are not using colored paper, paint the pattern pieces. Also paint the "bowl" the same color as the rest of the toilet.

3. Glue the rim of the "bowl" to the underneath side of the toilet seat.

4. Take the pattern piece for the toilet. Bend the front, back, and ends down. Glue flaps A to the front and flaps B to the back.

5. Take the pattern piece for the tank. Bend along the dotted lines to form a box. Glue flaps C to the ends, flap D to the back, flap E to the front, and flap F to the end.

6. Glue the tank to the toilet in the position shown in the drawing.

7. Pin and glue the map-pin handle to the toilet.

PAPER TOILET

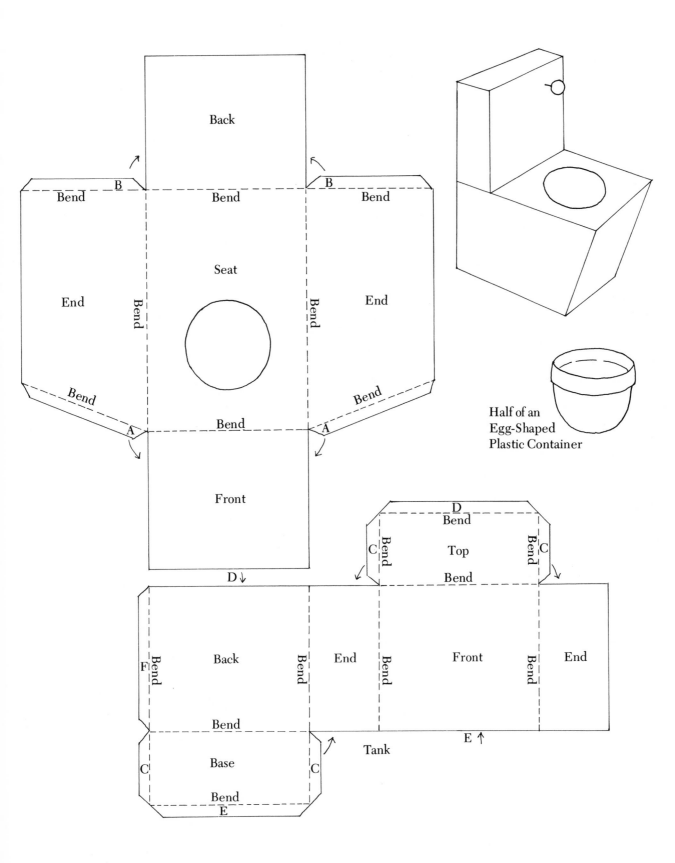

Half of an
Egg-Shaped
Plastic Container

My young daughter's idea of a dolls' house is an ever-changing arrangement of building blocks on the floor. She and her friends use the matchbox and paper furniture I've made and they have added furniture and bedding they have made themselves. The pillows are irregular rectangular shapes stuffed with paper tissues. The bed covers are scraps of fabric, the raw edges hastily turned down with giant, zigzag basting stitches. These little girls never wait for the glue to dry properly because of their impatience to get on with the game. I often overhear my daughter and her friends changing their voices to conform to the characters of their dolls as they act out fantastic domestic dramas in the "dolls' house." For me, and my friends who make dolls' house furniture, that kind of fantasy play is gone—along with childhood. But a different kind of pleasure has taken its place: the pleasure a craftsman takes in creating a miniature chair out of a piece of wood or a four-inch-by-six-inch quilt from odd scraps of fabric.

APPENDIX

Useful books, pamphlets, and magazines; where to get tools and materials; names and addresses of suppliers throughout the country.

Part I: Recommended Publications

BOOKS

Baker, Roger. *The Collector's Book of Dolls and Dolls' Houses.* New York: Crescent Books.

Bradford, Faith. *The Dolls' House* (booklet). Washington, D.C.: Smithsonian Publication 4641, 1965.

Bragdon, Allen Davenport, ed. *The Family Creative Workshop.* New York: Plenary Publications International, 1974. (An excellent series of books, well designed and clearly illustrated, with many drawings and color photographs. Step-by-step instructions on every imaginable craft and skill.)

Elliot, Mrs. *How to Make Dolls' Furniture and Furnish a Doll's House* (booklet). Reprinted from the Victorian edition by Carter Craft Doll House. Hyattville, Maryland. (Text and illustrations on how to make paper furniture.)

Greene, Vivien. *Family Dolls' Houses.* Newton, Mass.: Branford, 1973.

Ickis, Marguerite. *The Standard Book of Quilt Making and Collecting.* New York: Dover Publications, 1959.

Jacobs, Flora Gill. *A History of Dolls' Houses.* New York: Scribner's, 1965.

———. *Dolls' Houses in America.* New York: Scribner's, 1974.

Johnson, Audrey, *How to Make Dolls' Houses.* London: Bell, 1968.

———. *Furnishing Dolls' Houses.* London: Bell, 1972.

Latham, Jean. *Dolls' Houses: A Personal Choice.* New York: Scribner's, 1969.

Moore, Colleen. *Colleen Moore's Doll House.* New York: Doubleday, 1974.

Musgrave, Clifford. *Queen Mary's Dolls' House* (booklet). London: Pitkin Pictorials, 1973.

Ness, Evaline. *American Colonial Paper House to Cut Out and Color.* New York: Scribner's, 1975.

Newman, Thelma R., and Merrill, Virginia. *The Complete Book of Making Miniatures.* New York: Crown, 1975.

Thorne, Mrs. James Ward. *American Rooms in Miniature* (booklet). The Art Institute of Chicago, 1962.

———. *European Rooms in Miniature* (booklet). The Art Institute of Chicago, 1962.

Worrel, Estelle Ansley. *Americana in Miniature.* New York: Van Nostrand Reinhold, 1975.

Yarwood, Doreen. *The English Home.* London: Batford, 1956. (A comprehensive, copiously illustrated survey of interiors and furniture from the seventh century to Edwardian times.)

All the books on miniatures and dolls' houses can be obtained by mail order from:

Paul A. Ruddell, Bookseller
4701 Queensbury Road
Riverdale, Maryland 20840

Mr. Ruddell specializes in books on dolls, dolls' houses, toys, and antiques. He prints a detailed descriptive biannual catalog, which he sends free of charge upon request.

MAGAZINES

International Dolls' House News
56 Lincoln Wood
Haywards Heath
Sussex, RH161LH, England

Miniature Gazette
N.A.M.E., Box 2621
Brookhurst Center
Anaheim, California 92804
(Official publication of the National Association of Miniature Enthusiasts.)

Mott Miniature Workshop–News
P.O. Box 5514
Sunny Hills Station
Fullerton, California 92635

Nutshell News
Editor, Catherine B. MacLaren
1035 Newkirk Drive
La Jolla, California 92037

For subscription rates and other information, write to any of these publications, enclosing a stamped, self-addressed envelope.

Part II: Suppliers

The advertisements in the *Nutshell News* and *Miniature Gazette* are the best sources of information about dealers who sell supplies, as well as those who sell ready-made dolls' houses, dolls' house furniture, and accessories. I have bought supplies from the dealers listed below and have found them reliable. All these dealers have well-illustrated catalogs. (I have not included the prices of the catalogs, for they may change from year to year; but a letter to the dealer would get you the information.)

Architectural Model Supplies, Inc.
　115-B Bellam Boulevard
　P.O. Box 3497
　San Rafael, California 94902
Dowel
Assorted basswood moldings
Wood flooring
Window and door parts
Stair treads, risers, and stringers
Wood—all thicknesses from 1/32 inch up
Shingles
Plexiglas
Thin glass for windows
Small hinges
1/4-inch brass pins
Wallpaper
Victorian tile papers
Landscape materials

Constantine
　2050 Eastchester Road
　Bronx, New York 10461
Hand and power tools
Veneers
Carved wooden trim
Balsa wood—sheets, blocks, and strips
1/8-inch-thick plywood
1/8-inch-thick basswood
Dowel

Cotton Patch
　2121 E. 3rd Street
　Tulsa, Oklahoma 74104
Fabrics with tiny prints

The Dollhouse Factory
　Box 456
　157 Main Street
　Lebanon, New Jersey 08833
Basswood and mahogany strips and sheets from 1/32 inch thick
　up
Door and window parts
Assorted moldings
Flooring
Small hinges

1/4-inch brass pins
Small bricks
Electrical and lighting components
Wallpaper
Hand and power tools

Dremel Manufacturing Co.
　4915 21st Street
　Racine, Wisconsin 53406
All Dremel power tools

Federal Smallwares Corp.
　85 Fifth Avenue
　New York, New York 10003
Reprints of Victorian postcards
Printed paper "scrap" pictures
Old-fashioned die-cut seals

Green Door Studio
　517 E. Annapolis Street
　St. Paul, Minnesota 55118
Small hinges
Wallpaper

J. Hermes
　P.O. Box 23
　El Monte, California 91734
Wallpaper

Illinois Hobbycraft
　12 S. 5th Street
　Geneva, Illinois 60134
Electrical lamps and fixtures
Tiny bulbs, sockets, plugs, and switches
Information on wiring a dolls' house
Hand and power tools
Dowel
Door and window parts
Flooring
Assorted moldings
Wood
Brass sheets, rods, and tubes

The Jewel Thief
　2886 Blue Star Avenue
　P.O. Box 3597
　Anaheim, California 92806
Jewelry findings—bell-caps, jump-rings, filigree
Fine chain
Large selection of different beads
Ring and brooch settings (to use for picture frames)

The Miniature Mart
　1807 Octavia Street
　San Francisco, California 94109
Wallpaper
Victorian tile papers
Small hinges

The Miniature Mart (continued)
1/4-inch brass pins
Doors
Windows
Wainscoting
Paneling
Baseboard
Assorted moldings
Flooring
Drawer pulls
Faucets

Northeastern Scale Models, Inc.
P.O. Box 425
Methuen, Massachusetts 01844
Basswood and mahogany strips and sheets from 1/32-inch-thick
up
Assorted moldings
Baseboard
Flooring
Door and window parts
Picture frame

Polks Hobby Department Store
314 5th Avenue
New York, New York 10001
Hand and power tools
Dowel
Balsa wood strips, sheets, and blocks
Brass tubing

Shaker Miniatures
2913 Huntington Road
Cleveland, Ohio 44120
1/32-inch-thick to 1/4-inch-thick basswood and mahogany
1/8-inch-thick maple, cherry, and walnut
Hand and power tools

The Vermont Country Store, Inc.
Weston, Vermont 05161
Fabric: small calico prints

Walbead, Inc.
38 W. 37th Street
New York, New York 10018
Large selection of different beads
Sequins
Magnetic strip (comes on a roll like Scotch tape, and can be cut
to size)
Decorative pins
Metallic braid
Felt
Jewelry findings—bell-caps, jump-rings, filigree, etc.
Wire

X-acto
48-31 Van Dam Street
Long Island City, New York 11101
All X-acto products

INDEX

A Note on the Type

The text of this book was set, via computer-driven cathode ray tube, in Gael, an adaptation of Caledonia, a type face originally designed by W. A. Dwiggins. It belongs to the family of printing types called "modern faces" by printers—a term used to mark the change in style of type letters that occurred about 1800. Caledonia borders on the general design of Scotch Modern, but is more freely drawn than that letter.

Composed by Harold Black Inc., New York, New York
Printed by The Murray Press, Forge Village, Massachusetts
Bound by The Book Press, Brattleboro, Vermont
Photographs by J. Wesley Jones
Designed by Helen Barrow